CONSUMMATUM EST

CONSUMMATUM EST

*Eschatology and Church
in the Gospel of St John*

By
ALF CORELL

WIPF & STOCK · Eugene, Oregon

Wipf and Stock Publishers
199 W 8th Ave, Suite 3
Eugene, OR 97401

Consummatum Est
Eschatology and Church in the Gospel of St John
By Corell, Alf
Copyright©1958 SPCK
ISBN 13: 978-1-4982-9769-1
Publication date 4/28/2016
Previously published by SPCK, 1958

CONTENTS

AUTHOR'S PREFACE TO THE ENGLISH EDITION — ix

CHAPTER 1. THE PROBLEM AND THE TASK
1. The Starting Point — 1
2. The Idea of the Church — 3
3. The Peculiar Character of Eschatology — 5
4. The Connection between Church and Eschatology — 9

CHAPTER 2. THE CHURCH AND THE MINISTRY IN THE GOSPEL OF ST JOHN
5. The Doctrine of the Church in the Fourth Gospel — 12
6. The King and the People — 15
7. The Shepherd and the Flock — 23
8. The Vine and the Branches — 26
9. The Mission — 29
10. The Confession — 33
11. The Ministry — 36

CHAPTER 3. THE LITURGY IN THE FOURTH GOSPEL
12. The Relation to the Jewish Cult — 44
13. The Baptism of John and the Baptism of Jesus — 54
14. The Miracle of the Wine — 56
15. Born of Water and of the Spirit — 58

16. The Water of Life	60
17. The Sabbath	62
18. The Bread of Life	63
19. The Light of the World	67
20. The Washing of the Feet	69
21. The Vine	73
22. The Piercing with the Lance	74
23. The Relation of the Gospel to the Liturgy in the Primitive Church (Summary)	75

CHAPTER 4. ESCHATOLOGY AND THE CHURCH IN THE FOURTH GOSPEL

24. Results of Earlier Investigations	79
25. The Spirit and the Paraclete	85
26. The Character of the Johannine Idea of the Church	92
27. The Unique Character of the Johannine Eschatology	101
28. The Connection between Eschatology and the Church in the Fourth Gospel	109

CHAPTER 5. IMPORTANT THEOLOGICAL CONCEPTIONS

29. λόγος	113
30. ῥήματα	119
31. σημεῖα	122
32. ἔργα	126
33. πίστις, πιστεύειν	128
34. ζωή	139
35. χάρις	150
36. δόξα	152
37. χαρά	155
38. εἰρήνη	157
39. ἀλήθεια	159
40. κρίσις	162

CHAPTER 6. THE IDEA OF ELECTION IN THE FOURTH GOSPEL

41. The History of Exegetical Investigation 166
42. The Johannine Idea of Election and that of the Old Testament 186
43. Chosen by Christ 188
44. "Born of God" 193
45. The "Offence" 197

CHAPTER 7. CONSUMMATUM EST 201

ABBREVIATIONS 209

BIBLIOGRAPHY 213

INDEX OF AUTHORS QUOTED IN THE TEXT 239

AUTHOR'S PREFACE TO THE ENGLISH EDITION

ALTHOUGH THE critical investigation of the Fourth Gospel has still been going on since the publication of this thesis in Swedish in May 1950, the results have not in any essential point caused the present writer to change his opinions. On the contrary, he feels gratefully strengthened in his ideas. Rudolf Bultmann's theories of partition and redaction have been opposed by E. Ruckstuhl, *Die literarische Einheit des Johannesevangeliums* (Freiburg, 1951), and B. Noack, *Zur Johanneischen Tradition* (Copenhagen, 1954). In these works the unity of the Gospel is stressed on philological grounds and Ruckstuhl discusses the eschatology of St John in opposition to Bultmann, emphasizing the final eschatology in the Gospel. The Johannine eschatology, especially in relation to the conceptions of "Life", "Light" and "Glory", is treated in the exceptionally good *Essai sur la Christologie de Saint Jean* by J. Dupont (Bruges, 1951). But the most important contributions to Johannine literature of recent years has been made by English scholars. C. H. Dodd's marvellous book, *The Interpretation of the Fourth Gospel* (Cambridge, 1953), stresses the theological unity of the Gospel in an authoritative and powerful manner. In accordance with his idea of eschatology in the Synoptic Gospels, Dodd rejects every trace of final eschatology in the Fourth Gospel. The present writer disagrees with him on this point, as will be shown in the following pages. C. K. Barrett by his *The Gospel according to St John* (London, 1955) supplies the much needed modern English commentary on the Fourth Gospel. The reader will find that the main ideas of this thesis coincide with those of Dr Barrett. There is one point, however, on which the present writer disagrees with him, namely, his conception of predestination in the Fourth Gospel. As is shown in the sixth chapter of this thesis the texts do not permit of an interpretation of predestination in the philosophical sense of the word. The present writer maintains that the Johannine conception is more correctly expressed by the word "election". There may also be a slight difference between the English and Swedish interpretations of the word "predestination". To Swedish ears the word has a definitely philosophical meaning.

In comparison with the above-mentioned scholarly English works, this thesis is but a slight study of some problems peculiar to Johannine theology, but it is now presented to English students in the hope of stimulating the discussion and further investigation of the extraordinarily fascinating world of the Gospel of St John.

ALF CORELL

Gryt,
Sweden.
April 1956.

CHAPTER 1

THE PROBLEM AND THE TASK

1. *The Starting Point*

IF EVER anyone should undertake to write the history of the different interpretations of the Fourth Gospel it would, no doubt, prove to be at the same time interesting, and depressing. It would then become clear not only that it has been interpreted and estimated in different ways by different churches and theologians—all the books in the Bible have been treated in that way—but also that it has been the source *par excellence* for gnostics, mystics, and individual fanatics of all kinds. Here each one has sought support for his own favourite ideas and has found that "something" which, as yet, no one has been able to define in a satisfactory manner but which each has considered "typical of St John".

The theological problem in the Fourth Gospel can, of course, be approached from many angles. In this treatise, however, eschatology is to be the main subject of our study. Our choice here is not accidental. Eschatology has during the last few decades become more and more the centre of interest for students of the New Testament. Profound and careful treatises on the eschatology of the three Synoptic Gospels and of St Paul's Epistles have been made, but it has proved difficult to deal with the Fourth Gospel in the same way. That is partly because true eschatology has been connected traditionally with apocalypse. Here the Synoptic Gospels and, of course, the book of Revelation have provided scholars with excellent material whereas the Fourth Gospel has not. For a long time it was therefore considered that the Fourth Gospel lacked all trace of eschatology; the few passages about the "last day" were dismissed as editorial interpolations designed to bring the teaching of this Gospel into line with that of the Synoptics. Indeed, critics even went so far as to quote the Fourth Gospel as the best proof that the eschatological teaching contained in the Synoptic Gospels and in St Paul's Epistles was in the early Church gradually abandoned owing to the disappointment at the delay of the Second Advent.

Now at the outset it is obvious that the eschatological problem in the Fourth Gospel can be tackled neither by a combination of eschatology with apocalypse nor by regarding the Gospel as an eschatological work throughout. In his great Commentary on St John, Rudolf Bultmann has adopted the latter method of interpretation, maintaining it throughout with much force and consistency. However, although he firmly rejects any attempt to interpret the Johannine texts in a "spiritualizing" manner, he does, nevertheless, himself very often commit this very error: and this leads him directly into spiritualism and mysticism. For the real message of the Fourth Gospel, as he sees it, is that man through faith is to gain "self-knowledge", that is, man is to come to a clear perception of the eschatological situation in which he is standing. This, however, turns eschatology into mysticism. For the mark of mysticism is that the individual experiences the fulfilment, alone, here and now. True eschatology, on the other hand, looks forward towards a fulfilment in the future, and is concerned primarily not with the salvation of the individual but with that of the community as a whole (lit. the collective). Although eschatology has frequently been misused and made to serve the purposes of spiritual self-seeking it is, nevertheless, in its essence not an expression of the concern of the individual for his own future wellbeing. On the contrary, it expresses the care of the faithful for the salvation of their fellow-men. It is an attempt to find an answer to the question as to what will happen to the many who are ungodly and indifferent when this age comes to an end, and that which is to come takes its beginning.

The Johannine eschatology will remain misunderstood or a matter of doubt until we discover the "collective", that is the Church, in the Fourth Gospel. Then two alternatives remain, both of which are outlined above. There is, however, also a third method of approach, namely to consider eschatology in connection with the Church. It is hoped that this will show the eschatology of the Fourth Gospel to be true and that it will also prove fruitful towards a better understanding of the text of the Gospel as a whole.

2. *The Idea of the Church*

The Christian Church is a "collective" characterized by faith in Christ Jesus. Other human "collectives" such as race, tribe, family, language, state, party, and so forth are dependent upon "natural" or social factors. These factors are by no means lacking in the Church. They are capable of either supporting and stimulating or of seriously hindering her work in the world. But it is the faith in Christ that gives to the "collective" of the Church its peculiar character. This does not mean that the Church has no "exterior" marks of her existence. Faith has need of such "exterior" marks in order that it may be kindled and kept alive. If it is really alive it will itself, in its turn, inevitably bear witness to its existence. This is true both with regard to the faith of the individual and to that of the "collective". The main marks of the Church seem to be the following: the Cult, the Ministry, the Confession, and the Mission.

(a) *The Cult* is the truest expression of the life of the Church. For just as the Church is something other and more than the sum of the number of her individual members, so, too, her life is something other and more than the sum of their spiritual lives. The cult is the manifestation both to

God and to man of this common life of the Church. Already in the Old Testament we find that the cult was the primary means of communion between God and his Chosen People. The cult of the New Covenant has its foundation and its centre in the Eucharist which Christ himself instituted. It is also a continuation of that fellowship of prayer which he established with his disciples during his earthly life.

The cult is, however, continually underestimated by the representatives of two opposed schools of thought. On the one hand there are those who stress the importance of right doctrine (intellectualism); on the other hand those who stress the importance of right living (moralism). But in the liturgy both doctrine and life meet. It is, therefore, the most perfect expression of the faith of the "collective" and it is also the best means of kindling and furthering the faith of the individual. It is the expression of the Christ-life of the "collective", and it can therefore stimulate the Christ-life of the individual. It is perhaps possible to imagine individual Christians not dependent upon a Christian cult; but to conceive of a Church without a cult is impossible. Did such a Church exist, it would be well on the way to destruction and death.

(b) *The Christian Ministry* was not invented by the Church. It has been a mark of her peculiar character from the very beginning. It is a sign that the Church is created "from above" and not by men. It is a function belonging to her very existence, instituted by Christ so that the members of his Body may receive the right administration of the Word and the Sacraments. The ministry is to protect the sacredness of the Church's confession, and to guard that life which, according to the Lord's will, is to be the mark of his Church. It is also an expression of the unity of the Church and of her constant dependence upon Christ. For those who "minister" possess their power and authority neither in virtue of any personal qualifications nor in virtue of any human commission but solely in virtue of the commission given to them by the Lord of the Church and in the power of his promise, "Lo, I am with you always, even to the end of the world."

(c) The Church has been from the beginning a *confessing Church*: that is, she "confesses" always that Jesus Christ is her Lord. This confession is the adequate expression of the Church's faith and indicates her peculiar character as a "collective", namely that she is the possession of Christ. This confession is not created by the Church but is part of her essential character and given to her in the revelation through which she was founded.

(d) Finally, the sense of "*mission*" is one of the original marks of the Church. Here again the mission is not created by the Church: it is not an expression of her own pretentiousness or desire for power, nor of such a desire on the part of her individual members. On the contrary, it is the expression of the indwelling, expansive power within the Church, that power which from the beginning existed in the group of disciples who went forth from Jerusalem to conquer the world. This power is still present and active wherever the Church is full of faith and life. Church history teaches us that missionary activity is not only an expression of the Church's spiritual vigour but that, in its turn, it strengthens her faith and helps to perfect her life.

If we are to find any traces of thought about the Church or any consciousness of her existence in the Fourth Gospel, we must then first of all look for these marks of the Church: the Cult, the Ministry, the Confession, and the Mission. This, therefore, is the task with which we shall be concerned in the next two chapters.

3. *The Peculiar Character of Eschatology*

It is necessary first to attempt to clarify the meaning of the term eschatology. Already we have pointed out two misinterpretations which have given to the word a *superficial* and *ephemeral* meaning.

Eschatology has been given a *superficial* interpretation when it has been identified with apocalypse and taken to mean only "the doctrine of the last things". Much human wisdom and intelligence has been spent in trying to map out the events of the last days and of the world to come, although Jesus emphatically warned his disciples not to try to find out those secrets which are revealed not even to the angels in heaven. The most serious mistake in this so-called eschatology is, that it is detached from the present, the "now". Thus, while professing to have a message for men in the actual present situation, it is nevertheless concerned almost entirely with inquisitive speculations regarding a remote future. As a result of this, it has failed to throw any clearer light upon the problems of the Christian faith in general. It is also significant that, interpreted in this way, eschatology has by theologians been regarded as the least important part of Christian doctrine.

Eschatology has been "watered down" and made *ephemeral* when it has been detached from the future and regarded as experienced only in the present—that is, when it has been described as altogether "realized". In this case it has lost its real meaning and has become transformed into mysticism, to which it is in actual fact entirely opposed. For an eschatology which does not point forward towards the consummation is no longer worthy of its name. It may satisfy longings for an individual happiness but it leaves the individual unconcerned with his responsibility for his fellow-men and their fate. This so-called eschatology is a destructive force both in theology and in the Church.

True eschatology, we believe, must be related to the future as well as to the present. It belongs to the history of redemption and like all history it has a future as well as a present. But history has also a past and therefore true eschatology must likewise be related to the past.

(i) Eschatology must be related to the *future*. This is of primary and fundamental importance. It must always point forward towards the consummation and the coming of the new age. This is to be done, not by means of idle speculations about interesting details of the last things, but by means of persistent and serious reminders of the transient nature of this present world and of the approaching end of history. It follows that there is in this world, and also in history, a meaning and that they both move forwards to a definite goal: and clearly this will have certain consequences for the individual, as well as for the Church.

(ii) Eschatology must be related to the *present*. It must show the relation of the coming judgement and consummation to faith and life of the Christian today. But it must also show how the Christian in the Church today is living already in the age of consummation. Thus the Kingdom of God is not merely something that is to come: it has come already. Christ is not only the One who, in the last days, will come on the clouds of heaven to judge the living and the dead: he has come already as the living risen Lord. He gathers his people together in his Church and sits in judgement over them daily, a judgement for death or life.

(iii) Eschatology is also related to the *past*—that is, it is related to the time in which the promises of salvation were made: the time when prophets, scribes, and priests both in word and action bore witness to the Saviour who was to come into the world. But above all, eschatology must be related to that particular time in the past when Christ accomplished his redemptive work in the world. He belongs to history; he is its very centre: and without a firm connection with the facts of redemption, that is, with the life of Jesus on earth, his passion, death, and resurrection, all eschatology will of necessity deteriorate into pious but more or less fantastic speculations.

Eschatology is thus not a flight *away* from reality past, present, or future. On the contrary it carries with it a deepening perception of the meaning of reality. It is founded on the revelation which has been given in the past, it is experienced here in the present, and it points forward towards the fulfilment. The eschatology of the Fourth Gospel, therefore, will prove to be true eschatology only if it reveals the characteristics which we have just mentioned; that is, only if it is related to the history of redemption as a whole.

In order to avoid the uncertainty which has only too often marked the use of the term eschatology in recent discussion, we shall use it with the following distinctions:

(a) *Futurist Eschatology*

This may be exclusively concerned with the future, as for example in the sayings about the Second Advent and the Resurrection at the last day. But it can also, without losing its future aspect, be concerned with the present. For example, we may recall how the Jewish cult was not only an expression of the nation's ardent longing for the coming of the Messiah but was also an opportunity for the worshipper to experience in anticipation his advent. This latter type of eschatology, therefore, is designated by the term *anticipatory or proleptic eschatology*.

(b) *Realized or Fulfilled Eschatology*

This also is related to the future; if it were not so, it would not be true eschatology. It is different from the type of eschatology just described inasmuch as it is already wholly or partially fulfilled. For example, through Christ the Old Testament prophecies of the coming Messiah were fulfilled and in him the Messianic kingdom was realized; but this does not mean that the work of Christ is finished or his kingdom finally established. Yet in certain important respects the eschatological promises have already been fulfilled and we may therefore rightly speak of realized eschatology. When this realization is experienced by us in the present we may describe it as present eschatology. Examples of this may be found in sayings about the realization of the Christian life.

4. *The Connection between Church and Eschatology*

We have already pointed out that all true eschatology must be concerned with a "collective"—that is, with the people of God, the Church. Now, whatever be the relationship between the Church and the kingdom of God, it is obvious that in both cases the reference is to the Chosen People of God—a community called forth by him in order that he may use it as the instrument for the redemption of the whole of mankind. Thus the eschatology is indissolubly linked to the thought of the people of God: God's creation is also to become God's possession, and in his redemptive purpose the Church has her given task. To her the promises of redemption are given and through her they are to come to fulfilment. If related only to the individual, eschatology is transformed into its opposite, mysticism. Only through its relation to the Church does it become truly futurist—the final consummation of the people of God.

But the Church too needs eschatology as its complement. If the message of the Gospel were only for individuals those who were willing to receive it could be won and perfected here in this life, while those who did not receive it would have to be left to their own fate. The gospel is, however, directed to the Church as a whole and the Church has among her members both good and evil men. And it is this "collective" of good and evil that is to be saved. Only eschatology can solve the problem thus posed. And this is what we mean by true eschatology: that all questions—not only those concerning the personal life-problems of the individual, but the Church's own great question of redemption—are to be answered and all problems solved.

The connection between Church and eschatology may also be seen in the relationship of each to history. As we have already shown, eschatology is related to the past as well as to the present and the future. In it the aim and meaning of history are contained. The Church is the sacred history, continuing from the resurrection of Jesus until his Parousia. Thus the Church, like eschatology, is anchored in the redemptive work once performed by Christ, while she has a message to men in the present age and awaits her consummation in the age to come.

Our task will now consist of a study of the Church, the Ministry, and the Cult in the Fourth Gospel with a view to discovering the relationship of each to eschatology (Chapters 2 and 3). The conclusions at which we may arrive regarding the Johannine eschatology will be summed up in Chapter 4. Chapter 5 contains a study of the most important theological terms used by St John in an attempt to show to what extent they are coloured by eschatological ideas. Finally, in Chapter 6 we put forward an exposition of the evangelist's idea of election which may throw some light on his conception of eschatology and Church.

This study will not take into consideration the controversial question of the homogeneity of the Fourth Gospel, a question belonging mainly to the field of literary criticism. Bultmann's drastic idea of a variety of sources has aroused much opposition, in particular from Eduard Schweizer, who, by means of a meticulous philological investigation, has attempted to stress the homogeneity of the Fourth Gospel. For our purpose it is of greater interest to study the text as it is, that is, in the form in which it has been accepted and handed down by the Church, and to search for the intentions and the theological views of which this text is an expression.

There remains the problem regarding chapter 21 and its relationship to the Gospel as a whole. Boismard, having made a philological analysis of the words employed in chapter 21 as compared with those used in the rest of the Gospel, has come to the conclusion that, from a philological point of view, the reasons *for* are as strong as those *against* the evangelist's having written that particular chapter. He suggests, therefore, that chapter 21 was written down at the request of the evangelist, and in accordance with his directions, by one of his disciples. In the following chapters we shall refer to chapter 21 as well as to the rest of the Gospel, but the former references will not be considered as conclusive evidence in any argument.

As it is a matter of general agreement that the First Epistle was written by the author of the Fourth Gospel, this Epistle will, to a certain extent, be used as providing material for our study.

CHAPTER 2

THE CHURCH AND THE MINISTRY IN THE GOSPEL OF ST JOHN

5. *The Doctrine of the Church in the Fourth Gospel*

IN THIS Gospel, we shall not find a deliberately formulated doctrine of the Church, nor even a clearly-defined idea of the Church. This need not surprise us, however, since the author of the Gospel, and his Christian contemporaries, were actually living in that Church. Indeed, to them, she represented the natural way of living their spiritual life. She offered to them, not a religious and theological problem, but the obvious medium for the practical expression of their faith. In spite of this it would surprise us if there were no traces in the Gospel of the existence of the Church. And in point of fact, such traces do exist; for although we do not meet the word "*ecclesia*", nor such expressions as the Pauline "Body of Christ", yet both in individual passages and also in the Gospel as a whole, the reality of the existence of the Church is clearly implied.

Thus we find the author's conception of Jesus' work on earth portrayed as a consistent whole. Everything is seen, estimated, and explained in relation to his death and resurrection. These events are inseparable acts in the drama of redemption. Together they form that drama: and it is the central theme of the Gospel—the "lifting-up" or "Exaltation" of Jesus, towards which all his words and actions tend. Moreover his Exaltation is the key which gives significance to all that he does and says. Without it the Incarnation would be purposeless and unintelligible, whereas it is the first and all-important step in the journey of the Eternal Word through his human nature back to the bosom of the Father. Thus the Exaltation throws light upon the Incarnation, of which, indeed, it is the necessary corollary: and apart from the Incarnation it cannot itself be truly understood. Furthermore it provides the background for a right interpretation of the teaching of Jesus; it gives their proper significance to his miracles which are shown to be in very truth the works of God[1]; while, more important than all else, it provides the right foundation for faith.[2] The Exalted Christ is not only the Lord who founded his Church once upon a time at a definite point in history: he is her Risen and Ascended Master who still lives and works within her. For the Church of Christ came into existence through the death and resurrection of Jesus—those crucial acts in the drama of his "lifting-up"—and she awaits her consummation at his Parousia. It is only from within the Church, possessed by and possessing his interpretative Spirit, that the life and teaching of Jesus can be truly understood.

Let us turn now to St John's idea of the Church. We shall find it in his conception of the life of Jesus; for he realizes that that is not merely something which happened a long time ago, but that it is an ever-present reality. Thus he quotes Jesus as having said, "I, if I be lifted up from the earth, will draw all men unto me."[3] This saying contains the whole of the Fourth Gospel's "Church-theology". The Church is anchored in the death and resurrection of Christ. She is thus founded not on myth but on historical reality, called into being not by human hands but by the intervention of God Himself. The Church is built up when men gather round the Exalted One—Christ lifted up on the Cross, and lifted up in glory—and they so gather, not of their own accord, but drawn by Christ to himself. For the Church is nothing else than the continued presence of the Risen

[1] John 2.4; 5.21; 6.35; 9.3; 11.25.
[2] John 3.14, 15; 8.28; 12.32; 20.8. [3] John 12.32.

Lord with his disciples, still speaking to them in his words and acting on them through his sacraments.

This aspect of St John's Church-consciousness we shall be considering in the next chapter, which deals with the cult. Here, we should note, however, the eschatological view which St John consistently takes of every detail of Jesus' life on earth. Everything in his Gospel points forward to the great decisive "hour", the hour of suffering, death, lifting up, and glorification, which is at once the climax and the end of the earthly work of Jesus and also the beginning of his work in the Church. Thus we read: "Mine hour is not yet come"; "the hour cometh"; "his hour was not yet come". But in chapter 19, v. 27 we read: "And from that hour that disciple took her to his own home."

It is a serious mistake in theological thinking about the Church if we erect a sharp and insurmountable barrier between the death and resurrection of Jesus, and the life which he now lives in Heaven and within his Mystical Body the Church. Sacred history is often regarded as coming to an end at Christ's Exaltation, the development of the Church through his Apostles and their successors being frequently treated as though it were a series of events in ordinary history. The author of the Fourth Gospel, however, through the intimate connection which he sees between the hour of Christ's glorification in passion, death, and resurrection and his continued work in Heaven, in and on behalf of his followers, refuses to admit any such division. This is most clearly shown in the discourses in the Upper Room.[1]

We will now turn our attention to those passages in which Jesus speaks of himself as the King of his people, the Good Shepherd, and the True Vine; for it is here that we find most clearly expressed the relationship between Christ and his followers, a relationship which, in its turn, constitutes the very essence of the Church.

---

[1] John 14.12, 13, 19; 16.7, 23–28.

6. *The King and the People*

It is remarkable how often in this Gospel Jesus is spoken of as King—a title which appears more frequently in St John than in the Synoptic Gospels and which, moreover, is not confined to the story of the Passion. Thus, Nathanael acknowledges Jesus to be the King of Israel[1]; the multitude desire to make him their King after the Feeding of the Five Thousand[2]; at the Triumphal Entry he is hailed as the King of Israel.[3] Pilate asks, "Art thou the King of the Jews?"[4]; while at the very end of his earthly ministry the title "King" occurs in the superscription of his accusation placed upon the Cross.[5] Furthermore, Jesus himself does not repudiate this title of King; rather he accepts it, explaining at the same time that his Kingdom is not of this world.[6]

Now it is a well-known fact that, according to Jewish tradition, the Messiah was to spring from the House of David and that he would therefore be entitled to be called "King". Moreover, it was as a political usurper that Jesus was brought by his accusers before Pilate and it was as such that he was condemned by him to be put to death. It is, however, obvious that, to St John, the giving of the title of "King" to Jesus carried with it a deeper significance than was realized by either the enthusiastic crowd who thus hailed him, or the suspicious and wrongly-informed Roman Governor who thus condemned him. What was it, then, that inspired Nathanael's acknowledgement of Jesus as Israel's King? Why, again, after the miracle of the Feeding of the Five Thousand, were the people so ready to welcome him as their King? What was the meaning of that title of "King" which Jesus himself undoubtedly accepted and what, above all, was the significance of the trilingual superscription on the Cross?

Now according to prophecy when the Son of David, the Messiah, should at length appear, he would gather together

[1] John 1.49. [2] John 6.15. [3] John 12.13.
[4] John 18.33, 39; 19.14. [5] John 19.19, 21. [6] John 18.36.

the people of God that were scattered abroad and would reign as King over the new Israel thus established. To him, furthermore, both Moses and the Prophets had borne witness, whilst at his appearing, the great signs of the Messianic Age would take place. Among these signs would be the repetition of the miracle of the Manna[1]—the expectation of which explains why the multitude after the Feeding of the Five Thousand so spontaneously hailed Jesus as their King. It is clear, therefore, that St John is trying to show that in Jesus, the ancient Jewish longing for the Messiah was at last finding fulfilment.

Nathanael's confession, "Thou art the Son of God; Thou art the King of Israel",[2] is very important in this connection. It must be interpreted in relation to the term applied by Jesus to Nathanael[3]—an Israelite indeed (ἀληθῶς 'Ισραηλίτης) —a designation which may be taken to signify a member of the true people of God. Thus, the dialogue between Jesus and Nathanael shows how Christ, the King, acknowledges one of his subjects, and how, in his turn, this subject acknowledges Christ as King. The name of "Israel" in the Old Testament, however, signified not a political or racial but rather a religious group. Israel was God's chosen people, deriving her peculiar status from the covenant that he had established with her.

In the beginning this covenant relationship found its chief expression in the cult; but after the establishment of the monarchy it became centred round the person of the King, who at one and the same time represented the people to God and God to the people and who was proclaimed at his coronation to be God's Son.[4]

In the Fourth Gospel Jesus is acknowledged as the Son of God and as the King of Israel from the very beginning of his ministry. Now although in one sense the baptism of Jesus may be regarded as a kind of enthronement, it is, neverthe-

---

[1] Exod. 16.4.   [2] John 1.49.   [3] John 1.47.
[4] Ps. 2.7; 89.26–28; 110.1–3; 2 Sam. 7.14; 1 Chron. 22.10.

less, neither through it nor in virtue of it that he is both Son and King. These titles have belonged to him from before the foundation of the world. He is, from all eternity, God's preexistent Son. This conception in the Johannine writings is quite different from that of the Old Testament.[1]

Now this eternal Sonship of Jesus is the theme which dominates the whole of the Fourth Gospel. It is true that Jesus speaks of himself as the "Son of Man". More often, however, he refers to himself simply as "the Son"—an expression always used in close connection with the phrase "the Father". Nathanael and John the Baptist distinctly acknowledge him to be the "Son of God",[2] while the same title leads both to accusations from the Jews[3] and also to confessions of faith on the part of believers.[4] The conception of Jesus as the Son of God is not incompatible with the thought of him as the Messianic King; for in Jesus all Messianic expectations are fulfilled. This is the significance of Nathanael's confession.

When we turn from the title "Son of God" to the specific reference to Jesus as King, we find from recent studies in comparative religion that the so-called "King" ideology has left traces in the literature not only of the Hebrews but also of almost all mankind. It has been specially noted and studied in the Near East, where it has passed from generation to generation and from nation to nation in very varied rites and myths. Everywhere, however, the King is the central religious figure, who, representing God to the people and the people to God, is frequently referred to as God's "Son". Now the liturgical and mythological ideas are, as one would expect, very varied. Nevertheless, it has been possible to fix a "ritual pattern" containing the main features of the form of this "King" ideology. The pattern is as follows:

(1) A fictitious fight against enemies in which the King is victorious.

[1] John 1.1; 3.13, 31; 6.46, 62; 8.14; 13.3; 16.27; 17.5, 24.
[2] John 1.49; 1.34.   [3] John 19.7.   [4] John 20.31.

(2) The King is proclaimed conqueror of the world.
(3) The King is admonished to reign in righteousness.
(4) The regalia are given to the King.
(5) Food and drink for immortality are given to the King; he is baptised and is anointed with oil.
(6) The King is proclaimed the Son of God.
(7) The King is enthroned on the throne of God.
(8) The King celebrates the sacred wedding (ἱερὸς γάμος).

To this pattern may be added another common characteristic, namely:

(9) The supernatural birth of the King.

Traces of most of these ritual phases have been found in the Old Testament, especially in the Psalter, and it is obvious that all of these conceptions have influenced the Jewish cult and Messianic tradition. The cult ceremonies of the Feast of Tabernacles, in particular, seem to have helped to keep alive among the people the idea of the fighting and conquering King, so that this Messianic hope of the future continued in all its freshness. We shall deal in the next chapter with the question of the Jewish cult as the background of the eschatology in St John's Gospel. Here we will but draw attention to this cult and to the important part played by it in keeping alive among the people the expectation of the Messianic King.

Now in setting out to draw some parallels between the Fourth Gospel and the ritual pattern of the King ideology, we must make one point clear—namely that the life of Jesus cannot be pinned down to or confined within the limits of a liturgical pattern. Nevertheless, there are in this Gospel certain interesting points which seem to indicate that the Evangelist has arranged his material in a way which suggests the liturgical pattern of the King ideology. For example, the ritual fight fought by the King has its counterpart in Jesus' cleansing of the temple, an incident placed by St John in a prominent position at the very beginning of his Gospel[1]; while it is likely that the same fight is reflected in the heated discussions between Jesus and the "Jews" in the Temple at Jerusalem. Again the cult ceremony of the King's enthronement has its counterpart in Jesus' Triumphal Entry into Jerusalem,[2] where the palm branches bear a distinct resemblance to the procession with willow branches during the Feast of Tabernacles and where the multitude, quoting Ps. 118.26, cry out, "Blessed is he that cometh in the name of the Lord", significantly adding according to most MSS., "and the King of Israel". The water ceremony at the Feast of Tabernacles reminds us of the baptism of the King, an important feature in the ritual pattern; but it is lifted up and transformed by Jesus' proclamation of himself as the source of true and living water[3]; while the anointing at Bethany[4] corresponds to the ritual anointing of the King with oil. Here, however, St John makes an important commentary, namely, that this anointing is for Christ's burial.[5]

In one important point the Fourth Gospel differs from the liturgical pattern; for whereas in the ancient King cult the King who was to give his life in propitiation for the sins of the people and as a surety for a good harvest was replaced by a substitute victim, in this Gospel Jesus, the King, in very truth offers himself on behalf of his own. "The Crown of Thorns and the Purple Robe"[6] are his regalia: the scorn and mockery of the soldiers[7] is an acclamation of his royal dignity: and he is enthroned on the throne of the Cross.[8] The idea of the epiphany of the King might be traced in Jesus' utterances in the Upper Room when he repeatedly assured his disciples of his return.[9] Moreover, we might also venture to find in the words of St John the Baptist, "He that hath the bride is the bridegroom . . .",[10] a reference to the

[1] John 2.13–16. [2] John 12.12–19. [3] John 4.14; 7.37.
[4] John 12.1–11. [5] John 12.7. [6] John 19.2.
[7] John 19.3. [8] John 3.14; 8.28; 12.32.
[9] John 14.3, 18, 28; 16.22. [10] John 3.29.

union between Christ and the Church, the counterpart to the sacred marriage of the ritual pattern. Thus the "mystical marriage"—the union with himself which Christ may vouchsafe to individual members of his Body—is seen to have its roots in the very being of the Church herself. Finally, we may, perhaps, catch a glimpse of the idea of the unknown origin of the King in the following passages:

> 6.42. "Is not this Jesus... whose father and mother we know? How doth he now say, I am come down out of heaven?"
> 7.27. "Howbeit, we know this man whence he is: but when the Christ cometh, no one knoweth whence he is."
> 8.14. "I know whence I came, and whither I go; but ye know not whence I come, or whither I go."
> 9.29. "As for this man, we know not whence he is."

Later on we shall examine more closely those details in the ritual pattern that are especially connected with the Jewish cult. But when we see the interesting agreement between the Fourth Gospel and the King ideology, we cannot but ask whether this can be the result of mere coincidence, especially as this agreement is even greater than that which existed between the Old Testament and the ritual cult. Furthermore, can it be mere coincidence that the Fourth Gospel agrees with the ritual pattern to a much greater extent than do the Synoptic Gospels? Faced with these questions it is probably not too bold to suppose that St John has consciously arranged his material in this way, so as to stress the conception of Jesus as the longed-for King. Jesus is here portrayed as the King in whom, on the one hand, the long-delayed Messianic hope of the Jews found its fulfilment; and on the other hand, in whose person and work mankind's ancient longing for redemption was satisfied.

This theory finds support in the passage in chapter 4 where the inhabitants of Sychar acknowledge Jesus to be the Saviour of the world. This conception was entirely foreign to the Jews but quite natural to the more Hellenized Samaritans.

This study of the "King" ideology has given us a deeper understanding of the ancient unity between the King and his people; for in it, as in the Old Testament, the King represents not only the people to God but also God to the people. If we compare this conception of the King's function with the Old Testament idea of a race chosen to be God's instrument for the salvation of all mankind, we can realize something of what St John meant in proclaiming Jesus to be King.

The Fourth Gospel agrees with the Synoptists in quoting the superscription on the Cross, as naming Jesus, "King of the Jews". Unlike the Synoptists St John adds that this superscription was written in Hebrew and Latin and Greek[1]—a reminder to his readers that the kingship of Jesus was of significance not for Israel only but for the whole world. Loisy quite rightly speaks of this trilingual superscription as a proclamation of the universal royalty of Jesus: "Les trois langues signifient visiblement la royauté universelle du Christ." Thus Christ is seen to be the King of the House of David who, although rejected and condemned by his own, nevertheless fulfilled the promises concerning the Messiah that was to come. Furthermore, although scorned and put to death by the representatives of the Roman Empire, he, nevertheless, fulfilled the hope attached to the idea of King by the different races of this Empire in their several cults and myths. He is the King who, both when he accomplished his sacrifice of propitiation for the good of the people and also when he was exalted and glorified on their behalf, truly embodied them as their inclusive representative. Thus in him the eschatological expectation attached to the idea of "King" alike by Jews and Gentiles found fulfilment. That is why St John so pointedly speaks of Jesus as "King". His Kingdom, however, forms a sharp contrast, not only to the dreams of political power among the Jews—"My Kingdom is not of this world"[2]—but also to the mythological

[1] John 19.20.   [2] John 18.36.

speculations of the pagan world: "Thou sayest that I am a King: to this end am I come that I should bear witness to the truth."[1] The truth is reality as opposed to imagination and myth—historical reality which continuously points towards its fulfilment and which is, therefore, an eschatological concept. Thus the Kingdom of Jesus is neither subject to human imperfection and decay nor is it merely an illusory dream of the future. It is realized in the midst of this world but awaits its fulfilment in the world to come. It is the Church. Pilate's trilingual superscription on the Cross appears to be a scornful mockery of the man condemned to death as well as of his compatriots. In actual fact, without realizing it, the Roman Governor is, on behalf of the official Roman Empire, proclaiming Jesus as the real universally longed-for King and Saviour. Or does St John, perhaps, wish to indicate that, in some dim way, Pilate sensed this? His account of the Governor's repeated efforts to save Jesus, and of his refusal to alter the superscription on the Cross, may bear witness to this supposition. The answer to this we shall never know.

It is probably not too bold to suppose that the insistence in this Gospel on Jesus as King is also a protest against the Emperor worship of the Romans; this again is supported by the trilingual superscription on the Cross. The whole world must be made to know that Jesus is the real King—the King of the chosen Jewish nation and, therefore, the King of the whole world. Nevertheless, his Kingdom is not of this world[2]—a fact which in its turn means that, as regards kingly authority, he is above not only the Roman Governor but also above this Governor's Emperor.[3] Everyone who insists on the absolute supremacy of the Emperor must, therefore, be opposing Jesus.[4] With biting irony St John pictures the Jews uttering their protests of eager loyalty to the Emperor, in the hope that they might thus bring Jesus to the Cross: "If thou let this man go, thou art not Caesar's

[1] John 18.37.   [2] John 18.36.
[3] John 19.11.   [4] John 19.12.

friend: whosoever maketh himself a king speaketh against Caesar."

The royal dignity of Jesus is made manifest in his "lifting-up" on the Cross. The Caesars were exalted to the dignity of gods at their death and in the succeeding burial and apotheosis. The following words uttered by Vespasian when at the point of death bear a striking witness to this fact: "Vae, puto deus fio." And here, in opposition to the Roman Empire and its claims for worship of its dead—and, at times, even of its living—Caesars, the young Church placed the crucified Christ, bravely, and with unshakeable faith proclaiming, "Regem habemus."

Finally, the expression "the kingdom of God" which appears so frequently in the Synoptic Gospels is used only twice by St John, namely in chapter 3, verses 3 and 5. This passage we shall be studying more closely later on. Suffice it to say here that in this text we catch a glimpse of Christ as the King who gathers together to himself his subjects—by means of their being born again of water and of the spirit.

In chapter 18.37 we read: "To this end was I born. . . . Everyone that is of the truth heareth my voice." As King, Christ gathers together his people, namely those who hear his voice. Behind this picture we can discern St John's conception of the Church. Indeed it is more than a picture, it is a reality: the people of God gathered around its heavenly King. This King, however, does not merely gather the Church around his own person: he personifies this Church, thus revealing her eschatological character. Thus the Church is the fulfilment of the longing for the new kingdom of both Jews and Gentiles, while at the same time she is the promise of this Kingdom's consummation in eternity.

7. *The Shepherd and the Flock* (ch. 10.1–18)

Ἐγώ εἰμι in vv. 7, 9, 11, and 14 is, according to Bultmann, a formula of recognition, given in answer to the question,

"Who is the expected one, the looked-for one?" The same is true with regard to the corresponding expression in chapter 6.35, 41, 48, 51; in chapter 8.12, and in chapter 15.1, 5. The word ἐγώ in all these places is really predicate. Thus a correct translation would be "The good—that is the only true—shepherd, it is I." This, together with the solemn affirmation, shows the importance of the statement. For us the important question is, "What is the significance of Jesus thus proclaiming himself to be the only true shepherd of the sheep?"

The relationship of the sheep to the good shepherd is expressed in the words ἀκούει (they hear his voice); ἀκολυθεῖ (he goeth before them and the sheep follow him); οἴδασιν (they know his voice); σωθήσεται (shall be saved); and νομὴν εὑρήσει (shall find pasture).

Thus the word "sheep" stands for a group, the characteristics of which are hearing and following, etc.—activities which presuppose some sort of guidance and organization. This guidance is given by the shepherd who is described as entering in by the door (εἰσερχόμενος διὰ τῆς θύρας) (v. 2); who calls his own sheep by name (Φωνεῖ κατ' ὄνομα) (v. 3); who leads his own sheep out (ἐξάγει) (v. 3); who goes before them (ἔμπροσθεν αὐτῶν πορεύεται) (v. 4); and who finally even lays down his life for their safety (τὴν ψυχὴν αὐτοῦ τίθησιν ὑπὲρ τῶν προβάτων) (v. 11). These passages describing carefully the functions of both the shepherd and the sheep have been inserted by the Evangelist for the obvious reason of emphasizing the unique relationship between the shepherd and the sheep. A flock is something more than the mere sum of its individual members; it is guided and guarded by a shepherd. This gives security to the sheep and also demands their obedience. The flock is not just drifting along without a plan but is led to places for pasture and rest according to the shepherd's will. Furthermore, the members of the flock are intimately connected both with the shepherd and with one another. The shepherd knows his sheep and "calls them all by their name". It is quite clear that St John here wishes to give a picture of the Church, gathered together under the guidance and protection of her Lord, while fighting against the incursions of thieves and robbers (v. 1).

Now the thought of Jahveh as the Shepherd and of Israel as his sheep occurs frequently in the Old Testament.[1] There also occurs, however, in the Old Testament the thought of a shepherd whom God promises to send as his own representative to his people; and this shepherd is, as a rule, envisaged as the promised King.[2]

It is significant that the Shepherd passage in St John, chapter 10, also contains clear references to the death of Jesus. The general statement about the Shepherd's readiness to risk his life for his sheep is combined with Jesus' solemn declaration that he will die for his people. Here the King and the Shepherd pattern is woven together. For just as Christ the King wins his people and gathers them together through his death on the Cross, so also does Christ the good shepherd gather together his sheep by offering his life for them. This sacrifice is not an expression of weakness on the part of the shepherd, but rather of his power over life—over his own life as well as over that of his flock: "I have power to lay it down and I have power to take it again." This, then, is the same thought as that of the King's deliberate sacrifice of his life for the good of the people, a thought which recurs again and again throughout the Fourth Gospel. It is specially conspicuous at the betrayal, where Judas plays a very passive part, and the soldiers are overwhelmed with awe, while Jesus all the time retains the initiative and hands himself over to the enemy with the thrice-repeated proclamation ἐγώ εἰμι.

Thus Christ, the Shepherd, is also the King chosen by God to govern the chosen people of God. In Greek thought,

[1] Gen. 48.15; Ps. 23.1; 28.9; 77.20; 78.52; 80.1; 95.7; 100.3; Isa. 40.11; Jer. 23.1; Ezek. 34.11.
[2] Jer. 23.5; Ezek. 34.23; 37.24.

too, the King is sometimes spoken of as the shepherd of the sheep. This shows that "shepherd" ideology was known and loved among Jews and Gentiles alike, expressing as it did man's longing for order and security in a stormy and restless age.

Fascher takes "the fold" to mean Israel as fenced round by the Law. This interpretation gives to the passage a strong polemic character, the words about thieves and robbers in verse 8 being obviously directed against the rulers of the Jewish people. The two conceptions of Jesus as the Messiah and Jesus as the Redeemer dominate the Good Shepherd chapter. In all this it is easy to trace St John's idea of the Church, namely that those sheep which are enclosed in the sheepfold of Israel, as well as those that are scattered abroad in the Gentile world, are all to be gathered into one, so that there will be but "one fold"—or better, "one flock" —under the guidance of "one shepherd" (v. 16).

The final words in v. 16, μία ποίμνη, εἷς ποιμήν (one flock and one shepherd), picture the unity between Christ, the Shepherd, and his sheep. The unity is the reflection of that unity between the Father and the Son to which the Fourth Evangelist constantly refers. Thus, in the prologue to his Gospel, St John writes, "The Word was God", whilst elsewhere that unity is expressed in a variety of ways: for example, he records Jesus as having said, "He that hath seen me hath seen the Father",[1] and again, "... that the Father is in me and I in him".[2] The chief expression of this unity— Father, Son, and Church—is to be found in chapter 17.21: "that they all may be one; even as thou, Father, art in me, and I in thee, that they also may be one in us".

8. *The Vine and the Branches* (chapter 15.1–17)

Here we meet with the familiar words, "I am the true Vine", words which, according to Eduard Schweizer, cannot

[1] John 14.9.   [2] John 10.38; 14.10.

be derived from anything in the Old Testament but must be related to the myths about the tree of life, myths which appear so frequently in all religions. The conception of the vine, however, plays a very important part in the Old Testament. It is true that it signifies Israel as a whole and not simply the Messiah; and so far Schweizer is right in his theory: but since, as we have seen, the King personifies the people before God, we have every reason to take into account the Old Testament references to the vine if we are to come to a true understanding of St John, chapter 15. In the Old Testament, then, Israel is likened to "a luxuriant vine",[1] "a noble vine",[2] and to a "vine brought out of Egypt"[3]; while Isaiah describes her as a vineyard in the Lord's keeping.[4] Furthermore, Josephus speaks of a golden vine with clusters as tall as a man which adorned one of the porches of the Temple at Jerusalem. Now all these references indicate that the vine was a symbol often used and well known in Israel. Moreover, since the Messiah, God's Anointed One, and his chosen people were indissolubly linked together, it is most probable that Jesus' proclamation of himself as the "True Vine" was meant to imply that, in him, God's Israel had found its true fulfilment. Thus, in the person of Jesus, the Messiah, the true people of God is made manifest to the world.

Now a tree is something other and more than a mere collection of branches. Indeed, the latter are borne and sustained *by* the tree, provided that they have organic contact with it; if this contact is broken, the branches wither and die. Furthermore, it is by means of the common contact which they have with the tree that the branches have their contact one with another.

This description of the unity existing between Christ and his Church—a unity which St John speaks of in terms of the vine and the branches—is strongly reminiscent of St Paul's

[1] Hos. 10.1.   [2] Jer. 2.21.
[3] Ps. 80.8.   [4] Isa. 5.1, 2; 27.2, 3.

description of the Church as a body with many members.[1] What St John wishes to bring out by means of the vine imagery is apparently, on the one hand, the blessing that springs fron membership in the Church—καθαροί ἐστε (v. 3), φέρει καρπὸν πολύν (v. 5)—and, on the other hand, the great risk involved in severing oneself from her membership; for, according to St John, to break from the Church is not merely to cut oneself off from one's fellow Christians, but it is to cut oneself off from Christ himself. Furthermore, it is more than likely that in what is said here about the place of unfruitful members of the Church, we have not merely a foreshadowing of the judgement at the last day, but also a reflection of the discipline of the early Church; for another consequence of the eschatological nature of the Church is that in her, the final judgement is being realized in an anticipatory manner here and now. But such an ecclesiastical discipline naturally presupposes an organized common life with a ministry sanctioned to excommunicate the faithless. That the picture-language about the vine and the branches is meant to describe the relationship between Christ and the Church is further supported by the fact that we find in this passage an important reference to the death of Jesus: "Greater love hath no man than this, that a man lay down his life for his friends." Although it may seem that the picture of the vine and the branches is no longer being used, certain important words such as "tree", and "bear fruit" show that it it still occupying the Evangelist's mind. Furthermore, this way of presenting an idea is typical of St John. His reason for making use of it here, is that the vine cannot be taken as easily as can the good shepherd as an example of the true spirit of self-sacrifice unto death, while it is with the death of Christ above all else that, at this point in his gospel, the Evangelist is concerned. Indeed, the death of Christ is the last and most important thing that St John has

---

[1] Rom. 12.5; 1 Cor. 12.12, 13, 27.

CHURCH AND MINISTRY IN ST JOHN 29

to tell concerning him, whether he be pictured as universal King, Good Shepherd or True Vine.

The frequent use of the verb μένειν (to abide) in this passage (it occurs no less than ten times) also leads us to suppose that the Evangelist is referring here to the relationship between Christ and his Church: for μένειν, as will be shown in greater detail later on, is one of St John's favourite words when writing about the Church. It occurs in the well-known commandment of love (vv. 9–10), in the reference to his choice of the disciples to be his "friends" who are to bear fruit and whose fruit is to abide (vv. 15–16), in the description of the efficacy of the prayer of those who abide in him (vv. 7, 16) and finally in the joy, unfailing and abiding, which it is his desire that his disciples should possess (v. 11).

In many places and in various ways St John tries to express the joy of the eschatological Messianic age. Especially is this the case in the story of the marriage at Cana of Galilee[1] and in the account of the miracle of the Feeding of the Five Thousand.[2] It is, therefore, not unreasonable to suspect that the same Messianic joy is discernible in Jesus' reference to himself as the True Vine. Since the vine is the symbol of the joyful marriage feast, it therefore points to the joyful covenant which Christ has established with his Church—a covenant foreshadowed, indeed, in the Old Dispensation but fulfilled and transcended now in the Eucharist. This joy of the new covenant is vividly expressed in the words "... that my joy might remain in you, and that your joy might be full" (v. 11).

9. *The Mission*

The idea of "mission" is contained in the very conception of the Church. For if the Church is the eschatological Messianic Kingdom, it is essential that it be made accessible to all men. It is clear from the many sayings of Jesus implying a missionary charge that St John is very much alive

[1] John 2.1–11.   [2] John 6.1–14.

to the importance of this command of Christ. But since the Fourth Gospel is addressed to the Church, the missionary command is directed, not to the world nor to the whole of Israel, but to his own chosen followers. The words πέμπειν (to send) and ἀποστέλλειν (to send forth) are used, with reference both to the Father's sending the Son, and also to the Son's sending forth of his disciples. It is with the latter reference that we shall be concerned here. Thus:

> 4.38. "I sent you to reap that whereon ye bestowed no labour."
> 13.16. "Neither is he that is sent greater than he that sent him."
> 13.20. "He that receiveth whomsoever I send, receiveth me; and he that receiveth me, receiveth him that sent me."
> 17.18. "As thou hast sent me into the world, even so have I also sent them unto the world."

It is clear from these examples that the Father's sending of the Son is the motive and pattern of Jesus' sending of his disciples into the world. Similarly, as the Son is the Father's representative ἀπόστολος in the world, so too, in like manner, the disciples are the representatives—"apostles" of Christ. Thus missionary activity is a function of the continuing work of Christ in the Church.

The following have been pointed out as the most important "missionary" passages in the Fourth Gospel:

(1) "Behold the Lamb of God which taketh away the sin of the world" (ch. 1.29).
(2) "As Moses lifted up the serpent in the wilderness, even so must the Son of Man be lifted up, that whosoever believeth in him should not perish but have eternal life" (ch. 3.14–15).
(3) "And other sheep I have which are not of this fold; them also I must bring, and they shall hear my voice; and there shall be one fold and one shepherd" (ch. 10.16).
(4) "I, if I be lifted up from the earth, will draw all men unto me" (ch. 12.32).

(5) "Except a corn of wheat fall into the ground and die, it abideth alone; but if it die it bringeth forth much fruit" (ch. 12.24).
(6) "... that Jesus should die for the nation; and not for that nation only but that also he should gather together in one the children of God that were scattered abroad" (ch. 11.51–52).
(7) "Neither for these only do I pray, but for them also that shall believe on me through their word; that they may all be one" (ch. 17.20).

In each of these texts two thoughts constantly appear:

(1) The reason behind the Church's missionary activity of the "lifting-up" of Jesus.

(2) The aim of this missionary work is to gather together in the Church and to bring into one the children of God that are scattered abroad. The classical missionary passage in St John, however, is to be found in chapter 4.35–38. This passage about the sower and the reaper rejoicing together shows the missionary work of Christ's followers as an expression of the eschatological nature of the church (the eschatology here being both "fulfilled", that is, potentially realized, and yet also "futurist", that is, awaiting future consummation). The form of the word ἀπέστειλα shows that the statement is made from the point of view of the Church. It cannot be proved with certainty that ὁ σπείρων refers to Jesus. But it is certain that St John thinks of him as the foremost of those characterized in the words ἄλλοι κεκοπιάκασιν (others have laboured). The clearest understanding of this text is obtained when it is taken as a reflection of the missionary work of the early Church where, since the sowing and the reaping were experienced simultaneously, the disciples took part in an eschatological cycle of events, their contribution being at one and the same time both the fruit of someone else's effort—that is, of the effort of other disciples or of Jesus himself—and also the seed which was to produce the harvest of those who should come after. Such an interpretation, furthermore, throws light upon the meaning of that

otherwise incomprehensible acknowledgement made by the Samaritans, "This is indeed the Christ, the Saviour of the world."[1]

Another passage of profound missionary significance is found in chapter 7.37–38: "If any man thirst, let him come unto me and drink. He that believeth on me, as the Scripture has said, out of his belly shall flow rivers of living water." We cannot here make a detailed exegesis of this very difficult passage, the full meaning of which can only be appreciated in the light of its context. But these words were uttered by Jesus as he stood in the Temple at Jerusalem on the last and most important day of the Feast of Tabernacles when the solemn water ceremony was taking place. In them, he both declared himself to be the true well of life-giving water which would quench all thirst, while he also promised that those who came to him in faith would themselves become wells of life-giving water—that is, that they would become springs of eternal life, able to supply the needs of others. The same thought is found in chapter 4.14: "But the water that I shall give him shall be in him a well of water, springing up unto everlasting life." The liturgical aspect of this text will be studied more closely later on.

Yet another passage of missionary significance is found in chapter 12.20 ff, when some "Greeks", seeking Jesus, approach Andrew. This incident proves to be the prologue to that drama of the Passion which reaches its climax on the Cross: "The hour is come when the Son of Man should be glorified." For only through the death of Jesus could the Church be created and its mission begin. Clearly it is this mission for which the "Greeks" are asking. It is the Gentile world which demands the Gospel, but this cannot be given until it has itself reached its consummation through the "lifting-up" of Jesus. The same thought lies behind the words of Our Lord, "Except a corn of wheat fall into the

[1] John 4.42.

ground and die, it abideth alone; but if it die it bringeth forth much fruit" (v. 24), and again, "I, if I be lifted up from the earth, will draw all men unto me" (v. 32). Consequently, all missionary zeal is impossible and of no avail before Jesus' death and resurrection. Indeed, as Sundkler very well puts it, "Au sens le plus profond, le chemin de la Croix est celui de la mission." The suggestion of the Jews that Jesus might go out and on a mission among the "Greeks" is related by the Evangelist with considerable irony and is rejected as an impossibility, and as a new proof of the Jews' usual misunderstanding of the words and works of Jesus.

Missionary work, then, is a charge given to the disciples by their risen Master; an essential function of the Church whose task it is, during the time between the Resurrection of Jesus and his Parousia, to make both of these experiences living realities in their own lives, thereby gathering together into one the children of God that are scattered abroad so that there may be "one flock, one shepherd".[1] Thus, a deep sense of mission pervades the Fourth Gospel, a fact which may be taken as showing a strong Church-consciousness on the part of the Evangelist.

10. *The Confession of Faith*

The Church of Christ has always been a confessing Church; that is, she has always confessed her belief in Christ as her Lord and Saviour. The need for stating this confession in a definite form was felt very early in her history, while the reasons which prompted her to commit the content of her confession to writing have been summarized by Oscar Cullmann thus:

(i) Baptism and the Catechumenate.
(ii) Regular worship (Liturgy and preaching).

[1] John 10.16.

(iii) Exorcisms.
(iv) Persecution.
(v) Polemic against heresies.

Might we, perhaps, trace some of these motifs behind the "confessions" of faith in the Fourth Gospel, so as to see in them expression of a Church-consciousness? or are they simply expressions of individual belief? Let us consider the following:

(i) St John the Baptist: "Behold the Lamb of God, which taketh away the sin of the world" (ch. 1.29).
(ii) St John the Baptist: "This is the Son of God" (ch. 1.34).
(iii) Nathanael: "Thou art the Son of God; thou art the King of Israel" (ch. 1.49).
(iv) The inhabitants of Sychar: "This is indeed the Christ, the Saviour of the world" (ch. 4.42).
(v) Martha: "Thou art the Christ, the Son of God, which should come into the world" (ch. 11.27).
(vi) Thomas: "My Lord and my God" (ch. 20.28).
(vii) The purpose of the writer of this Gospel: "That ye might believe that Jesus is the Christ, the Son of God: and that believing, ye might have life through his name" (ch. 20.31).
(viii) The First Epistle of St John: "Every spirit that confesseth that Jesus Christ is come in the flesh is of God" (1 John 4.2).
(ix) The First Epistle of St John: "Whosoever shall confess that Jesus is the Son of God, God dwelleth in him and he in God" (1 John 4.15).

Cullmann has mentioned only the two latter quotations as examples of the confession of the early Church, the simple form of which was, "*Kyrios Christos*". Now these two passages from the First *Epistle* of St John seem merely directed against heresies. They are thus expressions of the apologetic activity of the early Church. What about the confessions in the *Gospel*, however, as distinct from those in the Epistles?

Several of the confessions in the Gospel when studied in

their context appear artificial in the mouth of the person uttering them and in the situation in which they are described. This is especially true of the following:

(i) Nathanael's confession which was seemingly called forth by Jesus' declaration that he had seen him already when he was under the fig tree (ch. 1.49).
(ii) The declaration made by the inhabitants of Sychar, after Jesus had been with them only two days, recognizing him as "the Saviour of the world" (ch. 4.22).

The strongest grounds for suspicion with regard to these, as also with regard to St Peter's confession[1] and Martha's declaration, "Thou art the Christ, the Son of God, which should come into the world",[2] is the fact that, according to the theology of the Fourth Gospel, the right faith in Jesus as the Messiah and, consequently, the confession inspired by this faith, are possible only after the death and resurrection of Jesus; that is, in the Church. All these confessions of faith in Christ, which, in this Gospel, are made before his "lifting-up", must therefore be considered as anticipations. In point of fact, they are the confessions of the early Church of faith in her risen Lord. Similarly, the confession of Thomas[3] must be regarded not merely as an expression of the affectionate faith of an individual disciple in his risen Master, but rather as the confession of the Church prostrate before her risen and exalted Lord.

The contents of the various confessions in the Fourth Gospel will be dealt with later, in connection with the Church's cult or liturgy. What has been of interest here is to point out the occurrence of these confessions and the peculiar form they take. For they are a further proof of the existence of the Church: and, moreover, they enable us to hear that Church confessing her faith in her Lord and Saviour.

[1] John 6.68, 69.   [2] John 11.27.
[3] John 20.28.

11. *The Ministry*

To the Church belongs also the Ministry. It is the backbone of her life, without which she would crumble and disintegrate. It is by means of the ministry that, through the Word and the Sacraments, the revelation committed to the Church is passed on to her members, for the furthering of whose faith and life the ministry is responsible. Can we now trace this ministry of the Church in the Fourth Gospel? Clearly we cannot expect to find it there as highly developed and graded as it appears later in Church history: we may, nevertheless, expect to find it in a more simple form.

It has been said already that in chapter 15.16 we seem to distinguish the discipline of the early Church and the ministry behind it. The best evidence for this ministry, however, is to be found in chapter 20, vv. 19–29, a passage more badly treated by all scholars alike than any other passage in the Fourth Gospel. Thus, Thomas is generally taken as the prototype of all doubting people—a frightening example; while the words, "Blessed are they that have not seen and yet have believed" (v. 29), are generally considered to indicate that "spiritual" faith which proceeds from hearing only, in contrast to that "lower" type of faith which asks for signs. This interpretation, however, not only leaves many questions unsolved; it also misses the main point of the whole passage.

First of all, then, we must ask the question, "Why should Thomas be the prototype of a doubting disciple?" After all, he asked only for that which had been granted unasked to the other disciples, namely that he might see the risen Lord. Moreover, since the first time that Jesus appeared to his disciples after his resurrection he did not utter a single word of reproach, why is it that he now demands of Thomas that, unlike the others, he should be able to believe without the help of sight? The explanation must be that something has come to pass between the first and second appearances of the risen Lord and that this something, in its turn, has justified and made possible the new demand to believe without seeing. And what has happened is this—namely, that the disciples have been given the gift of the Holy Spirit: "He breathed on them and said unto them, 'Receive ye the Holy Ghost'." This saying, then, is the key to the whole passage, the significance of which Thomas' doubting demand for tangible proof only serves to emphasize. Here, in other words, is the Pentecostal passage of the Fourth Gospel—the giving of the Holy Ghost which was to lead the disciples into all truth. This Holy Ghost was to make the Apostolic testimony credible when the disciples went out into the world to preach the Gospel in obedience to the command of the risen Lord and in his strength. The same Holy Ghost was to kindle faith in the hearts of the hearers.

It is significant that, in this Gospel, Jesus' giving of the Holy Ghost and his instituting of the apostolate are brought together. For there can be no doubt that it is the apostolate that is instituted by the solemn words, "As the Father hath sent me, even so send I you" (v. 21), and by the even more solemn declaration, "Whosesoever sins ye remit, they are remitted unto them; and whosesoever sins ye retain they are retained" (v. 23).

Furthermore, the Thomas incident is meant, above all, to answer the question, why does the risen Lord no longer appear to his disciples in visible form as he did on the first Easter Day? It would then be, they would say, easier to believe in his resurrection. Clearly this was a problem already in the early Church. St John wants to show that, by means of the gift of the Holy Spirit, the apostolic witness regarding the resurrection of Jesus is, in itself, worthy of belief, and that it can kindle faith in those who hear it.

This is the essential meaning of the words, "Blessed are they that have not seen and yet have believed" (v. 29). It is more blessed to live in the Church under the guidance of the Holy Spirit and so to come to faith in Christ, than to have lived before and outside the sphere of the life of the Church, and, therefore, not to be able to come to faith in the risen Lord.

From this important text, then, we can come to the following conclusions:

(i) The apostolate was, according to the Fourth Gospel, instituted simultaneously with the birth of the Church, namely when Jesus was "lifted-up" and the Holy Ghost was outpoured.

It is significant that the period of fifty days which, according to the tradition of St Luke, passed between Easter and Pentecost, is compressed in the Fourth Gospel to one single day, namely Easter Day. This need not surprise us, however, for St John thinks theologically, not chronologically, and to him it was clear that it was the death and resurrection of Jesus that brought the Church into being, while the outpouring of the Holy Ghost was the immediate and inevitable result of this his "lifting-up". The Church is that circle of his friends in which the risen Lord appeared on the first Easter-Day. Simultaneously with the Church, furthermore, the apostolate appeared before the world (v. 21), functioning among the Church's members (v. 23)—a fact which means that from the very beginning it belonged to her essential being, and was necessary for her very life.

(ii) The apostolate or ministry functions through the power of the Holy Ghost, from whose indwelling the Church herself derives her life.

(iii) The apostolate or ministry is the means by which, for all time, the Church is to spread throughout the world, while it is also the means by which she is to train her children towards an ever-increasing perception and practice of holiness.

"He breathed on them . . ." (v. 22). The exterior happenings at the outpouring of the Holy Ghost, as related in the Fourth Gospel, bear a striking resemblance to the creation of man as recorded in Genesis 2.7. This is surely no mere coincidence. What St John wants to point out is that the life once given to man in creation reaches its completion in the life given to him in the Church by Christ, through his Holy Spirit. Thus the material and the spiritual life, far from being opposed to one another, are, on the contrary, complementary—the Christ-life being the continuation of the creation life.

The Fourth Gospel says nothing about the risen Lord's again leaving his disciples; is this silence merely accidental? Or has that, too, a deep significance? We ourselves believe the latter to be the true explanation—namely, that by omitting to record the visible ascension, St John wished to indicate that the risen Christ has never left his disciples but that, on the contrary, he ever abides with them in his Church where, by means of the ministry which he has instituted, he speaks to them through his Word, forgives them their sins by his absolution, and acts with them in his Sacraments. No demand, therefore, can be made for further "appearances" of the risen Lord, since the whole life of the Church is the story of his continued and abiding Presence working through his own. This is the only serious argument against chapter 21 as belonging originally to the Fourth Gospel. Even if it has been written by the Evangelist himself, it is very probable that it has been added to the Gospel by one of his disciples who did not realize the deep significance of what we believe to have been the original ending— namely chapter 20. Such a theory might well prove the answer to the difficult question regarding the authorship of the final chapter of this Gospel.

The mark of the apostolate, however, is not only the fulfilling of the missionary charge and the holding of the keys of the Kingdom, but also the carrying on of Christ's work as the Shepherd of the sheep, an aspect illustrated in chapter 21.15-19. The thrice-repeated question, "Lovest thou me?" put to Peter by the risen Lord, and the Apostle's thrice-repeated affirmation of his love are taken by most scholars to be the apostle's restoration after his threefold denial. Bultmann, however, is inclined to see in them the instalment of St Peter in his apostolic task. These interpretations, far from being mutually exclusive, are obviously closely connected, for it is not until Peter has been restored from the degradation of his threefold denial of Jesus by a threefold affirmation of devotion made in the presence of the other disciples—that is, in the presence of the Church—that he can be established in his ministry as shepherd of Christ's sheep. The connection between this chapter and chapter 10.1–16 is obvious. It is for the Apostle to act as the envoy and representative of Christ and in his stead to shepherd the sheep. Like Christ, the Shepherd, he is not only to find pasture for the sheep, but he is also to be prepared to lay down his life for them.[1] Indeed, suffering for Christ's sake is one of the essential marks of the apostolate.

In the passages concerned with the feeding of the five thousand[2] and the washing of the disciples' feet[3] some scholars are inclined to see traces of the Church's diaconate. At the feeding of the five thousand St John does not expressly mention that the disciples took part in the distribution of the food; that they did do so can be taken for granted, since it is clearly stated in the Synoptic Gospels. Nevertheless St John is careful to tell us how, at the word of Jesus, they gathered up the fragments that remained. Since, moreover, the Synoptists also take care to relate this detail, we may assume that both they and St John saw in it a deeper significance than that of simply emphasizing the greatness of the sign. Indeed, the number of people who were fed would have been sufficient evidence for that. Rather is it meant to indicate the sacramental character of the meal. This point of view will be studied more closely in the next chapter. Here it is enough to point out that the Fourth Gospel shows the intimate relationship between the liturgy and the diaconate

[1] John 10.11; 21.18, 19   [2] John 6.1–15.
[3] John 13.1–17.

—a relationship which has existed in the Church from the very beginning.

The account of the Washing of the Disciples' Feet is usually taken, quite rightly, to be a lesson in humility and Christian service, given by Jesus to his disciples in the hour of their parting. This is indicated by his words in verse 15, "I have given you an example, that ye should do as I have done to you." The deepest significance of this text will be considered in connection with the liturgy in the Fourth Gospel. Here we will only consider whether the act of service rendered by Jesus as he washed his disciples' feet has any connection with the diaconate in the early Church. One writer talks of this washing as a "symbolic act, by means of which Jesus links the serving of the brethren to the Eucharist as an essential element in the Christian life of worship and fellowship". We shall show later on it is not right to think of the washing of the disciples' feet as a supplement to the Eucharist. It is an act, complete in itself, to be compared with Jesus' words to the disciples in St Luke, chapter 22.24–30, when during the course of their last evening together they were disputing as to who among them was the greatest. The word used in St Luke, chapter 22.26–27, is ὁ διακονῶν (deacon), while St John in chapter 13.16 has δοῦλος (slave). Both these expressions, however, might be be applied to a member of the Church's diaconate. In St John, chapter 13.16, ἀπόστολος corresponds with δοῦλος, while both these words are related to κύριος (lord) and ὁ πέμψας (he that sent him). This makes it all the more probable that we can here discern a trace of the diaconate. This probability, moreover, develops into a certainty when we note the fact that the washing of the disciples' feet is closely related to the death of Jesus, while the saying that it was not until after his "lifting-up" that they would be able fully to comprehend his action—"What I do thou knowest not now, but thou shalt know hereafter"—points in the same direction. Thus Jesus institutes the diaconate by performing the lowly and humble task of a slave—an action by which he simultaneously represents his own death and also sets an example to his disciples. Here, too, suffering is once again seen to be one of the essential marks of a minister of the Church.

Again, in chapter 12.26 there seem to be traces of the diaconate: "If any man serve me let him follow me; and where I am, there shall also my servant be." Here we meet with the forms διακονεῖν and διάκονος. Now, he who was the disciple of a rabbi was also responsible for the personal waiting on his rabbi, was his διάκονος: the original meaning of διακονεῖν was waiting at table, for example in chapter 12.2 (Μάρθα διάκονει), and the word was afterwards used with the wider meaning of being responsible for a person's livelihood. It was also customary for the servant of a rabbi to accompany him (ἀκολουθεῖν) on all his journeyings. Consequently, it is more than likely that here in chapter 12.26 we have a reflection of the ministry of deacons in the early Church. The service which is hinted at here is that which is given to the living Christ in his Church where, served in the liturgy and in the works of mercy among the brethren, he also asks of his disciples that they shall be prepared to follow him even unto death (cf. ch. 21.19, ἀκολούθει μοι). He promises, however, to those who are faithful, that they shall reign with him in glory. Discipleship with Jesus in his earthly life was, indeed, a type of this ministry within the Church. It is significant that the saying of Jesus which we have just considered is followed immediately by an allusion to his death. Thus we see again that the connection between the earthly life of Jesus and the continued work of the risen Lord within his Church is consistently emphasized throughout the Gospel.

To sum up, we have seen in St John's Gospel traces of the ministry of the early Church—in the apostolate and the diaconate. The following interesting facts have also emerged as a result of our study:

CHURCH AND MINISTRY IN ST JOHN

(i) Jesus did not institute the Church's ministry by means of mere proclamations or appointments, but he showed himself to be the first and, indeed, the one real bearer of the office, both as ἀπόστολος and διάκονος.

(ii) In this Gospel the institution of the ministry is constantly related to the death and resurrection of Jesus[1]; that is, to the very foundation on which the Church herself is built.

(iii) The work of the ministry is discharged in the service of the risen Lord; that is, in the Church's eschatological situation.

From this it is clear that the ministry is conceived by St John in a wholly religious and Christocentric way. The authority for it lies, not in the ordinances of man, but in the institution and commission of Christ himself. In the Church's ministry the most important factor is not the human holder of the office but Christ. He is the real Minister.

[1] John 20.19; 21.15; 13.1; 12.27.

CHAPTER 3

THE LITURGY IN THE FOURTH GOSPEL

12. *The Relation to the Jewish Cult*

THERE IS, in the Fourth Gospel, a very marked interest in the liturgy. This is shown by the many references to the Jewish cult. Thus, in a great number of cases, Jesus' teaching and work is connected with different cult feasts such as the Passover, the Feast of Tabernacles, and the Feast of the Dedication. It is in the Temple at Jerusalem also that, according to St John, Jesus gave most of his teaching; while there, too, his most violent controversies with "the Jews" took place. The Synagogue plays a much less important part in the Fourth Gospel, where the Temple is more often the scene of Jesus' activity. There are references to the cult as revealed in the Old Testament, to its prophecy[1]; to the Jewish ceremonies of cleansing[2]; to the preparations for the Passover[3]; to the cult sacrifices[4]; to circumcision[5]; and to the strict treatment of the excommunicated.[6]

Those earlier scholars who have interpreted the Gospel only along mystical and individualistic lines naturally could not find in it any resemblances to the Jewish cult. Modern scholars, moreover, such as Bultmann and Faulhaber, who interpret the Gospel from an anti-cult point of view, are forced by the nature of the text to adopt the hypothesis of

---

[1] John 11.49, 50; 18.14. [2] John 2.6; 3.25; 13.4; 18.28.
[3] John 19.31, 36, 42. [4] John 2.14; 11.51; 18.14.
[5] John 7.22. [6] John 9.22; 12.42; 16.2.

THE LITURGY IN THE FOURTH GOSPEL 45

divided sources—a method of exegesis no longer looked upon with favour by the majority of critics. Another method of interpretation has been that adopted by the school of comparative religion. These theologians, among whom are Bousset and Wetter, acknowledged the marked cult-character of this Gospel, but have seen in it, for the most part, the influences of Hellenistic or Persian religion.

Other theologians again have attempted to interpret the Gospel in the light of the Mandaean scriptures, Bauer tending towards a sacramental interpretation, Odeberg towards an allegorical and mystical one. Thus, for a long time, it has been considered an absurdity that the so-called "Greek" or "gnostic" Gospel should be thought of as possessing any close connection with Jewish cult and theology. During the last few years, however, there has been a definite reversal of opinion, a new approach to the problem which will probably lead to a deeper understanding both of the text of the Gospel and also of its theological peculiarities.

Thus it has recently been argued that, since the first Christian congregations appeared on Jewish ground, they would naturally have been organized after the pattern of the first congregation at Jerusalem, which we know held its meetings partly in the homes of its members and partly in the Temple.[1] Again, the liturgy of these first Christian congregations would have been strongly influenced by the language used in the Temple worship and by the phraseology of the Rabbis. The liturgy and the theological interpretations given in the Temple at Jerusalem, however, were very close to each other, not only as regards locality, the teaching being given, for the most part, under the colonnades of the Temple, but also as regards language. Now it is a feature of liturgy that it always makes use of set phrases in order to express the truths of religion; and theological teaching, which is mainly oral, similarly makes consistent efforts to give its doctrinal statements a set form. For while desiring to give

[1] Acts 2.46; 3.1.

adequate expression to the faith which is to be inculcated, it yet wishes, at the same time, to express that faith in such a way that it may be easily learned and assimilated. In order to attain this end, moreover, it employs certain artistic aids such as metrical or rhyming form, alliteration, assonance, etc. (cf. old national proverbs). Now it is wholly to be expected that just as the language of the early Christian cult was moulded to a large extent, especially in its use of the Psalter, by that of the Jewish cult, so also the form of Christian teaching will have been influenced very considerably by contemporary Rabbinism.

Now when we turn to the Fourth Gospel, we find that its language has been made the object of very careful study; for scholars, some of whom have favoured the hypothesis of a great number of different sources, whilst others have maintained single authorship throughout, have sought to verify on linguistic grounds their varied theories as to its origin. Burney, for example, has tried to prove that the entire Gospel is a translation from an Aramaic original, a theory which has met with but little approval, although Bultmann in his commentary favours the idea of an Aramaic source which he terms the σημεῖα source. Nobody, however, has as yet studied this Gospel seriously from the point of view of liturgy and doctrinal teaching, although several attempts have been made by Raney along these lines. He has tried to show that the following passages, chapters 1.1–18; 3.14–21, 31–36; 10.1–18, and the whole of chapters 14—17, are prose hymns, meant to be sung by a cantor or in choir, whilst the entire Gospel, according to his theory, has been written to be used at two or three successive cult proceedings. Now while not accepting this theory in all points, the present writer agrees with Raney in seeing, behind the composition of St John's Gospel, the existence of a Church with its life and worship; and in regarding the "prologue" and chapter 10.1–18 as cult hymns. In the other passages in which Raney sees cult hymns the present writer finds, instead, instances of

THE LITURGY IN THE FOURTH GOSPEL 47

the teaching of the Church at the time when the Gospel was written—teaching presented in the form employed by the Jewish rabbis, which was doubtless the form also used by Jesus himself. Now if this latter proves to be true, our confidence in the historical value of the Fourth Gospel will be greatly increased; for, thanks to the teaching technique employed here, many sayings of Jesus will have been preserved in their original form. Once formulated, these sayings will have been passed on and expounded by means of all the aids of the rabbinical teaching method—parallelisms, alliteration, synonyms, antithetical or synthetical forms, rhythm, rhyme, and with interjected remarks and questions, the last of which, while sometimes revealing a lack of understanding on the part of the hearer and bringing about the repetition and emphasizing of important points, at other times will have appeared simply in order to give to the account a more lively character. The significant thing about all this is, however, that it reflects the seething life of the early Christian Church, a life which found its main expression in liturgy and teaching. Let us turn then to consider this liturgy and teaching, paying special attention to the relation of the Christian liturgy to the Jewish cult.

The recent study of the King ideology as found among the peoples of Asia Minor has, more than ever before, focussed interest on the Jewish cult itself and on the articles expressed by it. Especially noteworthy in this connection is the Jewish Feast of Tabernacles with its ancient ceremonies. These are connected with the Feast of the New Year, traces of which are often to be found on Semitic soil. This feast was celebrated by the Jews, partly as Jahveh's enthronement feast, at which first the King and later the High Priest represented Jahveh, and partly as a fertility feast for the increase of the crops. This particular feast more than any other kept alive among the people the Messianic hope; for the Jewish cult as a whole, and the Feast of Tabernacles in particular, contained a great deal of "anticipatory" eschatology, the coming of the expected Messiah being anticipated in its rites. It is easy to see what a tremendous impression these annual cult feasts must have made on those taking part in them. Great multitudes of people from many different parts of the world surging together to the grand "stage" provided by the magnificent Temple and its courts, the numerous priests, the still more numerous levites and servants, the festal choirs accompanied by innumerable kinds of musical instruments, the solemn processions and, at night, the impressive lighting—all of these provided a powerful means both of expressing the nation's longing for the Messiah and also of stimulating and keeping alive that longing.

Now in order to understand aright the message of the Fourth Gospel we must keep in mind this ideological and liturgical background, since it is only against this background that we can grasp the significance of his frequent references to the Jewish cult and also of the importance attached by St John to certain incidents in the life of Jesus, incidents in which he sees a far deeper meaning than is apparent in the external course of events.

We have already noted that the water ceremony of the Feast of Tabernacles gave to Jesus an occasion of proclaiming the Well of Life.[1] The solemn Festival of Light, with which in the Court of Women this same great feast ended, similarly provided him with the opportunity of presenting himself as the Light of the World.[2] Furthermore, Jesus' entry into Jerusalem amid the ovations of the people and their waving of palm branches is psychologically inexplicable unless it be seen as a fulfilment of the Messianic expectation which had hitherto been expressed in the cult. This expectation, it must be remembered, had greatly increased in recent months as a result of the appearance of "signs" of the Messianic age—the feeding with manna, the healing of the blind, and the raising of the dead.

Here we may pay special attention to a small detail

[1] John 7.37. [2] John 8.12.

THE LITURGY IN THE FOURTH GOSPEL 49

typical of the Fourth Gospel. In chapter 12.13 it is recorded that the people "took branches of palm trees and went forth to meet him" The parallel versions in St Mark and St Matthew speak only of "branches" that were "strawed in the way"; while St Luke, in contrast to the other Evangelists, makes no mention whatever of this particular homage. Now the point of interest here is that, in the Jewish cult, those who took part in the procession on the last and greatest day of the Feast of Tabernacles likewise carried branches in their hands. It would seem, therefore, that St John was consciously correcting St Mark and St Matthew in order to bring out the parallelism between Jesus' triumphant entry into Jerusalem and cult-expression of the Messianic expectations of the Jews and to show that the people, though ignorant of the significance of their action, were responding instinctively to the presence of the Messiah in their midst. Thus St John saw in the Jewish cult an "anticipatory" eschatology.

In a similar way, if we regard the Jewish cult as preparing the way for the Christian Church, we get new light on Our Lord's words, "Destroy (λύσατε) this temple and in three days I will raise it up" (ch. 2.19). Here, too, a comparison with the text of the Synoptic Gospels is of interest:

> St Mark 14.58: "We heard him say I will destroy this Temple that is made with hands and within three days I will build another, made without hands."
>
> St Matt. 26.61: "At the last came two false witnesses and said, 'This fellow said, I am able to destroy the temple of God and to build it in three days.'"

No doubt the Synoptic tradition of the false witnessing is authentic and may be taken to refer either to a misunderstanding of the words of Jesus[1] or, alternatively, to a malicious misinterpretation of what he said. St John will have known this, but he also saw that the Jews, in their usual

[1] Mark 13.1, 2; Matt. 24.1, 2.

failure to understand Jesus' words—indeed *by* their very misunderstanding of them—were playing an important part in the fulfilling of the prophecy of judgement upon Jerusalem. Thus those who accused Jesus of evil devices against the temple, by the very fact of their driving him to the Cross brought destruction not only upon themselves but also upon their temple. In the Fourth Gospel, however, it is Jesus who is made to say, "Destroy this temple, and in three days I will raise it up." It is significant that the word used by St John is ἐγερῶ (I will raise up) as compared with οἰκοδομήσω (I will build) in the Synoptic Gospels; while as an explanation of Jesus' words St John adds, "He spake of the temple of his body."[1] This explanation, however, is more complex than, at first sight, it appears; for it is obvious that St John really had in mind also the destruction of the visible temple at Jerusalem, since this saying follows closely upon the narrative of the "cleansing" of that temple. As is often the case with St John, the words bear a double meaning. Thus they do refer to Jesus' bodily resurrection from the tomb; they also refer, however, to his establishing of the Church which is his mystical Body, the very Temple of his Spirit. That this saying was only understood in all its fulness by his followers after, and as a result of, his death and resurrection, verse 22 makes clear. So it came about that, just as in the Old Covenant the temple was the symbol of Jahveh's presence in the midst of his people, so now in the New Covenant, in the Person of Jesus Christ and through his Spirit, God still indwells his people, the new Israel—the Christian Church. This indwelling, furthermore, is accomplished by the fact that the risen and ascended Jesus, in his Body the Church, tabernacles with his own as truly as he tabernacled with them in the days of his flesh.[2] The saying in chapter 2.19 indicates that in killing Jesus the Jews were, in point of fact, preparing the way for his resurrection and were thus helping to bring into existence the Christian

[1] John 2.21.   [2] John 1.14.

Church. Indeed, by their action against him they were actually destroying their own temple which, when the Church of Christ had come into being, had no longer any mission to fulfil. Thus it came to pass that, in Jesus, the old cult was abolished, not because he was against it; on the contrary he cleansed it from its stain of human greed and profit-making; nor because its rites were wrong, or its hopes essentially false; rather it was abolished because all that it stood for he fulfilled, and transcended in such a way that only a new cult could express the union between God and man in him.

We meet with the same trend of thought again in chapter 4.20-21. Here the Samaritan woman takes up the long-standing controversy as to whether Jerusalem or Gerizim is the place where men should worship. Jesus replies that the *place* of worship does not matter but that the time would come—yea, had come already—when the true worshippers of the Father would worship him in spirit and in truth.[1] This, of course, does not mean, as certain "spiritualizing" interpreters of the Gospel throughout the ages have tried to persuade us, that Jesus wished to abolish all liturgical forms on behalf of an altogether "spiritual" (that is, non-liturgical) worship. On the contrary, the meaning of the text is simply this: that as a result of the life, the death, and the resurrection of Jesus, it is not the *place* of worship that decides whether the worship is legitimate or not. The mark of all true worship is that, centred round the Christ, it is permeated by his Spirit, and that, offered up in his Name, it is also in accordance with the truth; that is, with the true knowledge of God given to man in him. Thus the coming of Christ raised the whole problem to a higher plane, on which, as the Samaritan woman herself admitted, the Jerusalem versus Gerizim controversy became entirely out of place. Thus this passage also shows how the Jewish cult reached its fulfilment in Christ, and how, freed from its connection with a

[1] John 4.23.

certain place and a certain people—purified, perfected, and transcended—it became available for all mankind in him. There is a natural connection, therefore, between the incident of the Samaritan woman and the mission charge which immediately follows it.[1]

As we have seen, then, it was not Jesus' purpose to establish a new non-liturgical religion as a substitute for the old cult. Rather St John saw the old cult as attaining its fulfilment and perfection in and through Christ. All that the old Jewish cult had stood for and expressed was fulfilled in Jesus, who himself was the centre of the new Christian cult. The age of the promises, the age of the "anticipatory" eschatology of the Jewish Church, was thus fulfilled, while in Christ, the new age—the age of eschatology "realized" in the Christian Church—had come into being. The clearest expression of this coming of the new age is to be found in St John's treatment of the Passion, to which we will now turn our attention.

We need not discuss here the intricate question regarding the relation of St John's chronology of the Passion to that of the Synoptists. Suffice it to say that, according to St John, it was at the very hour when the Paschal Lamb was being offered in the temple at Jerusalem that Jesus died upon the Cross. Whether St John was historically correct in synchronizing these two events is a matter of but little importance. His Gospel was written in order to tell the story of the life and death, and resurrection of Jesus, in such a way as to bring out its most profound and eternal significance. St John, then, saw the death of Christ as the fulfilment of the Jewish cult with its numerous sacrifices. Indeed, all the sacrifices which through the centuries had been offered up in the temple at Jerusalem he saw as significant only in the light of this one great sacrifice towards which, as types, they all had pointed. Thus Christ was to him the "one perfect and sufficient Sacrifice" which made all other sacrifices

[1] John 4.35–38.

THE LITURGY IN THE FOURTH GOSPEL 53

unnecessary. He was the true Paschal Lamb[1] whose connection with the Paschal lamb of the Jewish cult was made clear by St John's recording of the fact that the bones of the dead Saviour were not broken.[2] It will be remembered that, concerning the Jewish Paschal lamb, it was prescribed in the Law that not one bone of it was to be broken.[3]

This investigation has revealed the reason for St John's many references to the Jewish cult, namely that he saw in that cult the forerunner of the Christian Church with her new worship centred in Christ Jesus. Our next task, therefore, will be to find out to what extent the worship of this Christian Church, as distinct from Jewish worship, is reflected in both the narrative and the theology of the Fourth Gospel. For this purpose we must first consider the part played by baptism and the Eucharist in "St John", since both of these sacraments are recognized throughout the whole Church as having been instituted by Christ himself.

What immediately strikes our attention is the fact that no account of the institution of either baptism or the Eucharist is to be found in the text of St John. This fact has caused many scholars to ignore its many oblique references to both of these sacraments and to regard it as an anti-liturgical and anti-sacramental work. Bultmann, in support of his non-sacramental theory, is forced, time and time again, to conjure up "*der kirchliche Redaktor*"—the ecclesiastical redactor —whom he makes responsible for various liturgical interpolations. When he finds this an impossible solution, he interprets the sayings in a "spiritual" manner. By most of the early Fathers, however, and by all medieval scholars, chapter 6 was regarded as referring to the Eucharist. Luther and his followers, with their often mechanical method of interpreting the Bible, disagreed with this, since, they argued, the Eucharist had not been instituted at the time when Christ fed the five thousand; but modern scholars, for

[1] John 1.29. [2] John 19.33, 36.
[3] Ex. 12.46; Num. 9.12.

the most part, agree with the early Fathers. It is also now generally accepted that in the washing of the Disciples' feet we have a symbolic reference to baptism. We will now deal with other passages of liturgical import in the order in which they appear.

13. *The Baptism of John and the Baptism of Jesus*
(St John 1.6–8, 15, 19–27, 32–34)

The Fourth Gospel agrees with the three Synoptists in beginning the story of the life and work of Jesus by recording the ministry of St John the Baptist. St John's account, however, consists mainly of a summing up of the Baptist's testimony to Christ. Cullmann points out that the priests and levites who were sent from Jerusalem to inquire into the identity of the Baptist indicate the liturgical character of this passage. The preparatory nature of the Baptist's mission is brought out in verses 6–8, 15, 26, 27, where it is stated emphatically that the Baptist's only task is to point forward to the coming Christ. Thus, his baptism is only a baptism in water (v. 26), whereas Christ's, when he shall come, will be a baptism in Holy Spirit (v. 33). John also declares, however, that Jesus is indeed the Christ who shall thus baptize, for he says, "I saw the Spirit descending from heaven, like a dove, and it abode upon him" (v. 32).

This passage, together with chapter 3.23–36, has often been taken as a violent polemic of the early Church against the baptism of John and against all those who would have proclaimed the Baptist as their prophet or Messiah—an interpretation to which the Mandaean writings have lent considerable support. Thus it has been argued that the author of the Fourth Gospel gives the maximum force to the Church's arguments by making the Baptist himself state his own inferior position in relation to Jesus. It would be wrong, however, to think of these texts as merely or even primarily polemical; above all, they are a positive pointer to Christ

THE LITURGY IN THE FOURTH GOSPEL

as the true Messiah. Clearly the Baptist appears in them as the representative of the old cult, while Jesus represents the new one. It is of interest, however, that neither the meaning of John's baptism in water nor the meaning of Jesus' baptism in "holy spirit" is precisely expressed. The one thing that the text does make clear is the fact that the old order and its cult must decrease, whilst the new one would increase,[1] since the time of fulfilment and of perfecting had drawn nigh. Thus Cullmann points out, quite rightly, that instead of John's baptism is placed, not Jesus' *baptism*, but rather Jesus himself, who, because he actually possesses and is possessed by the Spirit, brings in the new age, the age of the operation of the Spirit in the Christian Church. As a result of this, the Old Covenant with its rites and worship is superseded, its place being taken by the Christian Church with her new Christ-centred worship.

Unlike the Synoptists, St John emphasizes the fact that the Spirit remained on Jesus. Thus, the Spirit is depicted as an ever-abiding and continually operative force, not only in him but also in the new age which he inaugurated. The question which must now be faced is whether the Fourth Evangelist implies that Christian baptism was actually practised during the earthly ministry of Jesus. The present writer would reply in the negative, on the ground that according to this Gospel, it was only through his death and resurrection that Jesus' words as well as his actions attained to their full power and revealed their true meaning. This is made clear with regard to baptism by the Baptist's confession at the very beginning of Jesus' ministry: "Behold the Lamb of God, that taketh away the sin of the world." Baptism is here related to the sacrifical death of Jesus; and it is of the fruits of that death, namely the forgiveness of sin and life everlasting, that those who are baptised into Christ are made partakers. The Baptist's confession, no doubt, shows traces of the liturgy of the early Church, resembling

[1] John 3.30.

as it does a primitive liturgical formula. From the theological point of view there is unmistakable reference in it to the Suffering Servant of Isaiah.[1] It is, therefore, contrary to the whole conception of the Fourth Gospel that Jesus should have baptised during his earthly life, while any impression that he did so (see ch. 3.22, 26) is corrected by chapter 4.2. That correction, however, which states that it was not Jesus himself but his disciples who were baptizing, is intelligible only if seen against the background of the practice of baptism in the early Church. In point of fact, if any of the disciples of Jesus did actually baptize during his earthly life, they must have been former disciples of John who had come to Jesus and who were still carrying on John's baptism. In this case they bear witness to the continuity between the Old Covenant and the New. Passages in the Acts of the Apostles[2] seem to indicate that there was not always a clearly defined line between the disciples of John and the first members of the Christian Church.

14. *The Miracle of the Wine* (ch. 2.1–11)

There have been many attempts to master this difficult passage. Most scholars agree as to its sacramental significance, although it is often thought that it has been modelled on the pattern of the Dionysus-cult. Kundsin's theory that the miracle in Cana must be taken as a justification of the custom of using water instead of wine at the celebration of the Eucharist is most improbable, since it is the Jewish water of purification which is used by the Jews and is thus shown to be obsolete. The peculiar custom of saving the "not-so-good" wine until the end of a feast has also caused a great deal of discussion amongst scholars. Windisch has pointed out that it is very difficult to find any corresponding evidence in profane literature; he regards the passage as a merely legendary narrative, finishing in a clumsy and abrupt way

---

[1] Isa. 42.1; 53.7.   [2] Acts 18.25; 19.1–7.

as soon as the miracle has been performed. If, however, we consider it as a theological problem, rather than as a question of social custom, we find in ἕως ἄρτι (v. 10) the same eschatological "now" which we have already met in ἡ ὥρα (v. 4). Thus, the concluding sentence in the story, "Thou hast kept the good wine until now", gives the key to the whole passage. It is this that the narrative is intended to illustrate—the point to which it leads. Naturally, therefore, it ends when its climax has been reached.

The answer which Jesus gives to his Mother when she tells him that there is no more wine is of great interest. He replies, "Mine hour is not yet come" (v. 4). The "hour" to which he refers is not, of course, the moment when the water was turned into wine, for that hour manifestly had come. Rather, it is the great decisive "hour" towards which everything in this Gospel points—namely, the hour of his death which, paradoxically, was at the same time the hour of his "lifting-up" and glorification. The reference in this story to this particular "hour" is a clear proof of the sacramental and liturgical character of the passage, for if it were not the intention of the Fourth Evangelist to make a definite allusion to the Eucharist, there would be no reason whatsoever to refer to Jesus' death in this context—namely, at a marriage!

The harsh words τί ἐμοὶ καὶ σοί, γύναι; mark the distance between Jesus and his fellow men who have not yet understood his real task in the world, and the real miracle which he is to perform when his real hour is come. It is his death that is the necessary condition for the celebration of the Eucharist. By means of this miracle of the wine Jesus seems to show that the Jewish cult—here represented by the pots of the water of purification—must give way to the Christian worship, the centre of which is the Eucharist. Theologically this means that the Jewish ceremonies of cleansing are now useless and unnecessary, since Jesus, through his sacrificial death, has made atonement for the sins of the world. But it is not without significance that Jesus instead of rejecting the water of cleansing uses it to accomplish this miracle. By this, too, the Fourth Gospel shows that the great importance of the Jewish ceremonies has been their pointing forward towards the real "cleansing" and their keeping alive among the people the longing for such a cleansing. The final words "until now" which occur in v. 10 are the key-words to the whole passage, referring not to the miracle of the wine but to the death and resurrection of Christ—events towards which the whole Jewish cult, with its many prophecies, has pointed. Now, however, the eschatological expectations are fulfilled through the death of Jesus, while men are made partakers of the fruits of this death in the Eucharist of his Church. The scrupulous observance of the Jewish Law, moreover, is now replaced by the unconstrained happiness of the Messianic age—a happiness which we have been considering as essentially one of eschatological significance, based on a tradition the validity of which there is no reason to doubt.

15. *Born of Water and of the Spirit* (ch. 3.1–21)

"Born from above" and "born of water and of the Spirit" are the most important words in the conversation between Jesus and Nicodemus. To translate ἄνωθεν γεννηθῆναι as "born again" as in the English Authorized Version is very unsatisfactory, for that interpretation is quite foreign to the language and, indeed, to the whole theology of the Fourth Gospel. The word ἄνωθεν appears in three other places in St John; namely, in chapter 3.31 ("He that cometh from above", that is Christ), in chapter 19.11 (the power of Pilate is given to him "from above"), and in chapter 19.23 (Jesus' coat was "woven from the top throughout"). Thus, though this expression occurs in varied contexts, it always bears the meaning "from above". Furthermore, the conception of a wholly new life which is suggested by the translation "born again" is quite foreign to the thought of the Fourth Gospel, where the dualism is not spiritual life in contrast to physical life but, rather, life as against death. The well-known argument that the misunderstanding of Nicodemus (v. 4) seems to support the traditional translations of "again" or "anew" is easily repudiated by the fact that Nicodemus, being a Jew, would naturally think in the very realistic way typical of the Oriental mind. In his opinion, it is not the word ἄνωθεν but γεννηθῆναι that Jesus is stressing, while, to him, birth can only take place in a completely materialistic way. Thus, in a vivid picture, he shows the impossibility of that which he imagines Jesus to have proposed in his demand for a man ἄνωθεν γεννηθῆναι. But that very impossibility was an unmistakable indication that the birth of which Jesus was speaking was one brought about entirely by the action of the Spirit. The words ὕδατος καί (v. 5) (with water and . . .), which Bultmann dismisses as an ecclesiastical interpolation, Cullmann, on the other hand, retains. Traditionally this text has been interpreted as referring to Christian baptism. In another connection, however, Cullmann interprets verses 3-5 as correcting a misuse that had grown up in the early Church. Here baptism was often divided into two sacraments, a baptism in water which effected the remission of sins being followed by a laying-on of hands at which the Holy Spirit was given. The word ἄνωθεν Cullmann regards as having a twofold meaning, referring at once to the subjective as well as to the objective side of baptism. This subjective side of the Sacrament is the birth "from above" which is dealt with in the first few verses of the passage. Cullmann, however, in spite of *interpreting* ἄνωθεν in this way, keeps to the *translation* "born again"; understanding by it the incorporation of the individual into the Christ-life, that is, into the Christian Church. The objective side of baptism, dealt with in the second half of the passage, is indeed the necessary condition for baptism, namely, the "lifting-up" of Jesus. There is, moreover, in verses 14-16 a clear reference to the death of Jesus and to the Church which this death brought about. Consequently, it is only in this Church where the risen Lord works and bestows the gifts of the Spirit that baptism can take place. In verses 18ff the necessity of faith is brought out, for without faith in the risen Lord, even baptism itself is of no avail and man comes under judgement.

16. *The Water of Life* (ch. 4.1–15; 7.37–39)

The words in chapter 4.20ff, regarding worship "in spirit and in truth", have already been considered. We shall now, therefore, confine our attention to that part of Jesus' conversation with the Samaritan woman wherein he proclaimed himself to be the giver of τὸ ὕδωρ ζῶν (the living water, v. 10). It is well known, of course, that in Oriental languages "living water" means spring water. There was, therefore, a natural connection between the well whereon Jesus sat and the theme of their conversation. And, in accordance with St John's habit of using words with a twofold significance, a spiritual reality lies behind his use of this term. Bultmann interprets the phrase in a "spiritual" or non-sacramental way, calling it "the revelation which Jesus gives". To any realistically minded reader, however, it is obvious that we have here a reference to the water of baptism. Nevertheless it has been argued that, both in chapter 4.14 and in chapter 7.37, the act of drinking is meant, whereas in the Church it has never been a custom to drink the water of baptism, although such a practice has in point of fact existed in certain strange cults, for example, among the Mandaean believers. Nevertheless it was the drinking water in the well that gave rise to the subsequent discourse.

Here, then, Christ is depicted as the one who satisfies the human life-thirst, the strongest of all cravings, thus effecting the deliverance of mankind from the inevitable consequence of this thirst—namely, death. The type of this picture is to be found in Exodus 17.6ff; for, as Moses then gave water out of the rock to the thirsting people of Israel, thereby saving their lives in the desert, so now Christ, in like manner, gives to his people that living water which saves souls from eternal destruction.

"If any man thirst, let him come unto me and drink." These words, spoken by Jesus in the temple at Jerusalem on the most important day of the Feast of Tabernacles and with definite reference to the water ceremony that was then taking place, show how the Jewish cult, with its out-of-date and ineffective ceremonies, was destined to be replaced by the life-giving liturgy of the Church of Christ. The primary reference here is, of course, to baptism—but the passage implies the replacing of the entire old order by the new. Similarly, the fact that Jesus' conversation with the Samaritan woman took place beside Jacob's well—itself an ancient sacred site—emphasized the fact that the old order was now transcended by the new. Thus was Christ seen to be greater even than Jacob, the patriarch who had given the well, since he, in contrast to Jacob, bestowed that living water concerning which Jesus says, "Whosoever drinketh of the water that I shall give him shall never thirst". The Samaritan woman, in asking for this living water, was seeking, though she knew it not, the rite of Christian baptism.

In both of these passages water and the spirit are linked together—a fact which makes it still more probable that we have, in them, references to Christian baptism. Cullmann thinks that chapter 4.13ff indicates that baptism is a sacrament to be received only once, but Michaelis rightly argues that, if this be so, the same conclusion must be drawn with regard to the Eucharist (cf. ch. 6.35, 50ff): whereas according to the words of institution quoted by St Paul[1] this latter sacrament was certainly intended to be repeated. Cullmann does not approve of any allegorical interpretation of the five husbands of the woman but suggests, instead, that the purpose of this part of the narrative is to stress the fact that, if it is to be efficacious and to convey eternal life, baptism

[1] 1 Cor. 11.25.

must of necessity involve a complete turning away from the convert's old life—a life marked, in most cases, by sin and in many by heathen practices. When Cullmann goes on to suggest that the food referred to in chapter 4.31–34 is the Eucharist, his imagination seems to be a trifle too active. His reference, nevertheless, to chapter 6.38 in this context is of great interest; for in both of these passages Jesus speaks of himself as having come to do the Father's will. Thus, the sacraments are seen to be works performed by the risen Lord within his Church and in accordance with the Father's will.

17. *The Sabbath* (ch. 5.1–29)

Cullmann sees in the account of the healing of the paralytic at the Pool of Bethesda a reference to the sacrament of baptism. It is quite clear, however, that he is again being too zealous in seeking out a sacramental interpretation of the text. For it was not by means of bathing or washing but through the *words* of Jesus that the sick man was healed, while the admonition "Go and sin no more" (v. 14) does not provide sufficient grounds for seeing in the passage a reference to baptism. It is the question of the Sabbath, strict observance of which was a part of the Jewish cult, that is important in this story, for Jesus had acted against the Sabbath law not only by his own healing of the sick but also by his command to the paralytic to carry his bed. Now out of this Sabbath incident there arose a discourse regarding the right interpretation of the Law of Moses—a discourse which, on account of the eschatological significance of the claims made in it by Jesus, led to the wrath of the Jews and their consequent desire to take his life.[1]

Cullmann and Michaelis both see in this passage the polemics of the early Church against the Jewish Sabbath, but this interpretation is too negative and mechanical.

---

[1] John 5.16, 18; 7.1, 21–23, 30.

Instead, we have here instruction given to the early Christians regarding both the position of the Church herself and also the conditions of the new dispensation—the Messianic Age—which is now fulfilled in the Church. The healing of the paralytic (the importance of which healing is stressed by mention of his many years' illness, v. 5), the exercise of judgement by Christ (v. 30), and even the raising of the dead (v. 28) are all signs of the Messianic age. Thus, it is here not merely a question of the Jewish Sabbath versus the Christian Sunday; rather is it a question of the old dispensation versus the new. The old Sabbath was but a preparation for and a pledge of this new dispensation. Now, however, the time of fulfilment has come while the ancient eschatological promises are actually being realized in the works of Christ. Indeed, it was by an appeal to the nature of his works that Jesus refuted the Jews when they accused him of breaking the Sabbath—"My Father worketh even until now and I work" (v. 17). Thus he pointed out that, while the Law of Moses forbade that men should do their *own* work on the Sabbath, it could in no wise forbid or prevent the accomplishment of God's work on that day. He, himself, had come to do the works of God[1] which, being of eschatological significance, belonged to the Sabbath in a very special way (cf. circumcising on the Sabbath, ch. 7.22–23). Indeed, his very doing of these works was a sure sign that the real Sabbath of fulfilment had come. Since, moreover, the risen and ascended Christ lives and works within his Church, her life itself is one continuous Sabbath—a pledge and foretaste of the consummation and the great Sabbath of eternity.

18. *The Bread of Life* (ch. 6.1–71)

Almost all scholars now agree that the Eucharistic theology of the Fourth Gospel is to be found in its sixth chapter. Most, however, make the mistake of dividing the chapter into three

---

[1] John 9.4; 14.10.

parts: the miracle of the feeding of the five thousand; the discourse on the Bread of Life; and the sermon on the Eucharist. This is done by Cullmann and Michaelis, as well as by Bultmann who, as might be expected, refers the last of these parts to the activity of his ecclesiastical redactor. Cullmann, however, shows that even in the first of these sections, the actual story of the miracle of the feeding of the five thousand, there are sacramental features, since it was bread and apparently fish that characterized the celebration of the Eucharist in the early Church, while wine was not obligatory. The word εὐχαριστήσας (v. 11), too, reminds us of the Eucharistic prayer in that same Church. It is, moreover, on the miracle of the feeding (a miracle which is related in all four Gospels) that St John builds up his entire exposition of the Eucharist. At first, he mentions only bread, a fact partly due to the connection of the discourse with the preceding miracle, but partly to the question raised by the Jews referring to the ancient miracle of the manna (v. 31). Thus:

> 6.35. "I am the Bread of Life: he that cometh to me shall never hunger; and he that believeth on me shall never thirst."
>
> 6.48ff. "I am that Bread of Life. Your fathers did eat manna in the wilderness and are dead. This is the Bread that cometh down from heaven, that a man may eat thereof and not die. I am that Living Bread." (ὁ ἄρτος ὁ ζῶν)

The references in 6.35 to both hunger and thirst are parallel descriptions of that same longing which is now satisfied by Jesus who describes himself as the longed-for Bread of Life which preserves man to eternal life. In the same way Jesus claims to surpass the great miracle which God wrought through Moses—the feeding of the Israelites with manna in the wilderness—for whereas the manna could only save the Israelites from bodily death, Christ, the living Bread, bestows on his people that life which never dies. It is this

Bread of Life that the Christian receives in concrete form in the Eucharist of the Church.

In v. 53, "Except ye eat the flesh of the Son of Man and drink his blood, ye have no life in you", the wine is introduced, and thus the reference to the Eucharist becomes obvious; note that the bread from heaven is here called the flesh of Jesus. The choice of words in this passage shows the strong anti-docetic tendency of the Fourth Gospel, but above all we have a clear linking up with the prologue in 1.14, a fact which most scholars have ignored. The Eucharist is the continuation of the Incarnation; this is emphasized partly by the eschatological character of the text and partly by the offence caused by this discourse, to which the author emphatically draws attention.

Cullmann reminds us that, according to the tradition of the Jews, the miracle of the manna was to be repeated in the last days.[1] These eschatological expectations are now shown by St John to be fulfilled when the risen Christ in the Church's Eucharist offers himself to his disciples as the true and life-giving manna. But the condition for the resurrection of Jesus is his Incarnation: the two belong together: and St John attaches great importance to the insistence on the identity between the historical Jesus and the glorified Christ. Cullmann points out that the adverb πάντοτε (always—"evermore") in v. 34 is strongly emphasized by its position so as to make it quite clear that the gift which is called the Bread of Life is not given once only, as in the feeding of the five thousand or in the historical Incarnation—which is also a non-recurrent event—but that it is still to be given after the death of Jesus, i.e. in the Church. At the same time we are reminded about the new terminus which is now fixed for the eschatological expectations—since the hopes of the Old Testament have now been fulfilled—namely the last days (cf. vv. 39, 40, 44, 54).

The Evangelist draws attention to the strength of the

[1] Baruch 29.8.

offence given to those who heard Jesus speaking of himself as the true Bread of Life. In vv. 41–43, we hear that the Jews murmured against Jesus' claim, making contemptuous reference to his earthly ancestry, "Is not this Jesus, the son of Joseph, whose father and mother we know?" (v. 42). This is the stumbling block of the Incarnation. In v. 60 many of his disciples say: "This is a hard saying; who can receive it?" This is the stumbling block of the sacramental presence of Jesus, a presence accentuated through the startling choice of the words used (v. 54). Thus the offence of the Incarnation finds its counterpart in the offence of Christ present in and acting through the Sacrament, and thus, in the age of the Church, fulfilling the will of his Father (v. 38). And the answer of Jesus in the Fourth Gospel to both these offences is: "Doth this cause you to stumble? What then if ye should see the Son of Man ascending where he was before?" The great all-exceeding offence, then, is the "lifting-up" of Jesus, on the Cross and in his exaltation. It is this that gives to the historical as well as to the sacramental presence of Jesus here on earth its significance and its importance.

St John wants to make it clear that "the glorified Lord" is always present with his disciples in the Eucharist, giving them his eternal life, and therefore that the Eucharist is necessary for the obtaining of this life (v. 53). It is, however, not merely a matter of physical eating and drinking: only by faith can the disciple receive eternal life in the Eucharist: without faith it is just σάρξ (v. 63). This is the significance of that verse which is used over and over again to interpret the difficult words, "Except ye eat the flesh of the Son of Man and drink his blood, ye have not life in yourselves." These two passages are closely connected with each other and they show how the Eucharistic idea of the Fourth Gospel is at one and the same time both deeply spiritual and strongly realistic: conceived in a manner both sacramental and religious. Thus v. 63 tells us that the Spirit is essential to the celebrating of the Eucharist; the Spirit, however, is not given until after the "lifting-up" of Jesus, i.e. in the Church. Thus it is in the Church that the Eucharist can be celebrated, and outside her there can be no Eucharist. The Church is, furthermore, assuring us through the Spirit that the Sacrament really is the Bread from heaven, the bread which supplies eternal life, but on the one condition, that it is received in faith.

Cullmann is of opinion that the reference to Judas Iscariot as the traitor (vv. 70, 71) is to some extent a proof that chapter 6 contains St John's Eucharistic narrative. For if this be the case, the Fourth Gospel is made to correspond with the Synoptists in regard to Judas' taking part in the Last Supper—a participation which throws a still darker shadow over his betrayal of Jesus. The presence of Judas in this context is also a reminder that the mere exterior partaking of the Eucharist does not help a man, that is, does not guarantee his salvation.

19. *The Light of the World* (ch. 9.1–41)

"While I am in the world I am the Light of the world." Those words stand like a motto over the narrative of the healing of the man born blind. The place this story takes in the Gospel justifies our supposing that St John relates it as an illustration of the proclamation made by Jesus in 8.12: "I am the light of the world; he that followeth me shall not walk in darkness but shall have the light of life." We have already mentioned the connection between this text and the "baptismal passage" in 7.37–39, a connection which justifies us in supposing that in chapter 9, too, there are to be found traces of baptism in the early Church.

Cullmann does not include this passage with the rest of his "sacramental" texts, although he hints that in it there might be references to baptism. This is undoubtedly the case, more so than in the story of the impotent man at

Bethesda (ch. 5). For in chapter 9 the blind man is healed by means of washing in the pool of Siloam. It is possible that in v. 6 there is a reference to the laying on of hands which was used in connection with baptism in the early Church, right from the very beginning. In the early Church the name for baptism was φωτισμός and eventually there grew up the custom of handing a light to the newly-baptized person.

There is clear evidence in the New Testament that φῶς in the thought of the early Church has a connection with baptism. In Eph. 5.8 it is written: "Ye were sometimes darkness, but now are ye light in the Lord; walk as children of light"; while in the verses following there is mention made of "the fruit of light"[1] in contrast to "the works of darkness", which are "unfruitful".[2] This fruit of light is on the one hand a godly life while on the other it is Christian worship: "psalms and hymns and spiritual songs".[3] Thus the life of those who are baptized is put in clear contrast to that of the pagans; light is the atmosphere wherein the Christian lives, into which he is introduced through baptism,[4] while the existence of the pagans is pictured as a walk in the darkness.[5] And the Christians are not merely "children of light",[6] but they themselves are "the light of the world".[7]

In vv. 35–38 we may perhaps trace an ancient baptismal liturgy, the most important parts of which are the "baptismal question", "Dost thou believe on the Son of God?" and the confession given in answer to it, "Lord, I believe". The information that the Jews excommunicated the man (v. 34) does no doubt reflect their actual behaviour during the lifetime of the evangelist: those who believed in Christ and were received into the Church through baptism were excluded from the Synagogue.

[1] Eph. 5.9. [2] Eph. 5.11. [3] Eph. 5.18, 19.
[4] John 1.7. [5] Eph. 5.8, 11. [6] Eph. 5.8.
[7] Matt. 5.14; Phil. 2.15.

With the proclamation Jesus makes of himself as "the Light of the World" our thoughts are brought back to the tremendous words in the story of Creation, "Let there be light". For St John, too, this linking up comes quite naturally. Just as the light is the first created thing and the necessary condition for all life in the world, so also is Christ first in the renewed and redeemed Creation, i.e. the Church, and the condition for that perfect and eternal life which is a mark of the Church. John the Baptist, as compared with Christ, "the Light of the World", is only "the Lamp" in whose light men could rejoice for a short time, while Christ himself in the Church gives the true and abiding life.

The question of the Sabbath is also raised in chapter 9, but nothing further is added to what has already been said in chapter 5. We are reminded that the healing of the blind (the greatness of the sign is here emphasized by the man being *born* blind) was another of the marks of the Messianic Age.[1] It is clear that the Fourth Gospel is written to show that the world without Christ, i.e. outside the Church, is a world in darkness. In the Church Christ is to be found and the way to him is through baptism; this, however, is not merely an outward ceremony but an act of faith: baptism and confession of faith belong together (v. 38). He who is baptized and believes receives his sight; he sees and hears Christ (v. 37); but faith and baptism are not the work of men—they are the "works of God" (v. 3).

20. *The Washing of the Feet* (ch. 13.1–20)

There are few passages in the Bible which have been the object of so many varying interpretations as this one. Already the Fathers of the Church saw in it a reference to baptism. Modern scholars have interpreted the washing of the feet as an example of humility, an act which was continued to a certain extent in the early Church in imitation of the act

[1] Isa. 29.18; 35.5.

of Jesus. Bauer sees in it a protest against the many ceremonies of purification among the Jews and with a reference in it to the Eucharist; Hirsch thinks of it as referring to baptism and the mutual forgiveness of sins; while Bultmann, of course, dismisses all attempts at interpreting the text in a sacramental or liturgical way and declares that it is concerned with the reception of the ministry which Christ offers and performs through his word. Goguel calls the washing of the feet an allegory of the Eucharist; Kundsin considers it to be a new sacramental action; and Bertram has found in it an aetiological cult story. Eisler refers the washing of feet to marriage ceremonies and interprets it as the union of the heavenly bridegroom with the bride, i.e. the Church (here represented by the Apostles); while Henderson sees in the story a foreshadowing of the coming Passion of Jesus. Von Campenhausen and Craig see in the washing of the feet a defence of the system that grew up in the early Church of baptizing by means of "aspersion" when the catechumen stood in the baptismal "bath", the water reaching up only to the ankles! Lohmeyer states that the washing of feet does not represent baptism but that it is, with reference to the Eucharist, a dedication of apostleship. Belser considers it to be a form of shriving which Jesus used with his disciples immediately before the first Eucharist and which he asked them to go on using in the future. Cullmann regards the whole narrative as a polemic treatise against Anabaptists and interprets the meaning of it to be, that he who is once baptized is not to be baptized a second time; henceforth he is only to take part in the Eucharist. Michaelis has quite rightly pointed out that such an interpretation makes the Eucharist less important than baptism, a theory which cannot be justified either from the Fourth Gospel as a whole or from the theology of the Church. It is also clear that it would be quite contrary to the entire terminology and pictorial language of the Fourth Gospel to talk of the Eucharist as a washing of the feet.

THE LITURGY IN THE FOURTH GOSPEL

It seems as if the commentators have not paid enough attention to the position of this passage in its context and, above all, that they have not considered that any interpretation of it must not only tally with the pictorial language of the book as a whole, but also with the interpretation which is given in 13.12–20. Some scholars, among whom are Wellhausen, Schwartz, and Spitta, have sought a solution by means of the hypothesis of different sources. But it seems safest and best to study the actual text as it stands, taking into account the context in which the passage appears.

Jesus, when washing the feet of his disciples, performs the most despised of all menial tasks, one which was only given to the most inferior of the servants. This was bound to upset the disciples and, as usual, Peter speaks on behalf of them all in refusing to submit to the washing; and Jesus answers: "What I do thou knowest not now, but thou shalt understand hereafter" (v. 7). In this answer there is a clear pointer to the fact that the washing only receives its full meaning through the death of Jesus. A further proof of this is to be found in Jesus' words: "If I wash thee not, thou hast no part with me" (v. 8). Thus "to have part with Christ" means to partake of the fruit of his death, and it is just his approaching death which Jesus wants to illustrate by performing the meanest and most despicable of all the tasks allotted to a servant. The death of Jesus on the Cross still gives to the faithful forgiveness of sin and eternal life; Jesus here performs that sacrificial service in a symbolic way in the presence of his disciples immediately before he performs it in reality on the Cross. The meaning, therefore, of the washing of the feet can only be understood in the setting of the Church, and only by those who already have part in Christ; for to have part in Christ is to have membership in the Church. With regard to the Church it is also self-evident that ὁ λελουμένος (v. 10) must be interpreted as referring to Christian baptism, through which a man is taken into the Church and made partaker of the fruits of the death of

Jesus. Only with this interpretation can the text be considered as a polemic against the ritual washing of the Jews. For it would be unthinkable for Jesus to attack these customs by performing an action of the same significance himself. It is by means of his death on the Cross that he once and for all performs the "washing" of all men; through that baptism which unites men to Christ and gives them a part in the fruit of his suffering, all ritual washings are thus both fulfilled and superseded: that is the clear meaning of this text.

What, then, is the meaning of εἰ μὴ τοὺς πόδας νίψασθαι (v. 10)? The question whether the words εἰ μὴ τοὺς πόδας are original is of little importance, for in any case the meaning can only be one; baptism is to take place only once, just as Christ died only once. For baptism is a baptism into the death of Jesus[1] the sins committed after baptism are to be removed through confession and absolution. This must be the significance of νίψασθαι, which thus refers to the Sacrament of Penance. Such an interpretation corresponds with the words in v. 14: "If I then, the Lord and Master, have washed your feet, ye also ought to wash one another's feet. For I have given you an example. . . ." Through the washing of the feet St John wants to show how Jesus, by performing the task of a lowly servant, offers himself for his own, giving them by means of his own death the forgiveness of their sins. He, at one and the same time, gives to them the power of receiving this forgiveness through baptism in the Church, and of continually renewing this gift by confession of their sins and the reception of absolution. So the washing of the feet is closely connected with the institution of the Sacrament of Penance.[2] But this possibility of forgiveness of sins is only open to those who believe; Judas was present at the washing of the feet, but he nevertheless went to perdition.[3] His receiving the morsel of bread dipped in the wine, given to him by Jesus (to which St John pays more

---

[1] Rom. 6.3.　　　[2] John 20.23.　　　[3] John 13.30.

attention than do the Synoptists), further stresses his crime. Not even his participation in the common meal of the Last Supper (the equivalent of the Eucharistic communion of the Church) can save the man who has no faith. The sacramental "background" to the whole story can also be seen in the use of the verb ἀγαπᾶν (v. 1) and above all in δοξάζειν (v. 31 ff).

21. *The Vine* (ch. 15.1–17)

This passage has been treated above as an expression of the deep unity existing between Christ and his disciples in the Church. Here we must ask the following question: What is it that lies behind this proclamation by Jesus of himself as the true Vine? We have already seen that the references to the Vine in the Old Testament are not sufficient for our study and therefore we have tried to find further material in the religions of other nations.

Most scholars seem to think that this passage must be interpreted against the background of the idea of the tree of life which is common to most religions. The "tree of life" then, in our text, may be compared with that tree in the Garden of Eden described in Gen. 2.9. From this the deep significance of the passage immediately becomes apparent; for as the tree of life in Paradise once brought about the Fall of man, so that he was no longer able to live in Paradise, so now does the new tree of life, Christ, bring to man remission of sin and opens again to him the gates of Paradise. The curse of sin is taken away and creation reaches its perfection through the death and resurrection of Christ, i.e. in the eschatological age of the Church.

Now comes the question: "Is it merely accidental that the unity between Christ and his disciples is here pictured under the image of a vine?" Certainly not! For the vine is the symbol of joy; and in v. 11 mention is made of joy. Wine is the drink of the joyful marriage feast, and love is spoken of in vv. 9–10, 12. This love and joy come about because Jesus gives his life for his disciples (v. 13). It is also clear that in the words referring to Jesus as the true Vine there is also a reference to the Eucharist, which receives its power significance through the death of Jesus; this sacrament at one and the same time shows to the faithful the suffering of the Cross and gives them a part in the fruit of this suffering, and thus establishes a deep and real unity between them and Christ. But it is also the most perfect expression of the union of the disciples with Christ and with each other; it is the supreme cause for thanksgiving and at the same time the most perfect sign of their shared life and mutual love.

22. *The Piercing with the Lance* (ch. 19.34)

"Howbeit, one of the soldiers with a spear pierced his side, and straightway there came out blood and water." Bultmann, as usual, explains the latter part of this text by ascribing it to his "editor", while Cullmann and most other scholars see in it a clear reference to the two sacraments of the Church. The same thought recurs in 1 John 5.6–8, where it is even more clearly formulated from the point of view of the Church: "This is he that came by water and blood, even Jesus Christ ... and it is the Spirit that beareth witness, because the Spirit is truth." St John is everywhere at pains to point out that it is the Spirit that gives to the sacraments their validity. He thinks of the sacraments in an altogether religious and eschatological manner: all thoughts of magic or impersonal mysticism are entirely out of the question.

The statement in 19.34 emphasizes the true humanity and the actual death of Jesus as against any docetic heresies. The whole theology of the Fourth Gospel is built on the two basic facts of the Incarnation and the Reconciliation. Here the Evangelist shows that it is in the very death of Jesus that the sacraments, and thus the Church, take their origin and derive their strength.

THE LITURGY IN THE FOURTH GOSPEL 75

Attention has been called already to the deep symbolism of the fact that, in contrast to the treatment given to the two thieves, no bone was broken in the dead body of Jesus; he is the true Paschal Lamb. But there is here another complex of ideas which claims our attention, namely the Jewish belief that the rest of the dead body in the grave was a condition for its resurrection. The description of the forbearance of the soldiers towards the dead body of Jesus is inserted to point out that this body was meant to rise again. This may be taken as a further proof of the consistency with which St John shows the death and resurrection of Jesus to be one indivisible whole—his "lifting-up".

Again this incident brings out very clearly what is implied in the conception of Jesus as the true Paschal Lamb; with the death of Jesus the new Passover has come. As at the first Passover the children of Israel were delivered from the bondage of Egypt and given the chance to begin the journey to the promised land, so now the new Passover gives to all the children of God deliverance from the land of bondage of sin and death and the chance to begin their journey to the heavenly Canaan. The followers of Jesus, therefore, live in the age of the new Passover, that is, of the Christian Church, for it is from his death that the two life-giving wells of the Church spring up—baptism and the Eucharist. Thus we agree with Cullmann that 19.34 is a key-passage to the understanding of the whole theology of the Fourth Gospel; and this is emphasized by means of the solemn declaration of the truthfulness of the narrative in v. 35 ff.

23. *The Relation of the Gospel to the Liturgy in the Primitive Church*
(summary)

So far we have shown that the sacraments play an important part in the narrative and in the theology of the Fourth Gospel. Although we cannot agree with Cullmann's theory of the interrelationship between the sacramental passages, we must nevertheless admit that all these liturgically coloured texts bear witness to that strong sense of the *ecclesia* which is a mark of the Fourth Gospel and also to the importance attached to eschatology in the same Gospel. For the sacraments are dependent on eschatology; they show that the time of fulfilment is come, while at the same time they point onwards to the great fulfilment.

We must now ask what it is that induces the Evangelist to make such continuous references to the sacramental life of the Church in a narrative which, after all, mainly sets out to relate the earthly life of Jesus. For it is not very likely that in so doing he merely wants to show his interest in the Church and her liturgy. Again we must ask how it is that, in spite of this obviously keen interest, he does not mention the institution of either baptism or the Eucharist. The omission of the institution of the Eucharist, in particular, has greatly bewildered scholars of all schools, inducing them to draw all kinds of false conclusions. Bultmann sees in it a clear proof of the anti-sacramental character of the Fourth Gospel. According to him, the High-Priestly prayer (ch. 17) takes the place of the omitted Eucharistic account. Gaugler represents the common view that St John omits the narrative as being widely known. Moffat holds that St John represses the Eucharist in favour of the "meal of love" (ἀγάπη) because, he thinks, the Evangelist has a "deeper and more spiritual view of communion". Creed believed that St John omitted the narrative of the institution as well as that of the baptism of Jesus because he disliked representing material things as vehicles of the gifts of the Spirit. Both Moffat and Creed have clearly failed to realize that such a spiritualizing interpretation stands in sharp contrast to the anti-docetic tendency of the whole Gospel. Oehler states that the narrative of the institution has been omitted because the Gospel was written for pagans to whom the Eucharist would have been incomprehensible, so that a narrative about it would only give rise to blasphemous ideas. According to Huber, it is the "arkan discipline" that has kept St John from relating the institution of the Eucharist. In our opinion, the real reason for the omission of this account is that the Eucharist as well as baptism, both of which are vitally bound up with the risen life of Jesus, is impossible before the death of Jesus. In other words, it was not that St John was anti-sacramental but that, in his view, sacraments belong to the New Age ushered in by the death and resurrection of Jesus, and can therefore only be celebrated in the Church embodying the New Age. Why, then, is it that the Fourth Gospel mentions the sacraments at all in connection with the earthly life of Jesus? Would not every such reference seem to the Evangelist an unbearable anachronism? Cullmann's answer is, no doubt, the correct one: that the one aim is to link up in this way the earthly life of Jesus with the life of Christ who is alive and working in the Church; i.e. to state the identity between the Jesus of history and the Christ who is present in the Liturgy.

This chapter has mainly dealt with texts containing references to the sacraments or the sabbath. But there are other passages, too, which can be fully understood only when their liturgical character is taken into consideration. Among these is 1.51: "Ye shall see the heaven opened and the angels of God ascending and descending upon the Son of Man." The presence of the angels is a manifestation of the divine power and glory of Jesus and refers not only to his "signs" during his earthly life, nor to his coming as the Judge of the world at the end of time, but also to his presence in the cult which is an anticipation of the Parousia. In this context we must also consider such a passage as 3.29: "He that hath the bride is the bridegroom . . .", words which might well be an echo from the cult in the early Church in the same manner as the following liturgical formula which appears very frequently in the Fourth Gospel: "Verily, verily I say unto you".

Now we can advance a step further in the conclusions we

can draw from the Fourth Gospel's keen interest in the Jewish cult. The Gospel aims at showing how the expectations about the coming Messiah were fulfilled through Jesus Christ in his earthly existence, and how this existence is being fulfilled and perfected through his continuing work as risen Lord in the sacraments of the Church, until the Parousia, when the New Age of the Church ceases, and all promises will come to their final fulfilment. The whole line of thought is thus altogether eschatological. The proleptic eschatology of the Jewish cult is fulfilled in Christ, who in his turn creates in the Church a new eschatological position, which is experienced in the cult, and continually points onwards to the end of this age and to the great fulfilment.

CHAPTER 4

ESCHATOLOGY AND THE CHURCH IN THE FOURTH GOSPEL

24. *Results of Earlier Investigations*

WE NOTED in the very beginning of this thesis the important part played by Rudolf Bultmann in recent discussions, regarding the eschatology of the Fourth Gospel. There it was pointed out that Bultmann regarded it as a wholly realized eschatology, related only to the "present"; with no future significance. Thus, he maintains that man is always in the eschatological "now". It is *now* that he is brought into contact with the Word and forced to make a decision. Indeed it is of the essence of the faith of the Church that she understands and is aware of her eschatological position, and that as a result of this awareness she lives "offen für die Zukunft" ("open to the future"). But according to Bultmann, this future has no attributes—it is empty.

Now to some extent, the Fourth Gospel gives support to these views since the word "hope" (ἐλπίς) is altogether missing from it: while the verb (ἐλπίζειν) appears but once, and then in connection with the Jews' unfounded reliance on Moses.[1] But there are many sayings which necessitate a "futurist" eschatology. These Bultmann dismisses as editorial additions designed to bring St John into line with the teaching of the early Church. Thus he maintains that, according to the "realized eschatology" of the Fourth

[1] John 5.45.

Gospel, the Parousia has come about through the resurrection of Jesus; judgement takes place here and now when man is brought into contact with the Word, and is forced to make a decision; faith is the means by which man comes to self-knowledge while life is "das aus der Zukunft bestimmte Sein" ("the 'now' determined by the future"). The Paraclete is taken by him to mean the Word as preached in the congregation.

This theme is frequently varied by Bultmann and his followers. In order to support his theories, however, he is forced to cut the text of the Gospel in a very ruthless manner; and this leads to such a misinterpretation and watering down of Biblical ideas that they lose their realism and clearness and lead us into the cold and rarefied atmosphere of philosophical distinctions. The eschatology has thus been reduced to philosophical abstractions, and as he has divorced it wholly from the Church, i.e. from history, and from the future, Bultmann is bound to end in mysticism and spiritualism, however much he may deny it.

Johannes Schneider does not go so far as Bultmann in his denial of the eschatology of the Fourth Gospel, but he thinks that its eschatological expectations are no longer really alive. Nevertheless, it is from the soil of this "withered eschatology" ("abgelasste Eschatologie") that he sees the Johannine "mysticism" growing up. O. Michel states that the Johannine eschatology is "uberzeitlich und endzeitlich" (both pointing beyond time and fulfilled in time), thus seeking to give support to its forward-looking character.

H. Greeven, to whom the Johannine Christ is, above all, the advocate of the Christians before God, declares that the eschatology of the Fourth Gospel is impossible to define on account of its "gedankliche Unklarheit" (lack of clear thinking). In the end, however, he admits the future aspect in it.

Gustav Stählin has written a very instructive essay on the eschatology of this Gospel. In it, on the basis of its sayings about the coming Messiah, the relation to the present as well

ESCHATOLOGY IN FOURTH GOSPEL

as to the future of such expressions as κρίσις and ζωή, and finally the dualism which runs all through the Gospel and which demands a final solution, he states that the Johannine eschatology is in the majority of cases realized in the present: nevertheless he sees a definitely future aspect all through the Gospel. This twofold aspect of St John's eschatology cannot be explained as his attempt to conform to popular opinion, nor can it be regarded simply as an expression of his personal conception of the message and work of Jesus. Stählin criticizes Bultmann's theory and gives his own view as follows: "Alongside and interwoven are the 'already-now' and the 'not-yet'. The life in the 'now' and the life 'looked-forward-to' in the future belong together. That is the basis not only of Johannine devotion but of the New Testament as a whole." However true these conclusions may be, we consider that Stählin's view of St John's eschatology is extraordinarily colourless and lifeless. Yet it is just in its conception of "life" that this present eschatology should reveal its peculiar character. The mistake Stählin makes is that he does not confront the eschatology with the actual life in the early Church, which was so clearly marked by it; and it is always fatal to turn life into an abstraction. This life is not merely reflected in the Fourth Gospel: the Gospel is itself an expression of it. Although Stählin points out that St John wrote after the death of Jesus and from within the Church created by him he has not really made use of this opinion in his interpretation of the eschatology.

Gaugler, too, criticizes Bultmann's theory and emphasizes the tension between the present and the future as something characteristic of the Gospel as a whole.

Buri sees in the present character of the Johannine eschatology a proof of the influence of Hellenistic mysticism.

Dodd thinks that the future aspect has been pushed into the background by St John in favour of a "realized eschatology" which he emphasizes as belonging to the Christian message right from the beginning.

Huber's view is that St John has done away with the cosmological aspect of eschatology, and refers it solely to man, without thereby diminishing its force.

As regards the *ecclesia*, very few scholars have found any trace of it in the Fourth Gospel, for they have assumed that such an entirely "mystical" writing could have no place for organized Church life. The Archimandrite Cassian, however, in an essay on the New Testament doctrine of the Church refers to this Gospel in connection with the apostolate[1] and with the unity of the Church.[2] Thus, he saw in "the disciple whom Jesus loved" a symbol of the Church, which, at the foot of the Cross, was taken under the protection of the Virgin Mary, reverence for whom he considers to have its origin in the Johannine theology. Cassian, however, thinks of the Church in this Gospel only in terms of this present world: it was to him the Kingdom of God here and now. He expresses his views with regard to the Johannine eschatology in another work in the following words: "The Kingdom of God of the Synoptic Gospels has its counterpart in the Johannine 'life'." Hence to him the Johannine eschatology corresponds with that of the whole New Testament, the Kingdom of God being, on the one hand, realized in the Church; and on the other hand coming at the end of time—the Holy Spirit working in the Church here and now as well as in the eschatological fulfilment.

W. F. Howard acknowledges in the Fourth Gospel both a future eschatology and also a "Church-consciousness". The problem, however, is not further discussed by him, while no hint is given as to the connection between these two.

With H. E. Weber we meet a peculiar combination of eschatology and mysticism. Thus he writes: "The true meaning of 'Eschatology' lies in its relationship to 'mysticism': and the essence of 'mysticism' is to be found in its relation to 'Eschatology'." This combination is made

[1] John 20.30; 21.   [2] John 14—17.

possible because "Mysticism" is here taken in its widest meaning. Thus Weber speaks of *Glaubensmystik, Liebesmystik, Geschichtsmystik* (mysticism of belief, mysticism of love, mysticism of history), a fact which shows that the idea of *mystik* has been brought to bear on all sorts of religious manifestations, and is therefore of no use for scientific discussion. That Weber considers the eschatology of the Fourth Gospel to be both present and future the following quotation makes quite clear: "The present salvation is mystically interpreted pointing to God's plan in the future." Thus the dualism in the Fourth Gospel leads Weber to speak of its "apocalyptic" conception of the world—a conception, nevertheless, which he is obliged to admit is not pictured in detail.

Doris Faulhaber has seen evidence of the Church in the Fourth Gospel and defines it as follows: "a community of people living in the world whose lord is Jesus Christ, and in him is God". To prove this, she refers to the passages about the Good Shepherd and the Vine in chapters 10 and 15. We have already seen how the texts themselves correct her definition, which pictures the Church solely as a human organization. It is true that the author supplements her definition with the following explanation: "the Church is only there where Jesus is Lord"; but she gives no further direction as to where Christ is to be found, and in what way he exercises his rule. According to her own definition Christ's presence and his rule are not to be found in the Liturgy nor in the traditions of the Church, for she will not admit that there are any such marks of the Church in the Fourth Gospel. It must be seriously questioned whether the thought of the Church without a liturgy is possible, and still more, whether such a thought could possibly be realized. Indeed, when Faulhaber defines the Johannine idea of the Church as a community of people it follows that their communion should be in some way manifested. Now the foremost manifestation of such a communion has always been in its liturgy, and O. Cullmann has clearly shown what an important part the liturgy played in Johannine thought.

German romanticism flourishes in Wagenführer's interpretation of the Johannine idea of the Church. According to him, St John's is the picture of an ideal Church, the communion and unity in a small circle of disciples, undisturbed by hierarchical or administrative questions.

We now propose to follow the line of thought suggested by Scandinavian scholars such as H. Ludin Jansen, A. Fridrichsen, and Å. Ström, in an attempt to show the inevitable connection in the Fourth Gospel between eschatology and the Church. Kümmel, who, in his study of the Church in the New Testament, has left out the Johannine writings altogether, writes: "The idea in the mind of the primitive Church is quite clear and depends on the consciousness of the salvation which is already working but has not yet been completely fulfilled. Is this opinion also to be applied to the Fourth Gospel? If St John's eschatology is related only to the individual then we are faced with mysticism, not real eschatology. If, however, the Johannine eschatology is rooted in the doctrine of the Church, in her life, her confession and her orders, then being concerned with a community and with the experience of this community, it will be true eschatology."

The Fourth Gospel is rooted in history, a fact which has a bearing on its eschatology. Now the characteristic of all true historical writing, as distinct from the records of a chronicler, is a conviction that there is an inner connection between the varying events of history, and that history is not a mere matter of chance but that it is directed towards a definite goal; in other words, history is conditioned by eschatology. The Church *is* sacred history. It is the continuation of the work of Christ from the Resurrection till the Parousia. If then the eschatology of the Fourth Gospel is true eschatology, it will of necessity carry with it a strong "Church-consciousness".

25. *The Spirit and the Paraclete*

According to Christian tradition the Day of Pentecost is the birthday of the Church. We have seen in paragraph 11 that St John, when relating the events of Pentecost, makes them take place on the evening of Easter Day, thus causing Easter and Pentecost to coincide. His reason is clear, namely that it was through the death and resurrection of Jesus that the Church was created. Thus there was no *need* for a time of waiting, or for anything over and above the "lifting-up" of Jesus: nor indeed was any such lapse of time *possible*. The Church *was* the immediate and inevitable outcome of Easter. The intimate connection between the "lifting-up" of Jesus and the sending of the Holy Spirit is shown in 7.39: "But this he spake of the Spirit, which they that believed on him were to receive: for the Spirit was not yet given, because Jesus was not yet glorified." (N.B. The Swedish Bible reads instead of "glorified"—"risen from the dead".)

We have already seen the connection between the Spirit and the Church in those passages where the Spirit is connected with the sacraments, for example in the baptismal text of 3.5–6: "born of water and the spirit", where the new birth "of the spirit" is put over against the physical birth "of the flesh" and also in the eucharistic text of 6.63: "It is the Spirit that quickeneth; the flesh profiteth nothing: the words that I have spoken unto you are Spirit and are life." Thus it is through the Spirit that the Sacraments have their power and that the apostolic testimony, the word of Christ, has its credibility. Without the Spirit the sacraments are just "flesh" (σάρξ) and cannot mediate life (ζωή). This is expressed in 1 John 5.7–8: "There are three that bear witness: the Spirit, the water and the blood." It is the Spirit, too, that creates the conditions necessary for right prayer—"worship in Spirit and in truth".[1] Now in all these instances we may catch behind the conception of πνεῦμα (spirit) a

---
[1] John 4.23, 24.

glimpse of the Johannine Church with its liturgy and its preaching of the word. Through the Spirit the words of Jesus are "life", i.e. they are not merely the words of man but the words of God, for "God is a Spirit" (4.24). Therefore the testimony of the Church, the teaching of the exalted Saviour, is marked by the Spirit; it is none other than the word of God.

The account of the descent of the Spirit at the Baptism of Jesus has been regarded as opposed to the Logos-theology of the Fourth Gospel. St John firmly states that Jesus was from the very beginning the Incarnate *Logos*. Every possibility of an adoptionist interpretation is ruled out by the omission of the actual narrative of the act of baptism, while the descent of the Spirit upon Jesus is related indirectly in the form of the testimony of the Baptist. Thus St John suggests that this giving of the Spirit did not happen for the sake of Jesus, that is, in order to bestow on him a gift which he did not already possess, but rather for the sake of the Baptist, that he might be enabled to recognize him and bear witness to him.[1] The evangelist nevertheless stresses this descent of the Spirit on Jesus, for he refers to it twice, the second time with the addition "... the same is he that baptizeth with the Holy Spirit" (v. 33). This same passage emphasizes the fact that Jesus was prior to the Baptist, a thought which is brought out even more clearly in 1.6–9 and 3.25–36. Many writers see in these passages the struggle of the young Church against those who would have claimed St John the Baptist for the Messiah, and claim that the case for the Church was made particularly forceful by the Baptist's own declaration of Jesus' superiority.

The Fourth Gospel also emphasizes the idea of the Baptism of Jesus as a dedication to death. The words of the Baptist, "Behold the Lamb of God which taketh away the sin of the world", suggest the connection between the baptism of water and the baptism of blood. It is through the baptism of blood, "the lifting-up", that the Church is

[1] John 1.31–34; cf. 12.28–30.

created. Thus the words of the Baptist point forward beyond Jesus' baptism of water in the Jordan to his coming baptism of blood upon the Cross. The repetition of μένειν (1.32, 33) underlines the fact that the resting of the Spirit upon Jesus was not a momentary event limited to the time of his baptism but rather the abiding mark of the whole of his ministry. Thus the baptism of Jesus in the Jordan anticipates the age of the Spirit in the Christian Church. Indeed the Christian Church is already present in the world in the person of Jesus. He is the King in whom the people of God are realized. It is, however, only through his death and resurrection that the Church and her gifts (the Spirit) are made available to man.

In the text πνεῦμα ὁ θεός (God is a spirit, 4.24), πνεῦμα is the predicate. This passage does not describe the *personal* identity between God and the Spirit, but rather the "representative" identity between them—the same identity as there is between the Father and the Son[1] and between the Son and the Spirit.[2] This is an extremely important basis for the Church's doctrine of the Trinity.

St John's theology of the Spirit is complicated by the use of the two terms πνεῦμα and παράκλητος. The texts referring to the Paraclete[3] have been the object of much careful investigation. B. W. Bacon speaks about the two Paracletes, "the friend at court" (Christ) and "the friend from court" (the Spirit). S. Sasse distinguishes between two types of Paraclete-texts, the older one in chapters 15 and 16, where the references are due to the evangelist himself, and a more recent one in chapter 14, where a later hand had rounded off the discourse by identifying the Paraclete with the Holy Spirit.

The idea of paracletes found expression in angels, heavenly messengers and mediators, a characteristic feature of late Jewish and Gnostic speculation. The further thought of

---
[1] John 1.1.   [2] John 16.12–15.
[3] John 14.16; 14.25, 26; 15.26; 16.7–15; 1 John 2.1, 2.

angels as intercessors before God played an important part in late Judaism. S. Mowinckel believes that this conception, which owed its origin to Persian religion, had been associated with the Spirit who had thus been termed the Paraclete. This Spirit-Paraclete combination was already in common use, according to Mowinckel, before the compilation of the Fourth Gospel, so that the evangelist in speaking of the Spirit as the Paraclete only adopted a terminology ready to hand. Such a theory would explain the difficulty which has been felt in fitting the Paraclete-idea into the Fourth Gospel.

Bultmann, on the contrary, does not agree with this theory, but believes that the evangelist himself took over the conception of heavenly messengers, and applied it to the Spirit. Here Bultmann sees a trace of Gnostic influence. Against this N. Johansson maintains that the idea of the Paraclete is rooted essentially in Israelite soil. His further suggestion, however, that Jesus himself on some occasion identified himself with the Paraclete seems more dubious. But this identification of Christ with a Paraclete may be seen behind 14.16, ἄλλον παράκλητον (another paraclete), and is clearly shown in 1 John 2.1. The question still remains as to why the evangelist uses the words ὁ παράκλητος when speaking of the Spirit. παράκλητος really means advocate, "advocatus". The word "helper" used in the Swedish translation is colourless although not altogether misleading, as the functions of the Paraclete are very varied. A closer study of the Paraclete-passages gives the following result:

1. The Paraclete is called "the Holy Spirit" or, more frequently, "the Spirit of truth" (τό πνεῦμα τῆς ἀληθείας). Our investigation of ἀλήθεια later on in this book will show that this term includes the "lifting-up" of Jesus, and the Church which came into being through this event. Thus it is like πνεῦμα an ecclesiastical term.

2. The Paraclete stands in complete contrast to "the world", (κόσμος), which cannot receive him, because it

ESCHATOLOGY IN FOURTH GOSPEL 89

neither sees nor understands him (οὐ θεωρεῖ αὐτὸ οὐδὲ γινώσκει). It may well be that this "seeing" refers to the Christian cult, which is the meeting place for the Paraclete and the faithful.

3. It is in the Church that the Paraclete comes to be known and understood (ὑμεῖς γινώσκετε αὐτό), and this knowledge is the opposite of the false γνῶσις of the world.

4. The Paraclete abides (μένει) with the faithful, that is, in the Church. There is no doubt whatever that the verb μένειν is an ecclesiastical term, as we have seen already.

5. The Paraclete abides in the Church to all eternity (εἰς τὸν αἰῶνα), a fact showing us the eschatological function of the Paraclete.

6. The Father (or the Son) is to send out the Paraclete, (πέμψει), and the Paraclete proceeds, (ἐκπορεύεται), from the Father. The same verb, (πέμπειν), is used about the sending of the Paraclete as about the sending of the Son by the Father.[1]

7. The Paraclete is sent "in the Name of Jesus" (ἐν τῷ ὀνόματί μου). Here we may compare the passages about prayer "in the Name of Jesus".[2]

8. It is the function of the Paraclete to instruct the Church. Jesus said, "He shall teach you all things (διδάξει πάντα) and bring all things to your remembrance (ὑπομνήσει πάντα) whatsoever I have said unto you." Here the repetition of πάντα is of great importance, since it makes clear that the disciples, far from being impoverished through the "lifting-up" of Jesus, on the contrary, as a result of it, received the gift of the Spirit who is to show to them the whole truth.

9. The coming of the Paraclete is dependent upon the going away of Jesus, his "lifting-up" (16.17). This makes it clear that the Paraclete becomes available to men first in the Church.

10. The Paraclete is the driving force in the missionary

[1] John 6.44; 8.18; 12.49; 16.5.
[2] John 14.13, 14; 15.16; 16.23, 24, 26.

work of the Church: "He will convict the world (ἐλέγξει τὸν κόσμον) in respect of sin, of righteousness and of judgement"; sin is failure to believe in Christ, righteousness is Christ's redeeming work, and judgement is Christ's complete victory on the Cross over the "prince of this world". Thus we find here an argument against the moral and apocalyptic ideas of both Jewish and Hellenistic thought.

11. The Paraclete is the inspirer of prophecy: he will make known what is about to happen (τὰ ἐρχόμενα). The consummation of all things is foreshadowed in the Church.

12. The Paraclete will glorify Christ (δοξάσει). As will be pointed out later on, δόξα is a term which refers not only to the coming of Christ at the Parousia, but also to his coming now, in the cult.

13. The Paraclete reveals the unity between the Father and the Son: and this implies the same unity between the Son and the Paraclete. St John clearly wishes to mark by means of the term "Paraclete" the representative identity between Christ and the Spirit.

From this exposition it is clear that the word "Paraclete" as used in the Fourth Gospel is of an altogether ecclesiastical and eschatological nature. The Paraclete belongs to the Church, is necessary to the Church, and is to foster and guide the faithful towards the great fulfilment. Pointing back to Christ and to the facts of his first coming (i.e. to the historical revelation of God in him), the Paraclete at the same time points forward towards his second coming at the Parousia. Thus, making real in the lives of men the redeeming work of Christ which was accomplished once for all in time, he also is the pledge that this same Jesus who thus came once in time will come again, in great glory, at the end of time.

Apart from that suggested by Johansson, there are two other motives that might lie behind St John's use of the word "Paraclete" to designate the Spirit in the Church. As the Church grew and the Gospel was, therefore, "popularized" there was a great risk of the πνεῦμα-conception becoming either materialized or spiritualized. It would seem, then, that St John sets out to counteract both of these tendencies. Thus he consistently points out the importance of the Spirit at baptism,[1] at the Eucharist,[2] at the institution and administration of the Church's ministry,[3] at prayer,[4] and in preaching.[5] In this way St John is clearly fighting against tendencies to a superficial and vulgarized conception of the holy. Another dangerous tendency, and one often more difficult to detect, was that of a false spirituality such as characterized the Gnostics. This danger became acute when the Spirit began to be separated from the historical Christ and looked upon as an impersonal "power" at the disposal of man. This view of the impersonality of the Spirit gave rise within the Church to ecstatic and fanciful currents, which appeared very early in its history,[6] and before very long took on definitely schismatic and heretical characteristics.

Now it would seem to be against this danger that St John was trying to guard the Church when he linked the idea of the Spirit with that of the Paraclete, since the Paraclete had always been conceived of as a person. Thanks to him this personal conception of the Spirit has never been lost in the Church. Thus St John speaks of the Spirit as "proceeding" from the Father and the Son[7] and as "teaching" about very *real* things: sin, righteousness, and judgement.[8] The Spirit, moreover, is inseparable from Christ, his death, and his resurrection, for he is "the Spirit of truth" and can only be received and possessed in fellowship with Christ, in the Church. Furthermore, just as the Spirit of God, *ruach*, existed in the very beginning and as the *Logos* was in existence at the time of the creation of all things, so too the same

[1] John 3.5ff. [2] John 6.63. [3] John 20.22.
[4] John 4.23. [5] John 15.26.
[6] Acts 20.29ff; 1 Cor. 3.4; 2 Thess. 2.1–12; 1 Tim. 4.1–13; 6.3–5; 2 Tim. 4.3ff; 1 John 4.2ff.
[7] John 14.16, 26; 15.26; 16.7. [8] John 16.8–11.

Spirit is present at the fulfilment of that creation, that is in the Church, bearing witness to the final restoration and consummation: "He shall lead you into all truth" and "He shall make known unto you the things that are to come."[1] It was not the giving of random oracles to which Our Lord was here referring; rather he was pointing out the Spirit's essential function of preparing men for the age of consummation.

Another reason for St John's using for the Spirit the name "Paraclete", which had both Jewish and Gentile associations, was probably to show how in Christ and his Church lay the fulfilment of the hopes of both Jews and Gentiles. And finally, by adopting a non-Christian term, St John characteristically fills it with Christian meaning, thereby making it at one and the same time a channel for the expression of the Christian message and a new means of approach to the non-Christian world.

26. *The Character of the Johannine Idea of the Church*

Before we put together the result of our previous investigations regarding the Church in the Fourth Gospel, there are still a few more expressions which need to be examined.

The passage about the Vine has given us cause to note the frequent occurrence of the verb μένειν—to abide. Apart from a few places where μένειν is combined with some expression of place,[2] the word occurs more than twenty times in the Fourth Gospel, and just as often in the first Epistle of St John. It is used in the sense of abiding in Christ,[3] of abiding in the words of Jesus or in his love,[4] of the abiding of Jesus with his disciples, of the abiding of the Father in Christ, and of the abiding of the Spirit with the disciples.[5]

---

[1] John 16.13.
[2] John 2.12; 4.40; 11.6; 19.31.
[3] John 15.4, 6, 7.
[4] John 5.38; 8.31; 15.9, 10.
[5] John 12.34; 14.25; 14.10; 14.17.

But the term is also used to signify the remaining in darkness and sin of the unfaithful,[1] it is used in the parable of the son remaining at home,[2] and also of the enduring fruit in the life of the disciples.[3] In the first Epistle of St John μένειν is generally used of abiding in Christ; in God; in the words of Christ; in love; and of the abiding of God in us and reciprocally of the relationship between Christ and the faithful.

It is clear that in most cases μένειν is an expression of the unity between the disciples and Christ, and that the word is mainly used in the Last Discourse and in the Epistle. Therefore the reader may gather that the unity established between Jesus and his disciples during his earthly life was not a temporary and passing one even though it seemed to be broken by his death. The frequently repeated μένειν is a reminder that this unity is still there after the death of Jesus; or rather that it is coming to its real stature and perfection through his death and resurrection, i.e. in the Church. It is characteristic that the many texts containing μένειν in 15.1–17 are linked up with a clear reference to the death of Jesus and that the one in 6.56 definitely refers to the sacramental unity between Jesus and the disciples which is only possible in the Church. In 8.31, however, the reference is to the preaching of the word, for, as will be shown shortly, freedom is promised in 8.32 to those who abide in the words of Jesus; and this, too, is only realized in the Church.

The term φῶς next claims our attention. In the Fourth Gospel φῶς usually refers to the Christ revealed in the world[4] and the faithful are also called "the children of light".[5] Where Christ is, there is light also; and opposed to it is the darkness—the night. In two places the terms "day" and "night" are used in such a way that we may distinguish the twofold meaning: "I must work the works of him that sent me, while it is day: the night cometh, when no

---

[1] John 12.46; 9.41. [2] John 8.35. [3] John 15.16.
[4] John 1.4, 5, 8, 9; 3.19–21; 8.12; 9.5; 12.35, 36, 46.
[5] John 12.36.

man can work. As long as I am in the world, I am the light of the world."[1] "If a man walk in the day he stumbleth not because he seeth the light of this world; but if a man walk in the night he stumbleth, because the light is not in him."[2] Thus "the day" is the situation created by the "true light", or "the light of the world"—that is, Christ.[3] And this situation, which in 1 John 1.7 is called a walk in light in contrast to the walk in darkness which is sin (cf. 1 John 2.8–11), may be identified with life in the Church.

As more and more scholars are coming to think, it is mainly in the so-called Last Discourses that we shall find best examples of St John's conception of the Church. In 13.31 we come to a new phase in the narrative of the Evangelist. The traitor had gone out, after he had been warned by Jesus—or rather, after he had received from the Master direct admonition to go and accomplish his evil purpose. This means that the chain of events which inexorably led Jesus on to the death of the Cross had now its beginning. So Jesus opened his speech with the fateful "now" (νῦν). For now a new situation had begun, the first mark of which is—contrary to all human speculations—the δόξα of the Son of Man, his glory. In the discourses which, according to St John, Jesus gave at this time, we meet with several expressions which demand attention.

In 13.34 we have: "A new commandment I give unto you, that ye love one another (ἀγαπᾶτε ἀλλήλους); even as I have loved you, that ye also love one another." And the same admonition reappears in 14.15, 21–24; 15.9, 10. The secret regarding this "new commandment" which Jesus first gave to his disciples at the moment of farewell is revealed in 15.12–15; "This is my commandment, that ye love one another even as I have loved you. Greater love hath no man than this, that a man lay down his life for his friends. Ye are my friends if ye do the things that I command you.... I call

---

[1] John 9.4, 5.   [2] John 11.9, 10.
[3] John 1.9; 3.19; 8.12; 9.5; 11.9; 12.45.

you not servants . . . but I have called you friends." The prerequisite for the love of the disciples to each other is thus the love that Jesus first has shown to them. And that love found its perfect expression on the Cross. Only after Jesus, through his "lifting-up", has shown the real nature of his love, can he demand that the disciples should keep the "new commandment" to love one another. He has, then, himself kept his Father's commandment, even to the Cross, and has, thus, remained in his love. Therefore he can say: "If ye keep my commandments ye shall abide in my love." The time has come when Jesus no longer calls his disciples servants (δοῦλοι) but friends (φίλοι), because they now understand what their master does. For through the death and resurrection of Jesus the disciples are given full insight into the mystery of salvation; how the Father loves the Son and through him his disciples too[1]; the drama of the Cross has become good tidings of joy.[2] The new situation makes new claims, the "new commandment", but it also provides new possibilities of fulfilling them . . . "that ye love one another".[3] Thus the Christian "love of the brethren" can only be realized after the death of Jesus, that is, in the Church. Where this "new commandment" is really taken seriously it also becomes apparent to the "world", in which the Church of Christ takes shape—"By this shall all men know that ye are my disciples, if ye have love one to another."[4]

If 15.13 is meant not merely to refer to the death of Jesus but also to illustrate the behaviour of true disciples, then we have here a reminder of the reality of martyrdom in the early Church. To this true mind of the disciples belonged their readiness to give their lives for the brethren; that was the most perfect proof of their love of the brethren, practised in accordance with the example of the Master. Therefore it

---

[1] John 15.9; 16.27; 17.23–26.   [2] John 14.28.
[3] John 13.34; 15.17; 1 John 2.5; 3.10, 11, 14, 18, 23; 4.7, 11–21.
[4] John 13.35.

is written in 1 John 3.16: "Hereby know we love, because he laid down his life for us; and we ought to lay down our lives for the brethren."

From this survey it can be seen that "love" is intimately linked up with the Church. It is revealed in its fulness and greatness through the death of Jesus when the Church is created. In the Church the disciples become the friends and confidants of Jesus; but they are also put under the obligation of realizing the new possibility which is now given to them— to love one another.

Another expression of great interest in the final discourses is the phrase "in the Name of Jesus" which appears in varying contexts. It is always put in the mouth of Jesus himself in the formal phrase "in My name" (ἐν τῷ ὀνόματί μου), and generally in combination with the idea of prayer— "ask in My Name". That prayer is linked up with the promise of fulfilment[1] and it is made possible first through the "lifting-up" of Jesus, i.e. in the Church: "Hitherto (ἕως ἄρτι) have ye asked nothing in my Name; ask, and ye shall receive...." "In that day ye shall ask in my Name...." Certain scholars conclude from this that prayer in the name of Jesus must be referring to the corporate prayer in the congregation, that is the liturgical prayer, but it must be questioned whether such an interpretation is not too limited, especially in view of the statements about the Father sending the Spirit "in the name of Jesus"[2]; and about the world persecuting the disciples on account of the Name of Jesus[3]— that is, because of their membership in the Church. In 15.7 abiding in Jesus and in his word is made a condition of answer to prayer. Real prayer, which has the promise of answer attached to it, can only be made after the "lifting-up" of Jesus, that is, in the Church; and the expression "in the Name of Jesus" is to be understood as St John's way of referring to membership in the Church.

[1] John 14.13, 14; 15.16; 16.24, 26.
[2] John 14.26. [3] John 15.21.

The High-Priestly prayer in chapter 17 contains a more concentrated exposition of the "Church-thought" of the Fourth Gospel; we meet here with a few theological terms which will be specially examined later on: δοξάζειν, ζωή αἰώνιος, γινώσκειν, πιστεύειν, ἔργον, ῥήματα, χάρα, ἀλήθεια. Only two main thoughts in chapter 17 will be dealt with here; namely, the unity of the Church and the enmity of the world.

The idea of the unity of the Church has appeared earlier in 10.16 and 11.52; just as it is naturally suggested by the parable of the Vine and the branches. Now this thought reappears in 17.21: "that they all may be one; as thou, Father, art in me, and I in thee, that they also may be one in us."

And in 17.22 ff: "that they may be one, even as we are one: I in them, and thou in me, that they may be perfected into one" (τετελειωμένοι εἰς ἕν). From this it follows that the unity of the Church has its foundation in the unity between the Father and the Son, and in the unity which the Son through his death establishes between himself and the disciples, and which is depicted in the parables of the Shepherd and the Vine. It is likely that τετελειωμένοι in 17.23 corresponds to τετέλεσται in 19.30. In the words "that they all may be one", "that they also may be one in us", "that the world may believe that thou hast sent me", we have a threefold reminder that this unity is not a mere latent possession of the Church, but a possibility to be realized. Love is a necessary constituent of unity.[1]

The contrast between the Church and the world is described on the one hand in general terms: "They are not of the world even as I am not of the world" (ἐκ τοῦ κόσμου),[2] and on the other hand in more emphatic terms: "The world hath hated them (ἐμίσησεν) because they are not of the world, even as I am not of the world."[3] This hatred of the world is

[1] John 15.9; 17.26.   [2] John 17.16; see also John 17.9, 25.
[3] John 17.14; 15.18.

not so much the personal fate of disciples, as a logical consequence of the contrast between them and the world; a contrast which is, in its turn, identical with the one between the world and Christ, for he and his disciples are one. The contrast between them and the world goes down to the very roots (μισεῖν)—the world hates them. But even as the world in spite of all its evil is the object of the love of God,[1] so, in spite of its hatred of the disciples, is it the object of the loving mission of the Church[2]; and the success of that mission is made certain through the victory of Christ: "Be of good cheer, I have overcome the world."[3]

From our study of the Last Discourses and also of the Liturgy, of the Confession, of the Ministry, and of the Mission, three fundamental facts about the Church as St John knew it emerge: its unity, its universality, and its exclusiveness.

1. *The Unity of the Church* is implied in the parable of the Good Shepherd, "one fold and one shepherd"; in the conception of the King who gathers his people around him; and in the parable of the Vine and the branches; but above all, it is the first conclusion to be drawn from St John's theory that the Church has its foundation in the death and resurrection of Jesus. The unity of the Church is essentially a unity in Christ. He is the Shepherd who unites and guards the sheep, the King who gathers the people round him, and the Vine that gives life and strength to the branches. In all these passages, however—as indeed in the whole of this Gospel—there is an undertone, the teaching about the "one who is lifted-up" and who through his death and resurrection creates the Church, and through her gives to the faithful their part in life everlasting. In the High-Priestly prayer Jesus asks that this unity of the Church may be realized in the faith and life of the disciples. There is reason to suspect that bitter experiences of party spirit and sectarianism lie

[1] John 3.16.   [2] John 17.18, 20, 21, 23.
[3] John 16.33.

hidden behind this insistence on the unity of the Church and behind the frequent pleas of Christ that they should "abide" in him.

2. *The Universality of the Church*

St John makes this universality quite clear: the wall of partition between Jews and Gentiles has fallen. The question of the Jews' prerogative on the ground of being the chosen people of God, which was such a burning problem to St Paul, does not exist for St John. Christ is the Saviour of the whole world.[1] Our study of the cult in the Fourth Gospel has shown how Christ is represented not only as the fulfilment of the promises of the Old Testament regarding the coming Messiah, but also as the answer to the longing for salvation expressed in the cults and myths of the pagan world.

3. *The Exclusiveness of the Church*

This universality, however, does not preclude the *exclusiveness* of the Church. "The Jews" in the Fourth Gospel are not only mediators of the promises of the Old Testament but also, because of their unbelief, representatives of the "world" that is in opposition to Christ and his disciples. The hatred and persecution of the world is the lot of Christians, just as it was of their Master, and the Fourth Gospel emphasizes this enmity. Faith is not the possession of every man, nor is it something that man can obtain on his own. It is purely a gift of God, which he gives to whom he will. Thus the exclusiveness of the Church, unlike that of Judaism, is not based on membership of a particular race or nation, but it is the exclusiveness of faith, which has its foundation in the election of God.

These facts regarding the unity, universality, and exclusiveness of the Church in the Fourth Gospel correspond to three functions of the Church: namely, the Ministry, the Mission, and the Confession.

[1] John 4.42; 11.52; 17.23.

(i) *The Ecclesiastical Ministry* is an expression of the unity of the Church. It is not something set above the Church, but it is a function of the Church, instituted by Christ to administer his words and sacraments, which are the earthly means whereby the risen Lord is still "incarnate" in his Church. The Gospel of St John shows how the Ministry, from the very beginning, was a guiding and regulating factor in the life of the Church and how Christ himself is the original and real minister, through that "ministry" which he fulfilled on the Cross.

(ii) *The Mission* has a prominent place in the Fourth Gospel; it is a necessary consequence of its idea of the universality of the Church. The message about the Redeemer must be brought to everybody. The missionary task is not, however, a private matter for the individual but a function of the Church herself. And the missionary purpose is not to "convert" individuals or nations but to "gather into one the children of God who are scattered abroad".

(iii) *The Confession* is the outward expression of the exclusiveness of the Church. We have already seen that this exclusiveness is wholly that of faith. The first expression of faith is the clearly pronounced confession of faith in Christ. By means of this a definite borderline is drawn between the Church and the "world". For the mark of the "world" is just this, that it does not believe in Christ, and therefore does not know God either; it is entirely in the power of the devil. But in the Church it is Christ who rules. Through him the faithful have the true life and the hope of a share in his resurrection and in the great fulfilment.

The language, too, of the Fourth Gospel bears witness to the Church. The many sayings regarding cult and mission, ministry and confession imply the Church—a Church which is seen by the Evangelist, not as the work of men, but as a creation of God on earth, realized at that hour when Christ, in accordance with the will of the Father, was "lifted-up" on the Cross. And when we see how the Evangelist makes this "lifting-up" the absolute climax of the narrative of the life of Jesus, we understand that there is a definite connection between Church and eschatology in the Fourth Gospel.

27. *The Unique Character of the Johannine Eschatology*

In our study of the Fourth Gospel we have caught glimpses of eschatology in the most varying contexts. The evangelist sees in Jesus the fulfilment of the expectations of Jews and Gentiles alike with regard to a promised King (paragraph 6); and his interest in the missionary task (paragraph 9) suggests the underlying idea of a future consummation of all things. It is, however, in the many liturgical texts that the Johannine eschatology finds its fullest expression. But before we can venture on a summary, a few more terms must be considered.

We must first recall the relation of the Fourth Gospel to the Old Testament. Now although St John does not quote from it as frequently as do the Synoptists, we have noticed that he has a profound interest in the Jewish cult, the eschatological expectations of which he sees as having been fulfilled in Christ: for the great signs of the Messianic age, namely, the miracle of the manna, the bestowal of the living water, and the healing of the blind, are shown to have been realized, and the Messianic ideas connected with the Shepherd and the Vine, to have been fulfilled. Certain other features in the Fourth Gospel also demand consideration, as they reveal somewhat more clearly its relation to the Old Testament.

Abraham and Moses, each in his own way, were representatives of the Old Dispensation. Thus through Moses the law was given, while through Abraham came the promises. Now, over against the Law of Moses, St John places the "fulness" (πλήρωμα) of the revelation in Christ (1.16), while he makes Jesus proclaim in answer to the Jews' proud claim to be the children of Abraham—that is, heirs of the promises—"Before Abraham was, I am".[1] Abraham rejoiced to see the day of Jesus[2]—a fulfilment of Gen. 17—and Moses had written about him[3]; but the Jews dishonoured their forefather by seeking to kill Jesus, and their Lawgiver, Moses, by breaking the Law which he gave them and by not believing his words about the coming Messiah.[4]

In 4.5, 12 there are references to Jacob: mark well the words "*greater than* Jacob" in v. 12, an expression which recurs in 8.53, "*greater than* our father Abraham". This particular expression "greater than" is explained in the words of Jesus to Nathanael,[5] "Ye shall see the heaven opened and the angels of God ascending and descending upon the Son of man"; thus the dream of Jacob was realized in Christ. It is likely, too, that the thought of Jacob-Israel[6] lies behind Jesus' other words to Nathanael: "Behold an Israelite indeed, in whom there is no guile."

Now circumcision, given to the Jews by their "forefathers", might take place, according to the Law of Moses, even on the Sabbath.[7] This fact was seen by St John as an anticipation of the perfect Sabbath which is ordained by Christ and wherein he will make a man "every whit whole".[8]

Although the Jews were given so many and clear proofs that the time *was* now fulfilled and that the promised Messiah *had* come, they nevertheless did not believe the words of their Messiah but regarded him as a deceiver and transgressor.[9] This theme recurs again and again in the Fourth Gospel and strong emphasis is laid on the judgement which the Jews brought upon themselves by denying Jesus. In view of this it is not surprising that the Fourth Gospel shows a marked tendency to absolve Pilate from responsibility for the death

[1] John 8.33–39, 58.
[2] John 8.56.
[3] John 1.45; 5.39, 46.
[4] John 8.40; 7.19; 5.46.
[5] John 1.50, 51.
[6] Gen. 32.28; 35.10.
[7] John 7.22, cf. Gen. 17.10–14; Lev. 12.3.
[8] John 7.23 and chapter 9.
[9] John 5.18; 7.30, 42–44; 10.33; 11.53.

ESCHATOLOGY IN FOURTH GOSPEL 103

of Jesus and to lay this responsibility instead upon the Jews.¹ There is a theological reason for this and to speak of any opportunism on the part of the author would be quite out of place. To St John the great tragedy of the Jews was the fact that they did not understand the significance of Jesus' presence in their midst. Moreover, his dealings with the Jews, as recorded by St John, took place almost entirely within the Temple courts and their immediate neighbourhood. Thus they had no excuse for ignorance either of his person or his message. Now this underlining of the responsibility of the Jews shows that St John saw in the appearing of Jesus the fulfilment of the Old Testament promises and it thus bears witness to the vital connection between the Fourth Gospel and the Old Testament.

A still further proof of this is to be seen in St John's custom of quoting the name that Jesus used of himself, "Son of man" (ὁ υἱὸς τοῦ ἀνθρώπου). This title occurs in the Old Testament book of Daniel (ch. 7.13ff) and in the late Jewish speculations of the book of Enoch and the Apocalypse of Ezra. In the Fourth Gospel it occurs only twelve times; otherwise the expressions "the Son" or "the Son of God" are used. The term "Son of man" we meet in the following contexts: the lifting-up of the Son of man[2]; the glorifying of the Son of man[3]; his ascending into heaven[4]; the ascending and descending of the angels of God upon him[5]; his giving of the food of eternal life[6]; and his coming to judgement.[7] In all these cases "Son of man" is used in an eschatological way. Thus the "lifting-up", "the glorifying", and "the ascent into heaven" are all expressions for the death and resurrection of Jesus, while the descending and ascending of the angels on the Son of man functioning as judge bear witness to him as an eschatological figure. The same is the case when he is represented as the giver of eternal life

[1] John 18.38–40, 19.4–16.   [2] John 3.14; 8.28; 12.34.
[3] John 12.23; 13.31.   [4] John 3.13; 6.62.
[5] John 1.51.   [6] John 6.27, 53.   [7] John 5.27.

through the sacrament. It is only in one place that the eschatological link is hard to see, namely in 9.35, where Jesus asks the man born blind whom he has just healed: "Dost thou believe in the Son of man?",[1] and the man replies: "Who is he, Lord, that I might believe?" If the man born blind is the prototype of those who come to believe in Jesus and who, therefore, are punished by the Jews, we have here an exposition of the new age—a revelation of the position of those who "see", the first mark of whose "sight" is belief in the Son of man. To believe in the Son of man, the "lifted-up" and glorified Christ, is the mark of those who live in the age of fulfilment. But this age has not come without preparation, for the promises have been given in the Old Testament. Thus the idea of the Son of man is one more of the intimate links binding together the Old Testament and the Fourth Gospel.

Now when we compare St John's use of the title "Son of man" with that of the Synoptists we find an interesting contrast. The Christ of the Synoptic Gospels uses the title in the most varied situations: the Son of man has no earthly home, he eats and drinks, he is the Lord of the Sabbath, he scatters the seed of the word,[2] while the same term is employed in the narrative of the betrayal, the passion, the death, and the resurrection[3] and with regard to the Parousia,[4] to mention only a few examples, all from the Gospel according to St Matthew. In the Fourth Gospel, however, as we have already said, the term is used only in sayings of eschatological significance. This shows that St John preserves with greater faithfulness than do the Synoptists the link with the Old Testament tradition as expressed in Daniel 7.13 ff.

Our examination of the relation between the Fourth Gospel and the Old Testament has thus shown that the presence of Jesus in the midst of his people, that is, his life,

[1] R.V. marg.   [2] Matt. 8.20; 11.19; 12.8; 13.37.
[3] Matt. 17.9, 12, 22; 20.18, 28; 26.2, 24, 45.
[4] Matt. 10.23; 24.27, 30, 37, 39, 44; 19.28; 25.31; 26.64.

teaching, death, and resurrection, is the fulfilment of the Old Testament promises—in other words, realized eschatology. In contrast to this the eschatology of the Old Testament itself was but "anticipating" or "proleptic" as seen through the eyes of St John. We have noticed already the many references in the Fourth Gospel to time, such as "now" (νῦν used twenty-five times, ἄρτι used ten times), "already" (ἤδη used thirteen times), "hour" (ὥρα used twenty times), "moment" (καιρός used three times), "a little while" (χρόνον μικρόν used twelve times), and "the day" (ἡμέρα used fourteen times). Now this frequent repetition of seemingly unimportant references to time is worth noticing, for it is clear at the outset that they are not meant merely to determine the chronological sequence of events. Rather do they emphasize the theological significance of all that is related in the Gospel.

Thus while in the first half of the Gospel there are many sayings of the type: "mine hour is not yet come", in 12.23 we read "the hour is come", while in 19.27 we have the expression "from that hour". Obviously all these instances refer to one decisive "hour", the hour of the death of Jesus; that is, the hour of his "lifting-up" and glorification. Indeed, it is to this hour alone that all the sayings and events throughout the Gospel point and through which they receive their right interpretation and significance. Earlier in this treatise we noticed the expressions εἰς τέλος in 13.1 and τετελειωμένοι in 17.23. To these expressions we can now add the sayings about the Son who has come to "accomplish" the work of his Father (τελειώσω), that the Scriptures might be "accomplished" through him.[1] Now this "accomplishment" is effected at the hour of Christ's death upon the Cross, when the dying Saviour cries out his last word to the world: τετέλεσται "It is finished!"[2] There is no resignation in this cry, nor is it a mere statement of the

[1] John 4.34; 5.36; 17.4; 19.28. [2] John 19.30.

fact that the passion of Jesus has now come to an end, that his lifework is accomplished, although these thoughts are naturally implicit in it. On the contrary it is a proclamation of triumph and victory, a crying out to all ages and all peoples that the great hour has now arrived, the turning point of history is now come. Not only so, but the old dispensation is now at an end, the era of fulfilment is begun. It is the hour, moreover, wherein all the promises of the old dispensation are fulfilled; the hour, too, that sheds light upon the meaning of all that Jesus himself during his earthly ministry has said and done. It is the hour wherein the Son comes forth as the conqueror of the "world", obedient to the will of the Father to the very end, showing by his death both the true nature and the real significance of his own mission to the world. Surely it is not an exaggeration to think that τετέλεσται is the key word of the Fourth Gospel, the key to the solution of its theological problem.

The whole of the Fourth Gospel is really the story of the death of Jesus regarded as an eschatological fact. The Evangelist arranges his material and combines his exposition in such a manner that everything is subordinated to and points forward to the death of Jesus upon the Cross and the resurrection which follows it. Even in the Prologue we have a hint of the end: "His own received him not". The miracle of the wine, the cleansing of the Temple—practically every part of the Gospel—is in some way related to the death of Jesus, while it is very early in his ministry that the Jews begin to plan how they may get rid of him. The raising of Lazarus, the last and greatest of the miracles, is the very preparation for his own resurrection. The anointing in Bethany, the procession of palms, and the washing of the disciples' feet all witness to the fact that the end is close at hand. It is after the last discourse, however, and in the High-Priestly prayer that the real drama of the passion begins, the drama which reaches its climax and its end in the tremendous word from the Cross: "It is finished!" Thus it might be said that according to the conception of the Fourth Gospel Jesus' entire life on earth was but a prelude to his death upon the Cross.

How can we explain this? It may of course be said that it was essentially the death of Jesus which brought about man's redemption and that therefore his death is the central theme of the whole Gospel. This observation, however, though true, fails to account for the peculiar emphasis on the death of Jesus which we find in this Gospel, where it is made the object of a far deeper theological interpretation than is given to it in the Synoptic Gospels. The explanation, we would suggest, is simply this: St John all the time points beyond the earthly existence of Jesus, beyond his death and resurrection, to the new situation created through them.

This interpretation sheds new light on many obscure points in this Gospel. Thus the words "in that day", which occur so often in the last discourse, point forward to the new possibilities of knowledge and prayer that the disciples are to receive as a result of the "lifting-up" of Jesus. Similarly those difficult sayings in which the "hour" is represented as both about to come and yet already present (ἔρχεται ὥρα καὶ νῦν ἐστιν, 4.23; 5.25, 28, and ἔρχεται ὥρα καὶ νῦν ἐλήλυθεν, 16.32) are seen to signify, in the light of this eschatological method of interpretation, that the life and work of Jesus on earth is an anticipation of his work as the "lifted-up" Saviour. The cry τετέλεσται thus means:

1. that the work of Jesus on earth is accomplished;
2. that the eschatological expectations which were found in Israel and in the pagan world have now, in the new dispensation, reached their fulfilment;
3. that the new dispensation or age which has now come is in itself an anticipation of the final eschatological fulfilment.

It is important that due weight be given to the many passages in the Fourth Gospel that imply a future eschatology.

We cannot, with Bultmann and certain other critics, dismiss them as mere editorial additions reflecting current ecclesiastical conceptions. On the contrary, they are an organic part of Johannine theology, revealing as they do that St John's is a true eschatology. We may reckon among these passages many sayings regarding the resurrection "at the last day"[1]; the references to living "for ever"[2]; the passage in chapter 21 about judgement at the last day; and about the "coming" again of Christ[3]; the words to Nathanael, "ye shall see the heaven opened . . ."[4]; and finally in 1 John 4.17 the reference to the "day of judgement".

Now several of these texts contain not only a future reference but also an unmistakable mark of present or realized eschatology; for example: "Ye shall see the heaven opened and the angels of God ascending and descending upon the Son of man." If we consider these words in the context in which they were uttered during the earthly life of Jesus, we clearly see in them a future eschatology, a character which they retain even after his death. At the same time, however, in a very real way their meaning is realized in the liturgy of the Church. The same is true of the passage about "the dead" who shall hear the voice of the Son of God and "shall live"; of Christ's words in 6.58, "he that eateth this bread shall live for ever"; and in 16.16–19, "a little while and ye behold me no more and again a little while and ye shall see me . . ."; and finally in 16.22, "I will see you again . . .". In all of these we have examples of an eschatology which is realized in a preliminary way in the new dispensation which has come about through the "lifting-up" of Jesus, but which will be finally fulfilled at the Parousia.

Let us sum up, then, the results of our investigation into the peculiar character of the Johannine eschatology:

[1] John 5.25, 28, 29; 6.39, 44, 54; 11.24.
[2] John 6.58.   [3] John 21.22.   [4] John 1.51.

ESCHATOLOGY IN FOURTH GOSPEL

1. It is a *future* eschatology, i.e. it regards the Parousia, the resurrection, and the judgement as marking the end of this present world.
2. It is *proleptic*, i.e. it regards the eschatology of the Old Testament as an anticipating eschatology now fulfilled through Christ; while it regards the new dispensation that has been brought about through the "lifting-up" of Jesus as itself pointing forward to the great fulfilment, an anticipation of it.
3. It is *realized*. Thus the eschatological expectations of both Jews and Gentiles have reached their fulfilment in Christ.
4. It is *present*. By this we mean that it is continually being realized in the present situation, whether it be during the earthly life of Jesus or in the new dispensation brought about through his death.

Now when these features of Johannine eschatology are compared with the definitions of true eschatology as put forward in paragraph 3 we realize that we are justified in claiming that the Fourth Gospel contains such true eschatology.

28. *The Connection between Eschatology and the Church in the Fourth Gospel*

We have already seen that in the theology of St John eschatology and the Church are strangely intertwined. Furthermore, although in paragraph 27, concerning "The unique character of the Johannine eschatology", we deliberately tried to avoid making any mention of the Church—just as in the summary of the character of the Johannine conception of the Church we tried to avoid dealing with eschatology—nevertheless the close connection existing between the two was forced upon our minds by the very nature of the text. Thus it was found impossible to keep them apart since each clarified, corrected, and completed the other. Since the close connection has already become apparent all we propose to attempt here is a brief elucidation of the relationship existing between them.

When in the Fourth Gospel the Church is represented in terms of the King who gathers his people round him, the Shepherd who leads his flock, and the Vine which bears the branches, giving to them its own life, these conceptions are an eschatological reality—they have been realized through Christ. He is the "longed-for One", the Expected One, the One to whom both Jews and Gentiles alike have been looking forward, their eschatological hopes having been expressed in rites and myths. It is, however, in the cult—itself the most perfect expression of the Church's life—that, as we might expect, the close connection that exists between the Church and eschatology is best brought out. The many references to the cult are a very certain proof of Church-consciousness, since the cult is such an important part of the life of the Church. At the same time these cult-passages are an expression of St John's eschatology, for, as we have pointed out already, they show the cult connected with baptism, eucharist, and prayer as a fulfilment of the eschatological expectations of the Jewish cult and also as an anticipation of the eschatological consummation at the end of the present dispensation.

It is in the light of these facts that we must see the twofold meaning of many of the statements in the Fourth Gospel, which appear to the reader of the present generation as mysterious ambiguities, the significance of which he surmises rather than really understands, while they also lend themselves to an allegorical method of approach. Seen in their proper context, however, and in the light that we have thrown upon them, even these passages can be truly understood. Cullmann has opened up a way of investigation that should prove profitable, interpreting the ambiguity of such Johannine words as πνεῦμα, ἄνωθεν, ὑψωθῆναι, ἀκολουθεῖν, ναός, ὕδωρ ζῶν, ἄρτος τῆς ζωῆς, τυφλοί, ἀναστῆναι and the

ESCHATOLOGY IN FOURTH GOSPEL 111

prophecy of Caiaphas in the light of the redemptive, recreative purpose that links the Incarnate Logos with the Old Testament and also with the Church. These instances can be supplemented by several other sayings of Jesus in the contexts of which a twofold, sometimes threefold, meaning is expressed. Amongst such sayings are, "Hitherto have ye asked nothing in my name; ask and ye shall receive..."[1]; "Ye shall see the heaven opened..."[2]; "... the dead shall hear the voice of the Son of God; and they that hear shall live"[3]; "A little while and ye behold me no more; and again a little while and ye shall see me..."[4]; "I will see you again, and your heart shall rejoice..."; "And in that day ye shall ask nothing..."[5]; "I have both glorified it and will glorify it again"[6]; and lastly, "Now is the Son of man glorified... and God shall glorify him... and straightway shall he glorify him."[7] To these sayings should be added the "speaking in parables" during the earthly life of Jesus in contrast to the "open" speech which was to characterize his dealings with his disciples after his glorifying.[8] About the threefold meaning in τετέλεσται mention has been made already.

Now this ambiguity in the sayings of Jesus as recorded by St John is closely related to the Evangelist's eschatology and also to his conception of the Church. Thus the Church is represented, on the one hand, as a projection of the earthly life of Jesus (or, if one prefers to put it that way, the earthly life of Jesus is an anticipation of the Church), while, on the other hand, the Church is an anticipation of the final fulfilment. Similarly as regards eschatology, the expectations of the Old Testament are represented as fulfilled through Christ and in the Church created by his "lifting-up", while the Church in its turn is an anticipation of the consummation at the Parousia.

[1] John 16.24.   [2] John 1.51.   [3] John 5.25.
[4] John 16.16–19.   [5] John 16.22, 23.   [6] John 12.28.
[7] John 13.31.   [8] John 16.25.

From this we see that the connection between the Church and eschatology in the Fourth Gospel is rooted in the person of Jesus and, more particularly, in the central and dominating thought of the Gospel, namely his death and resurrection. Thus it was through the "lifting-up" of Jesus that the Church came into existence. We have noticed already, too, how the thought of the death of Jesus has kept recurring in all passages concerning the Church throughout the Gospel —in its conception of the King, the Shepherd, the Vine, the Ministry, and the Mission, but especially in its sayings connected with the liturgy. Thus through the "lifting-up" of Jesus there has come the new age wherein the eschatological expectations of the old dispensation have been fulfilled whilst simultaneously the faithful have been given the opportunity to experience in a proleptic manner the final eschatological fulfilment.

Now, if our exposition of the close connection between the Church and eschatology be correct and if the consequent conception of the Fourth Gospel be reliable, it also follows that new light will thereby be thrown upon certain Johannine ideas, which have always proved difficult of interpretation not only for the exegetical commentator but also for the preacher. In the following chapter therefore it is proposed to examine some of St John's more important theological conceptions in order to find out whether the above-mentioned theories about the Church and eschatology can in this way be verified.

CHAPTER 5

IMPORTANT THEOLOGICAL CONCEPTIONS

29. λόγος

ALREADY IN the Prologue we meet the most discussed term in the whole of the Fourth Gospel, namely, λόγος. Referring to the pre-existent Christ it appears in the Gospel only here and it also occurs in 1 John 1.1 and in Rev. 19.13. But in spite of the fact that it is used so few times this term is of the greatest importance for the whole Johannine theology and for a full understanding of the message and the purpose of the Gospel; the very fact that the term comes into the first verses of the Gospel and of the Epistle points to this.

"The Prologue" hardly deserves its name. It is not an introduction or a preface intended to help the reader to understand the thought of the Gospel. The Evangelist assumes that everything in the Prologue, including the λόγος-idea itself, is well known to the reader or at least to the extent that he is aware of the message which is now to be delivered, and which, in this hymn-like opening passage of the Gospel, receives its preparatory epitome and solemn wording. A more fitting word than "prologue" would therefore be "overture".

If, however, the λόγος-idea is comprehensible to the reader straight away, its conception cannot be attributed to the Evangelist himself. From which system of thought then is the term taken? For, with the significance here attached to it, it is unknown in the rest of the New Testament.

Most scholars now agree that the Johannine λόγος cannot be derived from the Hellenistic gnosticism, nor from Philo. The marked antignostic tendency of the Fourth Gospel as a whole rules out the former suggestion (cf. v. 3), and an argument against the hypothesis that it is due to the influence of Philo is to be found in the confession of faith in the incarnate λόγος in v. 14. On the other hand, there are references to types of the λόγος-idea in later Judaism; for there we find a strong tendency, while emphasizing the holiness and righteousness of God, to conceive of him as so exalted above the world and man that he becomes inaccessible to the speculations of the faithful as well as to their worship. Their theology attempted to bridge this chasm between God and the world by the use of hypostases, the most important of which were the Wisdom of God, *chokmah*, the Law of God, *torah*, and the Word of God, *memra*: the latter, however, only appears as a hypostasis of the Name of God, *tetragrammaton*. These expressions were used as though to indicate independent spiritual dignitaries, pre-existent in relation to this world, mediators of divine revelation. This development begins in the canonical and apocryphal books of Wisdom and is continued in the Targums.

It was natural that a Christian λόγος-speculation should grow up against the background of these types and in this spiritual atmosphere. It is not merely a product of the thought of the evangelist but something well known among those to whom he addresses his writing. Here we can dimly discern the work of the Johannine Church, attempting to produce a necessary counterpart to the mythological λόγος-idea of Hellenistic thought.

In view of all this it is the more surprising that Bultmann tries to prove that the Prologue was in the beginning a hymn to John the Baptist, composed by Jewish gnostics, which later on was taken over by the Evangelist and provided with editorial additions (the prose-parts in vv. 6–8, 15). But in a hymn originally written about John the Baptist, it would be

IMPORTANT THEOLOGICAL CONCEPTIONS 115

strange indeed for the very parts which expressly mention him to be a later addition! Bultmann has also an exaggerated idea of a polemic against the Baptist and his disciples, which he sees in the Prologue and in other parts of the Fourth Gospel, but of which there is no trace in the Synoptic Gospels. But in answer to Bultmann we must ask how a poem taken over from a Jewish gnosticism could so adequately express and sum up the essentials of the Fourth Gospel, in which the antignostic tendency is so clear throughout; and furthermore how came the λόγος-idea, if borrowed from a non-Christian world of thought, to be inserted in the very forefront of the Gospel with the assumption that it would be readily comprehensible to its Christian readers?

The Johannine λόγος-idea has the following attributes:

1. *Pre-Existence*. The emphasis in 1.1 is on ἐν ἀρχῇ as in Gen. 1.1 it is on ἀπ' ἀρχῆς. The existence of the λόγος is referred to as something self-evident. But now the important announcement comes: the λόγος was in existence from the beginning. The reference to Gen. 1.1 is obvious and deliberate: St John begins his writing by taking the reader back to the period before the creation of the world. There is a marked feeling of eternity in this repeated ἦν. The λόγος has no beginning, nor has it an end; it is a super-worldly and super-temporal entity which has, none the less, taken form in the world and in time—an eschatological conception. The interesting point is that the Johannine eschatology right from the very beginning is linked with "the protology".

2. *Divinity*. Καὶ θεὸς ἦν ὁ λόγος. In this sentence θεός is the predicate and the sentence seems to express complete identity between the λόγος and God. This, however, is quite contrary to the statement which has gone immediately before, ὁ λόγος ἦν πρὸς τὸν θεόν, and which is also repeated in v. 2. Attempts have been made to explain this peculiar sentence by making the word θεός, which has no article, equal to θεῖος. But this is an obvious weakening of the evangelist's meaning; for it is clearly his intention in this

context to use θεός in order to express a real identity between the λόγος and God, and the same thought reappears in 10.33. This phenomenon we will call "representative identity"; for even if this term seems to us moderns a logical contradiction, it is nevertheless very likely that it fitly expresses the meaning of the evangelist. The same type of identity meets us in 4.24, πνεῦμα ὁ θεός. The unity between the λόγος and God exists from the beginning and gives to the revelation mediated through the λόγος its loftiness and serenity.[1]

3. *Creative Power.* The thought of the λόγος as the instrument of God in creation is carried out by means of an antithetical parallelism in v. 3: "All things were made by him and without him was not anything made that hath been made." The reference to Gen. 1.3, "And God said . . .", is evident and is carried further by means of the terms φῶς, σκοτία, and ζωή; a fact that has often been neglected by scholars, who have been more inclined to seek the types for these expressions in gnostic writings. Thus the λόγος because of its co-operation in the Creation is put into a firm relationship with the world from the very beginning. The Saviour comes at the fulness of time, not, as in the gnostic world-religions, as a stranger—but "to His own": εἰς τὰ ἴδια ἦλθεν. καὶ οἱ ἴδιοι αὐτὸν οὐ παρέλαβον (v. 11). By οἱ ἴδιοι is not meant the Jews, of whom mention has not yet been made, and whose spiritual prerogative is not emphasized in any other way in the Fourth Gospel, but the whole of humanity as an expression of the totality of creation. St John saw humanity as one whole rejecting the λόγος. But because this rejection was realized by the Jews they are all through the Fourth Gospel spoken of as the representatives of sinful and unrepentant humanity, instead of representatives of God before man.

4. *The Source of Life and Light.* The term ζωή in the Fourth Gospel will be specially dealt with later on. In this context it will only be pointed out that ζωή and φῶς are not

[1] cf. John 10.30, 38; 12.45; 14.9-11; 17.11, 21.

IMPORTANT THEOLOGICAL CONCEPTIONS 117

metaphysical terms, as in the mystery-religions, but entirely religious conceptions. In v. 4 it is written: "In him was life and the life was the light of men." The thought of the light as the condition for all life clearly refers to Gen. 1.3. The λόγος is "the true light", τὸ φῶς τὸ ἀληθινόν (v. 9); which not only gives rise to the life of creation but also to that of salvation. The φῶς is here spoken of as the fulfilment of the ancient prophecy about the great light which shall shine over the peoples.[1] In other words, the term expresses the continuity between creation and salvation; between the work of God at the beginning of the world and the work he carried out in the Church. The significance of ἀρχή is realized when the λόγος becomes σάρξ. This thought is even more clearly expressed in 1 John 1.1–7, 14, where the same terminology is used again: ἀρχή, λόγος, ζωή, φῶς, σκοτία, θεάομαι, μαρτυρεῖν. "To walk in the light" is that unity (κοινωνία) which is realized in the Church, which is the fulfilment of creation.

5. *The Incarnation.* Καὶ ὁ λόγος σὰρξ ἐγένετο, καὶ ἐσκήνωσεν ἐν ἡμῖν (v. 14). σάρξ signifies the earthly and human existence in contrast to the eternal and spiritual (πνεῦμα). When the λόγος becomes incarnate it does not, of course, cease to be λόγος, but St John does not use that term any longer, once it has entered on its earthly existence. The new term is Jesus Christ, which appears already in v. 17 as the first acknowledgement of the incarnate λόγος. Jesus talks of himself both in the Fourth Gospel and in the Synoptics as the "Son of Man" (for the first time in 1.51), or more often still as "the Son"; this term always stands over against "the Father" and refers to his continuous relationship to him. As "the Son", the incarnate λόγος is the representative of "the Father" on earth and in the Church. As "the Son of Man" he is the representative of humanity before God. The verb ἐσκήνωσεν (dwelt or tabernacled) does not, as some scholars say, refer only to the momentary and short stay on earth of

[1] Num. 24.17; Isa. 9.2; 42.6; 60.1–3, cf. Luke 1.78.

the λόγος but is linked up with the Old Testament thought of the tabernacle as the symbol of Jehovah's presence with his people.[1] With the Rabbis, *shekinah* is the term for that glorious light which makes known the presence of God; thus ἐσκήνωσεν corresponds to the following δόξα (glory), a term which will be the object of further investigation later on.

There are different opinions regarding ἐθεασάμεθα. Does the word refer to eyewitnesses of the earthly appearance of Jesus, or is it only meant to convey the idea of "a vision in faith" after the death of Jesus, i.e. within the Church? The obvious reply is that it refers to them both. In the Fourth Gospel this verb is used to denote physical as well as spiritual sight, and it is a thought stressed throughout the whole Gospel that the latter is impossible without the former. Witness to this is borne, among other things, by the keen sacramental interest of this Gospel. The author definitely claims to have been an eyewitness of what he is recording,[2] and in reference to the Incarnation the actual sight of the earthly form of Jesus is included. "The Jews", too, saw Jesus with their own eyes, and also the signs that were done by him, and yet they remained in unbelief. For St John, however, the work of Jesus does not cease at his death and resurrection but is continued among the disciples in the Church; and in the Church it is the liturgy that is the foremost expression both of the gathering of the faithful round the Saviour and of his continued dealings with them. In the liturgy they hear him speak in his word, and they see him performing his works in the sacraments. Thus the faithful are made to know that the Word of God still "dwells among them". Thus we have an obvious answer to our question, "Who are they who 'saw'?" It was not merely eyewitnesses of the earthly appearance of Jesus, not the little group of disciples who saw the risen Lord at the first Easter,

[1] Ex. 25.8ff; 29.44ff; Lev. 15.31; Num. 5.3; Ezek. 37.26; cf. Rev. 21.3.
[2] John 19.35; 21.24; cf. 1 John 1.1–3.

nor a selected circle of especially favoured "initiated ones" as in the mystery-religions, but the whole Johannine Church, whose united witness to Christ the Fourth Gospel will now attempt to interpret: "We beheld his glory, glory as of the only-begotten from the Father, full of grace and truth."

Why, then, has St John confined the use of λόγος to the pre-existent Son? The answer is close to hand, since λόγος was a familiar term in both Christian and non-Christian circles. It represented the attempt of the surrounding pagan world to interpret the way of the divine revelation to man: it also had a place in late Jewish speculations. By linking his conception of the λόγος to the Story of Creation in the Old Testament, St John aims at revealing the Incarnate λόγος as the fulfilment of the hopes and expectations of the Old Covenant, as they had been expressed in cult, in prophecy, and in theological thought; and, by using a term well known in Greek philosophy and in Hellenistic aspirations after God, he is also trying to show that the divine revelation thus given fulfils the expectations of the pagan world as well as of the Jews. Everything reaches its fulfilment in Christ, the λόγος by whom the world was once created; who, at a certain point in human history, "became flesh" and accomplished the work of Redemption among men; and who is still carrying on this work in the eschatological situation of the Church, until the end of this aeon and the coming of the great fulfilment. Through the λόγος the whole history of redemption acquires its meaning and is led on towards its joyful end; in this term is summed up the continuity and the whole sequence of creation, redemption and final fulfilment.

30. ῥήματα (words, sayings)

ῥήματα—always found in the plural—occurs only twelve times in the Fourth Gospel and not at all in the First Epistle. It is, without exception, used to signify the words of Jesus or of the Father which are, in reality, one and the same thing

Once it is put into the mouth of Peter[1]; once it is uttered by the people[2]; and once it is said by the evangelist himself; but it always refers to the teaching of Jesus. In all other places it is used by Jesus himself referring to his message.

In addition to ῥήματα the Fourth Gospel makes use of λόγος (apart from the Prologue) thirty-two times; λόγοι four times. In some places it refers to prophecy[3]; or to the teaching of the disciples about Jesus.[4] In exceptional cases it refers to the words of men[5]; everywhere else it refers, like ῥήματα, to the words of Jesus or of the Father.

1. *Jesus' Words are God's Words*

   3.34. "For he whom God hath sent speaketh the words (ῥήματα) of God."
   5.38. "And ye have not his word (ῥήματα) abiding in you: for whom he sent, him ye believe not."
   8.55. "But I know him, and keep his word (λόγος)."
   14.10. "The words (ῥήματα) that I say unto you I speak not from myself."
   14.24. "The word (λόγος) which ye hear is not mine, but the Father's who sent me."
   17.8. "For the words (ῥήματα) which thou gavest me I have given unto them."
   17.14. "I have given them thy word (λόγος)."

2. *Through the Words of Jesus Faith is kindled and Unbelief is revealed*

   2.22. "And they believed the Scripture and the word (λόγος) which Jesus had said."
   4.41. "And many more believed because of his word (λόγος)."
   4.50. "The man believed the word (λόγος) that Jesus spake unto him."
   5.47. "But if ye believe not his writings, how shall ye believe my words (ῥήματα)?"
   6.60. "This is a hard saying (λόγος); who can hear it?"
   8.31. "If ye abide in my word (λόγος) then are ye truly my disciples."

---

[1] John 6.68. [2] John 10.21.
[3] John 4.37; 10.35; 12.38; 15.25.
[4] John 4.39; 17.20. [5] John 19.8; 21.23.

IMPORTANT THEOLOGICAL CONCEPTIONS 121

8.37. "Yet ye seek to kill me because my word (λόγος) hath not free course in you."

8.43 ff. "Why do ye not understand my speech? Even because ye cannot hear my word (λόγος). Ye are of your father the devil...."

8.47. "He that is of God heareth the words (ῥήματα) of God."

3. *The Words of Jesus bring Judgement to those who will not hear*

12.47.48. "And if any man hear my sayings (ῥήματα) and keep them not I judge him not; for I came not to judge the world, but to save the world. He that rejecteth me and receiveth not my sayings (ῥήματα) hath one that judgeth him; the word (λόγος) that I spake the same shall judge him in the last day."

4. *The Words of Jesus give Eternal Life*

5.24. "He that heareth my word (λόγος), and believeth him that sent me, hath eternal life, and cometh not into judgement, but hath passed out of death into life."

6.63. "The words (ῥήματα) that I have spoken unto you are spirit, and are life."

6.68. "Lord, to whom shall we go? Thou hast the words (ῥήματα ζωῆς αἰωνίου) of eternal life."

8.51. "If a man keep my word (λόγος) he shall never see death."

15.3. "Already are ye clean because of the word (λόγος) which I have spoken unto you."

15.7. "If ye abide in me, and my words (ῥήματα) abide in you, ask whatsoever ye will and it shall be done unto you."

5. *The Words of Jesus are the Pattern for the New Life*

14.23. "If a man love me, he will keep my word (λόγος): and my Father will love him."

15.20. "If they kept my word (λόγος), they will keep yours also."

17.6. "And they have kept thy word (λόγος)."

17.17. "Thy word (λόγος) is truth."

1 John 2.5. "But whoso keepeth his word (λόγος), in him verily hath the love of God been perfected."

1 John 2.14. "Because ye are strong, and the word (λόγος) of God abideth in you."

From this we see that both ῥήματα and λόγος signify the word revealed through Christ. It is the means whereby the Incarnate λόγος makes contact with the world, firstly during his earthly life and afterwards in the Church. These "words" contain his gift (life eternal) and his claim (the commandment of love). Witness to the situation in the Church is borne by the connection between the Word and the Spirit; the Word and answer to prayer; and the Word and love.[1] Thus the words of Jesus are not merely spoken once during his earthly life, but they are still spoken by him in his Church and there reveal their true significance and power.

This is emphasized by the theological connection between ῥήματα and λόγος and between ἔργα and σημεῖα. The verb σημαίνειν (signify) in 12.33; 18.32; and 21.19 bears witness to this connection. In 6.63 ῥήματα refers not only to the previous discourse about the bread of life, but also to the great miracle of feeding which was behind it. Also in 5.36, 38; 10.36–38; and 14.10–11 the words ῥήματα and ἔργα are so close in meaning to each other, that they are almost synonyms.

By his words and works throughout his earthly life, Jesus bore witness to the Father in heaven, to himself as God's Son, and to the longed-for Messianic age which had begun with him. By them he kindled faith in the hearts of his disciples and by them he revealed the unbelief of others. St John is concerned to show how the glorified Christ in the Church continues to speak his words and perform his works. Thus in the eschatological situation of the Church both ῥήματα and λόγος have their given place, and in that situation they continue to express the revelation that gives eternal life.

31. σημεῖα (signs)

The word σημεῖον occurs seventeen times in the Fourth Gospel and σημαίνειν three times. The sign at Cana is

[1] John 6.63; 15.7; 14.23.

IMPORTANT THEOLOGICAL CONCEPTIONS 123

called ἀρχὴ τῶν σημείων (beginning of signs) and the healing of the son of the nobleman[1] δεύτερον σημεῖον (a second sign). This has given rise to the theory that the Fourth Gospel was built on a previous document, "the σημεῖα-source", wherein a number of signs done by Jesus had been written down and recorded chronologically. Nothing, however, can be proved about this. The Fourth Gospel implies a number of signs[2] but mentions only a few and these, working up to an increasing significance, are presented as manifestations of the longed-for Messianic age, already typified in Moses.

1. *σημεῖα is the technical term for the signs of the Messianic age.* It is used of the wedding feast at Cana; of the healing of the nobleman's son; of healings in general; of the great feeding; and of the raising of Lazarus.[3] The same word is put into the mouth of Nicodemus, and also of the Pharisees in reference to the great signs of Jesus in general,[4] and to the demand of the Jews that Jesus should give by means of "signs" a clear proof of his claim to be the Messiah.[5] The common people point out that John the Baptist did no signs and ask whether the Messiah, when he comes, will perform more signs that Jesus had already done.[6]

2. *Many are brought by means of the signs to faith in Jesus as the Christ.* Although the sign at Cana cannot be considered as a decisive factor leading to the faith of the disciples, St John nevertheless stresses the fact that many believed when they saw the mighty works of Jesus. Jesus himself speaks about the signs as necessary for faith: "Except ye see signs and wonders ye will in no wise believe." There is, however, as we shall show in another connection, no reproof in these words. If there were, then why should Jesus continue with his signs? It is absolutely certain that St John does not consider the signs of Jesus to be merely concessions to the primitive

[1] John 2.11; 4.54.
[2] John 2.23; 3.2; 20.30.
[3] John 2.11; 4.54; 6.2, 14, 26; 12.18.
[4] John 3.2; 9.16.   [5] John 2.18; 6.30.   [6] John 10.41; 7.31.

desires of the people. Instead, they are regarded as the ratification of belief in Jesus as the Messiah, proofs of the coming of the longed-for Messianic age. These signs are a consequence of the Incarnation, for through them the Messianic power and glory of Jesus is made manifest. Thus St John 4.48 is an explanation of the sign that follows, lifting it up into the Messianic light. This is emphasized by the threefold repetition of ὁ υἱός σου ζῇ and by the conversion of the father and his household to belief in Jesus. The words of Jesus in 6.26 *are*, however, a reproof: "Ye seek me not because ye saw signs, but because ye ate of the loaves and were filled." This expression would remain insignificant if σημεῖα is taken as meaning merely an inexplicable work done by Jesus. That was how the people looked on the feeding, and that is where they were wrong; they saw in it only an amazing "miracle", not a "sign" of the coming of the Messianic age. This superficial conception of the work of Jesus is evidence of the unbelief of the people, and it is against this unbelief that Jesus directs his reproof. The same reproof is repeated in 12.37.

3. *To those who believe, the signs are a proof of the Messianic glory of Jesus.* This is apparent in 1.14: "We beheld his glory", and it is the aim of St John to point out this testimony in the signs.[1] In contrast to this, there is great stress on the unbelief of "the Jews" who, in spite of the signs, rejected the Messiah and brought him to the death of the Cross. The very signs which to the chosen disciples were decisive proofs of the Messianic character of Jesus, caused anger and offence among those who did not believe, and finally became the driving motive of their desire to kill him.[2] Thus in a way "the Jews" themselves, because of their unbelief and their rejection of Jesus, help to bring about "signs"—the death and resurrection of Jesus—through which all the others receive their true meaning.

4. *The death and resurrection of Jesus are the greatest signs of all.*

[1] John 20.30, 31.   [2] John 5.18; 7.19, 25; 8.37, 40; 11.50.

IMPORTANT THEOLOGICAL CONCEPTIONS 125

St John throughout regards these as one theological whole, as shown in the terms ὑψωθῆναι or δοξασθῆναι. They are not definitely spoken of as a σημεῖον. Logically, however, the "lifting-up" of Jesus *is* a sign, for it is the decisive proof of his Messianic character and therefore the foundation for the belief of the disciples. This is confirmed by the interesting use of the verb σημαίνειν in the Fourth Gospel: it only appears three times, twice when Jesus is predicting his own death, and once when he predicts the martyrdom of Peter:

> 12.33. "But this he said, signifying (σημαίνων) by what manner of death he should die."
>
> 21.19. "Now this he spake, signifying (σημαίνων) by what manner of death he should glorify God."

With the death of Jesus as an example, and also as the decisive sign of his being the Messiah, martyrdom became for the Church not only a sign of the enmity of the world but also a witness to the living Lord, who was calling his disciples to believe in him and to follow him.[1] It was also the sign of his leading them onwards to the goal in eternity. Thus σημεῖα and σημαίνειν are of eschatological character. All the works of Jesus receive their power and significance from the sign which he gave on the Cross[2]; all the mighty works done by him during his earthly ministry, e.g. the raising of Lazarus, were merely types of, and a preparation for, this sign. But the sign of the death and resurrection of Jesus is carried on in the Church through the σημεῖα which are done by the now risen Lord in the sacraments. The Evangelist is anxious to point out that Jesus does not allow men, even those closest to him, to make unconditional use of his power.[3] This is a reminder that the risen Lord also refuses to allow himself to be directed by men when he performs his mighty works in his Church.

[1] John 12.26; 21.19. [2] John 2.4.
[3] John 2.4; 7.3; 11.6.

32. ἔργα (works)

ἔργον (generally found in the plural, ἔργα) and ἐργάζομαι are used thirty-five times in the Fourth Gospel and twice in the First Epistle of St John. It applies on the one hand to the good or evil works of men, to the works of Abraham, and to the works of the devil,[1] and on the other hand to the works done by the Father through the Son. It is the latter which we are here to examine.

1. ἔργα *are the works done by the Son at the bidding of the Father*

4.34. "My meat is to do the will of him that sent me, and to accomplish his work."
5.17. "My Father worketh even until now and I work."
5.36. "The works which the Father hath given me to accomplish, the very works that I do . . ."
9.4. "We must work the works of him that sent me while it is yet day; the night cometh when no man can work."
14.10. "But the Father abiding in me doeth his works."

2. *The works of the Son will kindle faith*

The people asked: τί ἐργάζῃ? (6.30). The brothers of Jesus, who did not believe in him, said: "Depart hence and go into Judaea that thy disciples also may behold thy works which thou doest" (7.3).

Jesus himself says:

10.25. "The works that I do in my Father's name, these witness of me" (also 5.36).
10.37. "If I do not the works of my Father believe me not. But if I do them, though ye believe not me, believe the works."
14.11. "Or else believe me for the very works' sake."

3. ἔργα = σημεῖα

6.30. τί οὖν ποιεῖς σημεῖον = τί ἐργάζῃ
7.21. "I did one work and ye all marvel."

---

[1] John 3.19; 7.7; 1 John 3.12, 18; John 8.39, 41.

IMPORTANT THEOLOGICAL CONCEPTIONS 127

9.3. "... but that the works of God should be made manifest in him."

5.20. "And greater works than these will he show him, that ye may marvel."

10.32. "Many good works have I shewed you from the Father; for which of those works do ye stone me?"

15.24. "If I had not done among them the works that none other did, they had not had sin."

4. ἔργα *is a term summing up the whole life-work of Jesus*

7.3. "... that thy disciples also may behold thy works which thou doest."

17.4. "I glorified thee on the earth, having accomplished the work which thou hast given me to do."

The word τελειώσας (having accomplished), of course, corresponds, like τελειώσω in 4.34, with the great final word from the Cross: τετέλεσται.[1] In 7.3 the brothers of Jesus admonish him to go to Jerusalem and without knowing it they, therefore, encourage him to go to his death, to accomplish the purpose of his life, and to do the greatest of his works.

5. ἔργα *is the work of God in men—faith*

6.29. "This is the work of God, that ye believe on him whom he hath sent."

14.12. "He that believeth on me, the works that I do shall he do also; and greater works than these shall he do; because I go unto the Father."

It is now obvious that ἔργα, on the one hand, means the same as σημεῖα, but that, on the other hand, it has a wider meaning, including the whole life-work of Jesus. Thus it refers to the works done by the risen Lord in the Church just as σημεῖα does.[2] ἔργα serve both to kindle faith in men and also to reveal their faithlessness. The faithful are promised that in the power of the risen Lord they will be able to do "greater works" than he himself did among them during his earthly ministry. This refers to the works in

[1] John 19.30. [2] John 5.20; 14.12.

the Church, which find their chief expression in missions, in the preaching of the Word, and in the administration of the sacraments. For the works of Christ and of those who believe in him are identical. In the Church Christ does his works through the disciples; and the works of the disciples receive their power and their significance through Christ, until in the age to come still "greater" works will be wrought. Therefore ἔργα in the Fourth Gospel can only be understood if it is interpreted on an ecclesiastical and eschatological basis as the work of the risen Lord and his disciples both in the Church and in the time of fulfilment.

In the Septuagint ἔργον is used to signify the creative work of God[1] and the continuation of his work in the chosen people and their history.[2] The fact that St John is so anxious to point out that Jesus does the works of the Father on earth must mean that he takes part in the creative work of God. Thus the work of Jesus during his earthly ministry and in the Church is seen as the fulfilment of creation, and like logos, the ἔργα bear witness to the continuity which binds together creation, redemption, and fulfilment. The whole story of redemption is summed up in and realized by Christ.

33. πίστις, πιστεύειν (faith—to believe)

It is an extraordinary fact that the word πίστις does not occur at all in the Fourth Gospel, and only once in the First Epistle of St John. The adjective πιστός, however, is used once in the Gospel (in 20.27, where Jesus says to Thomas: καὶ μὴ γίνου ἄπιστος ἀλλὰ πιστός), and once in the Epistle (in 1.9, relating to Christ: πιστός ἐστιν καὶ δίκαιος). On the other hand, the verb πιστεύειν appears ninety-nine times in the Gospel and nine times in the Epistle and is one of the most important and frequently used terms in Johannine theology. The meaning of πιστεύειν is in most cases to believe in Jesus or to believe in God: in a few cases the

---

[1] Gen. 2.2, 3; Ps. 8.3. [2] Ex. 34.10; Deut. 3.24; 11.3, 7.

IMPORTANT THEOLOGICAL CONCEPTIONS 129

reference is to another object, e.g. Moses in 5.46; and "every spirit", 1 John 4.1. It always refers to the faith of men and does not at any time signify the relation of the Son to the Father. Only once does Jesus stand as subject of πιστεύειν in 2.24: "Jesus did not trust himself unto them" (the Jews). This is also the only instance when the meaning is clearly that of *fiducia*. Often (about thirty times) the meaning of πιστεύειν is absolute, i.e. in the sense of "coming to believe", e.g. in 1.7. We also find the expressions ἐλθεῖν πρὸς με,[1] λαμβάνειν αὐτόν,[2] and ἀκολουθεῖν,[3] which have the same meaning as πιστεύειν.

From a study of the many sayings in the Fourth Gospel concerning faith the following conclusions may be drawn:

1. *Faith is a Work of God*

   6.44. "No man can come to me except the Father which sent me draw him."
   1 John 5.1. "Whosoever believeth that Jesus is the Christ is begotten of God."
   1 John 5.4. "For whatsoever is begotten of God overcometh the world: and this is the victory that hath overcome the world, even our faith."
   1.12ff. "But as many as received him, to them gave he the right to become children of God, even to them that believe on his name; which were born, not of blood ... but of God."

The last example throws light on the above-mentioned identity between πιστεύειν and λαμβάνειν αὐτόν. The last three examples speak of the kindling of faith as a birth brought about by God; and call the faithful the children of God, all of which further emphasizes the idea of faith as a work of God.

2. *Faith is kindled through the words of Jesus*

   4.41. "And many more believed because of his word."
   8.30. "As he spake these things many believed on him."

---

[1] John 6.44, 65; 3.21.   [2] John 1.12.
[3] John 12.26; 13.36; 21.19.

3. *Faith is kindled through the works of Jesus*

2.23. "Many believed on his name, beholding his signs which he did."
4.53. "(The nobleman in Capernaum) himself believed and his whole house."
6.36. "Ye have seen me and yet believe not."
10.38. "But if I do them, though ye believe not me, believe the works."
14.11. "Or else believe me for the very works' sake."

There are other similar examples in 2.11; 10.41–42; 11.42, 45, 48; 12.11.

4. *Faith might also be kindled through the words of the disciples*

4.39. "And from that city many of the Samaritans believed on him because of the word of the woman."
7.38. "He that believeth on me, as the Scripture hath said, out of his belly shall flow rivers of living water."
17.20. "Neither for these only do I pray, but for them also that believe on me through their word."
19.35. "And he that hath seen hath borne witness . . . that ye also may believe."

This is in accordance with the interpretation earlier given to 7.38, a missionary charge, speaking of the possibilities for the faithful to take the life-giving faith out into the world.

5. *The content of the faith is this confession: Jesus Christ is the Son of God*

16.27. ". . . and have believed that I came forth from the Father."
17.8. ". . . and they believed that thou didst send me."
20.31. "But these are written, that ye may believe that Jesus is the Christ, the Son of God, and that believing ye may have life in his name."
1 John 3.23. "And this is his commandment that we should believe in the name of his Son Jesus Christ, and love one another even as he gave us commandment."
1 John 5.5. "And who is he that overcometh the world, but he that believeth that Jesus is the Son of God?"

This faith actually involves a new conception of God. He is no longer the Lawgiver of the Old Testament, but the

IMPORTANT THEOLOGICAL CONCEPTIONS 131

God who has sent his Son into the world to give men the gift of eternal life.

6. *Faith gives eternal life to man*

   3.16. "... that whosoever believeth on him should not perish, but have eternal life."
   3.36. "He that believeth on the Son hath eternal life; but he that obeyeth not the Son shall not see life, but the wrath of God abideth on him."
   6.47. "He that believeth hath eternal life."
   1 John 5.13. "... that ye may know that ye have eternal life, even unto you that believe on the name of the Son of God."
   7.39. "But this spake he of the Spirit, which they that believed on him were to receive."
   11.40. "... if thou believedst, thou shouldest see the glory of God."

There are other examples in 5.24 and 6.35, 40.

7. *Unbelief is sin*

Jesus has no use whatever for the faith of the Jews:

   5.37. "Ye have neither heard his voice at any time, nor seen his form."

Jesus speaks of himself as the only true revelation of God:

   14.9. "He that hath seen me hath seen the Father."
   10.38. "... that the Father is in me and I in the Father."

If anyone continues in unbelief, he must be prepared to take his punishment:

   3.18. "He that believeth on him is not judged; he that believeth not hath been judged already, because he hath not believed on the name of the only-begotten Son of God."
   9.41. "But now ye say, we see: your sin remaineth."
   8.24. "For except ye believe that I am he, ye shall die in your sins."

The absolute ἐγώ εἰμι in the latter example, as also in 13.19, is probably a reference to the Old Testament tetragrammaton and expresses the continuity of the revelation as well as the close relationship between the Father and the Son, emphasizing the fulness of the divine revelation given by Jesus.

8. *The possibilities of faith in the new life*

14.12–13. "... he that believeth on me, the works that I do shall he do also; and greater works than these shall he do; because I go unto the Father. And whatsoever ye shall ask in my name, that will I do, that the Father may be glorified in the Son."

This is a picture of the situation of the Church and it is stressed further in 14.28: "If ye loved me ye would have rejoiced, because I go unto the Father; for the Father is greater than I." It is in these circumstances that faith reaches its fulfilment and that the "greater works" can be done by prayer in the name of Jesus, i.e. through the prayer of the Christians in the Church, which, of course, means in the liturgy.

Has, then, the Fourth Gospel no recognition of different kinds of faith or of different degrees of faith? In 12.42 ff, it is said that many of the scribes believed on Jesus, but that they did not admit it because they were afraid of being put out of the Synagogue. After the account of the miracle in Cana, it is noted in 2.11 that "His disciples believed on him", but already in 2.22 we find that it was after his resurrection that the disciples believed fully, for the first time, "the Scripture and the word which Jesus had said" ("Destroy this temple and in three days I will raise it up"). The same thought comes back in 12.16. In 6.60 "many of his disciples" take offence because of the "hard saying" of the Master, and fall away, while others confess their allegiance to him. In 16.30 ff the disciples confess their faith, but Jesus answers: "Do ye now believe? Behold, the hour cometh, yea, is come, that ye shall be scattered. ...." He, thus, foretells that they will fall away from their faith. Thus both among the scribes and among the disciples there seems to have been a

IMPORTANT THEOLOGICAL CONCEPTIONS 133

faith which falls short; which did not, or could not, dare to make a whole-hearted confession of faith in Jesus and which, therefore, in a critical moment came to nothing. What is the relation of this faith to the right and true faith which is pictured by St John? Is the difference one of degree or of kind?

The question is solved in 16.30 ff, where the disciples confess that Jesus is come out from God (ἀπὸ θεοῦ ἐξῆλθες). Quite unexpectedly Jesus gives the following ironical answer: "Do ye now believe?" followed by the prediction of their falling away. The confession just made by the disciples showed clearly that they had not yet come to a true faith. The contents of a true faith Jesus has pointed out in v. 28: "I came out from the Father and am come into the world: again, I leave the world, and go unto the Father." This last point, the return of Jesus to the Father, the disciples had not yet grasped and therefore they could not believe it: thus their faith was imperfect. The same trend of thought appears in 6.61 ff: "Doth this cause you to stumble? What then if you should behold the Son of Man ascending where he was before?" This "lifting-up" of Jesus, his return to the Father through the shame and abasement of the Cross, is the real test of faith.

πιστεύειν signifies not merely faith in the Incarnate Lord but also faith in Christ lifted up and glorified through suffering and death. It follows that the true faith can only be experienced by the disciples after the resurrection of Jesus, i.e. in the Church. Thus it is from the point of view of the Church, with her certain knowledge of the presence of the risen Lord, that all the Johannine statements about the faith must be seen. The "faith" which might be shown by the disciples before the death and resurrection of Jesus must be thought of as a preparatory faith, a faith in the Christ who had come from God, but not a faith in the Christ who must return to God. Only in the Church, in union with the risen Lord, does faith reach its fulfilment and deserve to be called faith. In the Gospel we see how the timid rulers are rehabilitated after the death of Jesus,[1] how Peter, after denying his Master, is reinstated in his office[2] when, as a representative of all the disciples who had fled from Gethsemane because their faith had collapsed, he confesses his Master and regains his confidence.

Faith and confession of faith go together; and judging by what has just been said it was not possible to make a full confession of faith in Christ until after his death and resurrection. This fits in very well with what has also been said about the faith as only fully developed in the Church. πιστεύειν has been defined as meaning "to be a member of the church". This is only correct if by "member of the Church" is meant not only the exterior adherence but the open confession of Christ made in thought, word, and deed. No doubt St John knew members of the Church who were spiritually dead and faithless[3] and in other places we find words of warning directed to them. Faith, however, is not thought of as an individual spiritual quality, but as a gift of God, which can only be received and possessed in the Church; and which can only be preserved if the disciple remains in personal communion with Christ in his Church. Thus in 8.31 we read: "Jesus therefore said to those Jews which had believed him: if ye abide in my word then are ye truly my disciples . . ."; and again, in the story about the true vine, the word "abide" is dominating. In the Fourth Gospel faith is presented as man's possibility of possessing eternal life. To a certain extent it is actually identical with that life which is beginning already in the Church, and which at the Parousia will reach its fulfilment in the new age. Thus the conception of faith in the Fourth Gospel is altogether ecclesiastical and eschatological.

Hence it is pointless to ask whether faith in the Fourth Gospel is more inclined towards the idea of *fiducia* (trust)

---
[1] John 19.38, 39.   [2] John 21.15.
[3] John 6.60; 12.42; 15.6.

IMPORTANT THEOLOGICAL CONCEPTIONS 135

or *notitia* (knowing). The link between πιστεύειν and γινώσκειν (to get knowledge of), which we shall consider shortly, may seem to indicate that *notitia* is the aspect particularly stressed. But because the Johannine idea of faith is entirely conditioned by the Church and her eschatological situation, it is not possible to define it philosophically: it is altogether a religious conception.

It is commonly pointed out that faith based on signs, according to St John, is inferior to faith based on the words of Jesus. Reference is made to 4.48 as a proof of this: "Except ye see signs and wonders, ye will in no wise believe." But there is not necessarily any reproach in these words; it is unlikely that it is meant as a rebuke, since it was directed to the father of the sick boy. It is a mere statement of the fact of man's inability to believe without signs. It is thus an explanatory introduction to the following sign, the main purpose of which was not merely to restore physical health to the boy but also to kindle faith and awaken new life in those who, by witnessing this sign, were brought in contact with the life-giving power of Jesus. The threefold ὁ υἱός σου ζῇ is worth noticing.

In St John 12.37 there is, indeed, a reproach concerning the lack of faith, but there is nothing in this to suggest that signs should be an inferior motive for faith. From the interpretation given at an earlier stage to Christ's words to Thomas: "Blessed are they that have not seen and yet have believed",[1] it follows that this particular text cannot be taken as a proof that faith through hearing is superior to faith through seeing. Our examination of σημεῖα and ῥήματα and the relation we have discovered between these two expressions show that it was not possible to evaluate faith in the Fourth Gospel on a basis of seeing as opposed to hearing: both are equally necessary and equally justifiable ways of reaching a faith in the risen Lord.

In 6.28–29 we read: "What must we do that we may work

[1] John 20.29.

the works of God? Jesus answered and said unto them: This is the work of God that ye believe on him whom he hath sent." The question is formulated in accordance with the characteristically Jewish idea of the relation between God and man, a relationship characterized by its stress on what man can achieve: "What must we *do*?" The answer given by Jesus indicates the entirely different relationship with God into which man has been brought by him, for the works demanded by God from man are faith in Jesus. The faith, however, can never be man's own achievement. When the Jews go on to demand that Jesus should show the validity of his claim by means of signs, he speaks of himself as the Bread that comes down from heaven, with an obvious reference to the miracle which he had just performed; and directs a few words of reproof to his listeners: ". . . ye have seen me and yet believe not". In v. 40 we read: "For this is the will of my Father, that everyone that beholdeth the Son and believeth on him should have eternal life, and I will raise him up at the last day." To "behold" the Son is not synonymous with to "believe"; it is rather the condition of belief. We realize, however, that what is meant here is not merely physical sight, the seeing of Jesus in his earthly existence: it is rather the liturgical seeing of Christ which St John is showing to be the foundation of faith—the seeing of Christ in the Eucharist. The same meaning is explicit in the words "we beheld his glory".[1] The disciple by the open tomb "saw and believed".[2] To believe is to see the glory of Jesus revealed in and through his deep abasement on the Cross: "What then if ye should *see* (R.V. *behold*) the Son of Man ascending where he was before?"[3] The Cross is the final consequence of the Incarnation, and its consummation. It is the risen and glorified Christ who is manifested in the Church, in its Liturgy, and above all in the Eucharist, through the medium of simple earthly things. These things are the channels which make it possible for Jesus to say: "He that beholdeth

[1] John 1.14.   [2] John 20.8.   [3] John 6.62.

IMPORTANT THEOLOGICAL CONCEPTIONS 137

me beholdeth him that sent me", and "He that hath seen me hath seen the Father."[1] Thus according to the Fourth Gospel perfect faith is only possible through the revelation which Christ gives in the Church, in his words and sacraments: and because faith is so very firmly attached to "eternal life" and the resurrection at "the last day", it is an altogether eschatological conception. By means of his faith the disciple experiences here and now proleptically what he will finally experience in eternity.

In the Fourth Gospel there is a definite relationship between πιστεύειν and γινωσκεῖν. The most typical example of this is to be found in 6.69, where Peter confesses: "We have believed and know (πεπιστεύκαμεν, καὶ ἐγνώκαμεν) that thou art the Holy One of God"; γινώσκειν here seems to represent a higher degree of faith, but in other places, e.g. 17.8 and 1 John 4.16, the order is the opposite. Therefore the terms appear to be synonymous. It might possibly be argued that γινώσκειν underlines the intellectual side of faith. "Information", or gnosis on mystic-spiritual lines, is out of the question, as the evangelist is markedly antignostic in his approach. Thus his connecting πίστις with γνῶσις may well be taken as a sign of his antagonism to gnosticism.

The noun γνῶσις is as little used in the Fourth Gospel as πίστις, while γινώσκειν appears more than fifty times in the Gospel and twenty-three times in the Epistle. Very often it is used in the sense of "to know Christ",[2] "to know God",[3] "to know the Truth",[4] and reciprocally about the Father and the Son.[5] When used about "the Son knowing the Father" γινώσκειν is different from πιστεύειν, which never has Christ as its subject.

Prucker has shown that while γινώσκειν is very common in religious language during Hellenistic times, the term

[1] John 12.45; 14.9.
[2] John 1.10; 6.69; 10.14, 15, 38; 14.7, 9, 20, 31; 16.3; 17.7, 8, 23, 25.
[3] John 8.55; 10.15; 14.7; 16.3; 17.3.
[4] John 8.32.   [5] John 10.15.

γνῶσις θεοῦ first comes into use with the beginning of religious syncretism. By that time, however, γνῶσις had lost all meaning of logical knowledge and become equivalent to χάρις, a gift of God. Later it was used to express the doctrine of the way of salvation; and finally it became the term used for that magic wherewith the mystagogues tried to control the supernatural powers.

In the Old Testament, however, *yada'* signifies not merely an act of the intellect but includes the whole personality. It is an ethical concept and is used to express man's knowledge of God as well as God's knowledge of man. According to Prucker the term γνῶσις in the writings of St Paul contains a speculative, a voluntary, and an "existential" element. It is always linked together with πίστις and therefore cut off from gnostic mysticism. πίστις stands for the beginning or foundation of fellowship with Christ, γνῶσις for its fulfilment. Prucker, however, in his interpretation of γνῶσις in St Paul's writings seems to have over-emphasized the individualistic side of it.

In the Fourth Gospel γινώσκειν is used in more or less the same way as in the Pauline writings, but the ecclesiastical character of the term becomes increasingly prominent, so that the formula "to know Christ" appears most frequently in chapter 10 and in the final discourse, i.e. in passages implying life in the Church. St John's habit of co-ordinating γινώσκειν and πιστεύειν points in the same direction. By his use of γινώσκειν St John is emphasizing that in contrast to the false γνῶσις of Hellenism the Christian revelation has a true and pure γνῶσις which involves the personal engagement of the entire man in the faith in "the only true God" and him whom he did send, Jesus Christ. It has already been pointed out that St John boldly adopts gnostic terms and fills them with a Christian content in order to make of them useful weapons in the battle for the true faith. It is, therefore, reasonable to suppose that his use of γινώσκειν is meant to serve the same purpose, and that behind this ex-

IMPORTANT THEOLOGICAL CONCEPTIONS

pression we can see the young Church engaged in a keen fight against the most dangerous of all her opponents, gnosticism. To St John, γινώσκειν, as well as πιστεύειν, is never just the property of the individual, but always a knowledge which belongs to all in common, just as faith does. Both faith and knowledge can only be obtained and kept in the corporate faith and life of the Church, while it is, nevertheless, all the time the question of a personal faith in a personal God won by a personal Saviour. Herein lies the great difference between the true and the false γνῶσις.

34. ζωή (life)

ζωή appears thirty-five times in the Fourth Gospel and thirteen times in the First Epistle. It is used as an alternative to, and with the same meaning as, ζωὴ αἰώνιος. Consistently ζῆν and ζωή are used to signify the "spiritual" life—life in and through Christ as opposed to the purely physical life. The latter is mostly covered by the term ψυχή; e.g. in 10.15, 17, Jesus lays down his life for his sheep; in 13.37, Peter wants to give his life for Jesus. The difference between ψυχή and ζωή is clearly shown in 12.25: "He that hateth his life (ψυχή) in this world shall keep it unto life eternal" (εἰς ζωὴν αἰώνιον).

In the story of the healing of the nobleman's son,[1] ζῆν is used throughout and this confirms our idea that the three-fold ὁ υἱός σου ζῇ has a deeper meaning than merely the physical health of the boy. In 11.26 also we find that ζῆν does not stand for physical life alone: πᾶς ὁ ζῶν καὶ πιστεύων εἰς ἐμὲ οὐ μὴ ἀποθάνῃ εἰς τὸν αἰῶνα. Here ὁ ζῶν can only refer to the life which comes through that faith whereof the previous verse is speaking: to suggest that physical life alone is meant would be nonsense, as the dead cannot believe. ζῶν and πιστεύων are here co-ordinated and the consequences common to both of them are expressed in the words "... shall never die".

[1] John 4.46 ff.

From the many sayings about ζωή in the Fourth Gospel the following conclusions may be drawn:

1. *The origin of life is God (Christ)*
    1.4. "In him (*logos*) was life."
    5.26. "For as the Father hath life in himself, even so gave he to the Son to have life in himself."
    6.57. "As the living Father sent me, and I live because of the Father; so he that eateth me, he shall also live because of me."
    1 John 5.11. "God gave unto us eternal life, and this life is in his Son."
    1 John 5.20. "... his Son Jesus Christ. This is the true God and eternal life."

It appears to follow from the latter example that St John identifies Christ with God as well as with eternal life. The Johannine sayings, however, can never be treated as logical definitions. Thus from 1 John 5.20 we can only gather the absolute affinity which always exists between God, Christ, and eternal life. In this connection it is well to consider St John's expressions for the birth into this life, where man is spoken of as "born of God"[1] or as "born from above".[2]

Ζωή in the Fourth Gospel is not opposed to physical life: it is life in its perfection, including physical life. For there is only one "life"—life given in creation. The birth of which St John speaks is no metaphysical re-creation, but the realization and fulfilment of created life: God's creation, spoilt through sin and death, becomes God's possession. St John 1.4 and indeed the whole Prologue stresses the continuity between created life and redeemed life: the latter is the fulfilment of the former.

2. *Life is given in Christ*
    5.21. "... even so the Son also quickeneth whom he will."
    10.10. "I came that they may have life, and may have it abundantly."

---

[1] John 1.13; 1 John 2.29; 3.9; 4.7. [2] John 3.3, 7 (R.V. marg.).

IMPORTANT THEOLOGICAL CONCEPTIONS 141

10.28. "I give unto them eternal life, and they shall never perish."

17.2. "... that whatsoever thou hast given him, to them he should give eternal life."

1 John 4.9. "God hath sent his only-begotten Son into the world, that we might live through him."

Thus, according to St John, there is no life except through Christ. This is not contradicted by 6.63, where the Spirit is spoken of as the life-giver (τὸ ζωοποιοῦν); for the Spirit represents Christ. Through the Spirit the continued revelation of Christ is realized—and that constitutes the Church.[1] No man can possess life without faith in Christ.

3. *Life is given to those who believe*

3.15. "... that whosoever believeth may in him have eternal life."
3.36. "He that believeth on the Son hath eternal life."
6.40. "... that everyone that beholdeth the Son and believeth on him should have eternal life."
6.47. "He that believeth hath eternal life."

As faith in the Fourth Gospel is always faith in the risen and glorified Christ, it follows that life, i.e. real and eternal life, can only be had where faith is possible, namely, in the Church. This corresponds to what we have already said about the Spirit as the life-giver.

4. *Those who do not possess life are given over to death*

The antithesis of life is death. In the Fourth Gospel θάνατος and ἀποθνήσκειν are used alternately to signify physical or spiritual death. We are here, of course, concerned with the latter significance.

5.24. "(He that believeth) hath passed out of death into life."
8.51. "If a man keep my Word he shall never see death."
1 John 3.14. "We know that we have passed out of death into life."
1 John 5.16. "There is a sin unto death" (ἔστιν ἁμαρτία πρὸς θάνατον).

[1] John 14.26; 15.26; 16.12-15.

In the same sense ἀπόλλυμι, is used:

6.39. "... that of all that which he hath given me I should lose nothing, but should raise it up at the last day."

The life which St John here puts over against death is not immortality in the ordinary sense. Terms like ἀθανασία ἀθάνατος, ἀφθαρσία, and ἄφθαρτος, do not occur at all in the Fourth Gospel or in the Epistle, an omission which is surely due not merely to chance. On the contrary, we believe that St John has deliberately avoided these words in order to emphasize that ζωή is not a metaphysical or philosophical term but a purely religious one: life with Christ; life with God. This is particularly clear in 3.36, where the opposite to life is the wrath of God: "... he that obeyeth not the Son shall not see life, but the wrath of God abideth on him" (ἡ ὀργὴ τοῦ θεοῦ).

In the Old Testament "death" is spoken of as the very worst thing that can happen to a man in life, a greater calamity than illness, imprisonment, persecution, or even desertion by God. Thus "death" is not only the actual loss of life, but also the loss of those assets and possibilities which belong to life. For in the land of the dead there is only complete darkness and utter loneliness. There is no freedom of action and no hope for the future. Even eating and drinking are denied to the dead, for it is the mark of the living. It is as seen against this background that we can more fully understand some of the statements about ζωή in the Fourth Gospel.

Christ is the *Light of Life* (τὸ φῶς τῆς ζωῆς): "I am the Light of the world: he that followeth me shall not walk in darkness, but shall have the light of life."[1] Just as light is the prerequisite condition for all earthly life,[2] so Christ is the light, the very source of life, which is the condition of all human existence. To limit the significance of τὸ φῶς τοῦ κόσμου, as Pribnow does, to a purely intellectual enlighten-

[1] John 8.12; 9.5; 12.46.   [2] Gen. 1.3.

IMPORTANT THEOLOGICAL CONCEPTIONS 143

ment which makes men susceptible to life, seems to narrow unjustifiably the whole idea.

Christ is the *Water of Life* (τὸ ὕδωρ ζῶν). This is expressed in 4.14: "But whosoever drinketh of the water that I shall give him shall never thirst; but the water that I shall give him shall become in him a well of water springing up unto eternal life" (εἰς ζωὴν αἰώνιον).

Christ is the *Bread of Life* (ὁ ἄρτος τῆς ζωῆς). Thirst and hunger are the two most elementary human cravings. If they are not satisfied human existence is not possible. In the Fourth Gospel, Jesus is spoken of as the one who alone can satisfy the cravings of man and fulfil his expectations; the one who gives him that life which alone deserves the name of life.

How is the significance of this life to be understood? Lindblom interprets ζωή as a peculiar synthesis of Hellenistic and Jewish thought, so that ζωὴ αἰώνιος is to be interpreted as a purely Jewish formula filled with Hellenistic hope of immortality. Thus to Lindblom ζωή becomes "a metaphysical power" which expresses itself "on the one hand in religious and ethical perfection, and on the other hand in metaphysical-physical immortality and incorruption". We have already noticed that any reference to immortality and incorruption in the metaphysical sense is altogether alien to the Fourth Gospel. St John has not promised "physical" immortality, nor have later generations experienced any such thing. Neither is there in this Gospel any indication that ζωή should be taken to refer to religious and ethical perfection. Such trends of thought belong to the mystery religions. St John does not even use expressions such as "growth in faith" and his emphasis on the ethical side of ζωή is very slight. If indeed it is possible to trace any Hellenistic influence in the Johannine ζωὴ αἰώνιος it might be that St John—quite contrary to Lindblom's theory—has adopted a Hellenistic formula which he has then filled with ideas from the Old Testament and later

Jewish thought. This latter supposition would entirely agree with the manner in which St John deals with other theological concepts, such as λόγος.

Pribnow supposes the essential meaning of ζωή and σωτηρία to be identical; the latter term only appears once in the Fourth Gospel, in 4.22, while it is not found at all in the Epistle. Pribnow describes eternal life as complete communion with Christ and God, together with missionary activity and ethical action. Let us see whether we can arrive at a more satisfactory definition.

Is ζωή in the Fourth Gospel a purely immanent life, or is it a supernatural life, or is it a synthesis of both? Can it be achieved now, or does it belong altogether to the future? Von Schrenck states that ζωή in the Fourth Gospel usually implies something wholly present, and that the few places which actually mention a future life are a concession made by the Evangelist to satisfy an earlier and primitive but popular eschatology. Lindblom, however, considers ζωή to be a timeless state, an expression for the "mysticism" which earlier exegetes were so anxious to read into the Johannine texts. But Pribnow admits that ζωή at times signifies something present, and at other times something still in the future, something eschatological. This opinion is shared by Smilde. Bultmann and other representatives of the dialectical theology see in ζωή an adequate expression for "realized" eschatology: and therefore they consistently do away with all passages of futurist eschatology as being later editorial insertions. By doing so, they arrive at the "de-mythologized" present eschatology which is considered typical of ζωή in the Fourth Gospel. This simply means adapting the Johannine passages to the favourite theories of each particular theologian.

Even a hasty examination will convince us that ζωή is both life that can be possessed in the present age and also life given in the age to come. This is also the meaning of the adjective "eternal". For a life which is limited to the present

IMPORTANT THEOLOGICAL CONCEPTIONS 145

or to the future cannot be eternal. The most important of the sayings in which ζωή signifies life in the present are texts about faith in Christ as the condition for the obtaining of life,[1] or about Christ having come down from heaven to give life to the world.[2] In other places, ζωή αἰώνιος is spoken of as something belonging to the future.[3] In some cases it is not clear whether the life is thought of as present or future,[4] while in others we find that the two meanings appear side by side.[5] As the word ζωή cannot very well refer now to life in this world and now to life in the world to come, its significance must be so wide as to include both meanings. This may seem contradictory, but it nevertheless tallies with what has been said above about the twofold significance of the word in the Fourth Gospel: not spiritual life *contra* physical life, but life *contra* death. The solution to the problem of the relation between its two meanings is found in the resurrection. It is noteworthy that in both the passages in which ζωή is represented as something both present and future, the thought of the resurrection is obvious. For as the resurrection of Christ links up his earthly life with his life as the glorified Lord, and moulds these two "lives" into one unity which cannot be dissolved, so also is the earthly life of him who believes in Christ bound up with his life in the world to come. By means of this his personality is preserved so that he lives a real life with both body and soul, here on earth and afterwards in eternity; in other words it is the eschatological ζωή. The resurrection belief is here not a foreign addition to St John's ζωή-conception in either of the ways suggested by Lindblom and Bultmann. On the contrary, it is the obvious consequence of that thought. For ζωή is, whether present or future, a definitely eschatological conception. The ζωή of futurist eschatology has been stripped of the apocalyptic garments wherewith the early

---

[1] John 3.36; 6.47; 5.40.
[2] John 6.33; 10.10, 28; 17.3.
[3] John 14.19; 5.29; 12.25.
[4] John 6.51, 57; 12.50; 1 John 2.25.
[5] John 11.25, 26; 5.24, 25.

Church so eagerly covered her thought about the world to come. It may be that by so doing it has lost something of its imaginative lucidity, but on the other hand it has gained in religious power and sincerity, while gaining a new and more realistic lucidity—in the Church.

This view of ζωή accords well with the conclusion to which Cullmann has come in his examination of the Hellenistic and the biblical conception of the idea of time. He points out the great difference between the "linear" idea of time which is typical of the biblical revelation, and the "cyclic" one which clearly marks all Hellenistic thought. To philosophical (Hellenistic) thought, eternity means timelessness, while Jewish-Christian revelation, in a "naïve" and unphilosophical manner, sees eternity as the infinite extension of time. On this infinite line of time the Creation and the Parousia form two important points between which the present age lies. This particular part, and therefore also the whole line of time, is divided in the centre by the redemptive work of Christ—by his death and resurrection. The line between the resurrection and the Parousia is, however, the age of the Church, and there man is given the possibility of possessing in faith ζωή αἰώνιος, which afterwards, through the resurrection, will continue beyond the limit of this age.

Already Joachim Jeremias had pointed out the difference between the biblical and the modern conception of time, but he defines the latter as rectilinear and ascending, while the former is said to be "the over-ruling of the holy God who reveals himself in the circle of events". Cullmann quite rightly finds this view of time as a circle including the Creation and the Parousia, "confusing". Lyons defines the meaning of "eternal" in the sense that it has "neither beginning nor end", while Cullmann points out that, although it is true that ζωή αἰώνιος has a beginning, it certainly has no end. Wendland objects to the conception of eternity as timelessness and speaks of Christ as "the fulness of time, the centre of history". He does not, however, explain the

IMPORTANT THEOLOGICAL CONCEPTIONS

relationship between this time and eternity. It would seem that Cullmann has here really come to conclusions of lasting value.

We must now examine more fully the conception of ζωή as the realization of eternal life in the present if we are to attain to a more definite conception of it.

It is clear that the life which Christ gives to those who believe must take some form or other, and it seems natural to think first of the ethical life which should be lived by the disciple in obedience to the commands of the Master. The Fourth Gospel, however, contains remarkably few sayings concerning the Christian ethic; the sanctification spoken of in 17.17 does not appear to be in the first instance of an ethical character. On the contrary, we often find passages about ζωή which have a decidedly cultic significance; for example, the texts about the Water of Life which clearly refer to Baptism, and those about the Bread of Life which as clearly appear connected with the Eucharist. These are the two sources from which the Johannine ζωή springs—the sacraments which are necessary for the Church's life and therefore also for the life of the individual Christian. The sacraments, however, only hold life-giving power for those who believe in Christ, for according to St John, faith and life cannot be separated from one another. Through the sacraments Christ is revealed to faith as the true Saviour, the Mediator of the true knowledge of God and of real life. This is the content of 17.3: "And this is life eternal, that they should know thee the only true God, and him whom thou didst send, even Jesus Christ." Life, as it is represented in the Fourth Gospel, can never be separated from the Church. For in the Church by means of the sacraments the right condition for obtaining and preserving this life is to be gained. But by his strong emphasis on the necessity of faith for attaining to life, St John is trying to prevent the idea that life is independent of personal responsibility and personal effort.

There are several interesting parallels between the passages about the Water of Life (ch. 3 and 4) and those on the Bread of Life (ch. 6).

1. Christ is the giver of life.
2. Life is given through material elements—water and bread.
3. The working power is the Spirit ("born of the Spirit", "the Spirit maketh alive (R.V. quickeneth)").
4. Faith is necessary for the receiving of life.
5. It is Christ glorified who gives life.

> ("And no man hath ascended into heaven but he that descended out of heaven . . . and as Moses lifted up the serpent in the wilderness, even so must the Son of Man be lifted up. . . ." (3.13, 14.)
> "What then if ye should behold the Son of Man ascending where he was before?" (6.62))

6. The discourses about the Water and the Bread of Life give rise to dispute and offence.
7. The Water and the Bread of Life are the great signs of the Messianic age, typified by the smiting of the rock by Moses, and the miracle of the manna.
8. The deepest needs of man are satisfied by the Water and the Bread of Life for which man longs (4.15 . . . the woman asks for the Water of Life, i.e. Baptism; 6.34 . . . the Jews ask for the Bread of Life, i.e. the Eucharist).

From a consideration of these passages it becomes clear that ζωή is altogether an eschatological and ecclesiastical conception. The life goes out from the risen Lord and is received by the believer in the sacraments of the Church. The "created" life finds its fulfilment in this "redemptive" life wherein the believer, in an anticipatory manner, experiences eternal life in its perfection.

This conception of ζωή is not affected by the passages in the Fourth Gospel which have no direct reference to the sacraments; e.g. 6.63: ". . . the words that I have spoken

IMPORTANT THEOLOGICAL CONCEPTIONS 149

unto you are spirit and are life . . ." This refers to the word of Christ as administered by the Church. Mention of the Spirit indicates that the Church is already a realized fact, and the perfect tense λελάληκα shows that Jesus' own earthly mission of preaching the word is now something accomplished. As has been already shown there is in this Gospel no difference in principle between σημεῖα and ῥήματα In the same way there cannot be in the Church any fundamental difference between the life which is mediated by the word and the life mediated by the sacraments, for in both cases the life comes from the risen Lord. Thus ζωή or ζωή αἰώνιος is the eschatological life which through faith in Christ is received and lived in the Church, and which afterwards through the resurrection reaches its fulfilment in the world to come.

What, then, does the Fourth Gospel think of physical death? To a great extent it is treated as a nonentity, as a conquered enemy, to which the faithful must submit, but only momentarily—as was the case with the Lord himself. Thus it is written in 11.25, 26: "I am the Resurrection and the Life." (This is a "hendiadys" for the "risen" life.) "He that believeth on me, though he die, yet shall he live; and whosoever liveth and believeth on me shall never die." The story of the raising of Lazarus and above all the importance attached to the resurrection of Jesus himself in St John's theology bears witness to this. As Jesus himself has conquered death, so has he also conquered it on behalf of the faithful. His resurrection, foreshadowed by the raising of Lazarus, is in its turn the presage of the resurrection at the last day. Against this background death is powerless and no longer fills the faithful with fear. Only when death involves the loss of the real life, i.e. the eternal life, is it terrible. But Jesus has come to call to life those who are spiritually dead—for that is the significance of οἱ νεκροί in 5.25. Note the present tense in the sentence: "The hour cometh and now is, when the dead shall hear the voice of the Son of God; and they that hear shall live." As a consequence of this, St John avoids speaking of the departed as "dead", and in 5.28 we read: ". . . the hour cometh in which all that are in the tombs (πάντες οἱ ἐν τοῖς μνημείοις) shall hear his voice." This saying is referring to the future alone, for what is meant is the resurrection at the last day. All those who are in the tombs are not "dead" in the sense in which St John uses this word. In the resurrection at the last day the good will rise to life (ἀνάστασις ζωῆς), while the evil will rise to judgement (ἀνάστασις κρίσεως). St John always uses κρίσις as equivalent to κατάκρισις (condemnation). Those who believe possess life already and do not come under condemnation.

Is there, then, no ethical qualification of ζωή in the Fourth Gospel? The saying in 5.29 quoted above speaks of οἱ τὰ φαῦλα πράξαντες and οἱ τὰ ἀγαθὰ ποιήσαντες, but just before we also find ὁ τὸν λόγον μοῦ ἀκούων καὶ πιστεύων τῷ πέμψαντί με (v. 24). Thus works are intimately related to faith. Direct ethical sayings are very rare in this Gospel and this must be because St John sees faith and works as an indissoluble unity.[1] The same unity is emphasized in the Epistle, although there the ethical side is also stressed. Thus we find in 1 John 3.14: "We have passed out of death into life because we love the brethren. He that loveth not abideth in death."

35. χάρις (grace)

The term χάρις is used only in the Prologue to the Gospel and it does not occur at all in the Epistle.

χάρις καὶ ἀλήθεια in vv. 14 and 17 are a hendiadys signifying "the grace full of truth" or "the truth full of grace". Some commentators on χάρις ἀντὶ χάριτος in v. 16 have thought that the first χάρις refers to the revelation by Moses in the Law, while the second and more important χάρις refers to the revelation in Christ. This cannot be correct,

---

[1] John 3.20, 21.

IMPORTANT THEOLOGICAL CONCEPTIONS 151

for in the following verses Moses and Christ are spoken of in contrast to each other. Verse 14, too, makes it clear that χάρις can be connected only with Christ. Consequently χάρις ἀντὶ χάριτος must mean grace that is always increasing, grace without limit. Because of this, the expression takes on a strongly eschatological emphasis. Grace is wholly opposed to the Law (νόμος), which is only valid in the old dispensation and impresses its mark on life there. Grace is the gift given by Jesus to his own in the new dispensation, that is, in the Church. "Grace" and "truth" are the marks of the Person of Jesus (v. 14) and of his work (v. 17). This χάρις is in the Fourth Gospel expressed in many varying contexts and in different ways: "God so loved the world. . . ."[1] "Not to condemn the world; but that the world should be saved through him . . ."[2]; "The Father himself loveth you . . ."[3] As the Law was given to the old Israel and was valid for its own period, so now Christ gives his grace in the new Israel, the Church. Through this, νόμος too receives eschatological emphasis; it becomes the promise which points onward to χάρις, to the fulfilment. And χάρις in its turn not only signifies the "fulfilled" grace, but is also continually looking forward to that grace which knows no limit. This χάρις, which was revealed during the earthly life of Jesus, was a preparation for and a promise of that χάρις which belongs to the great fulfilment.

The full significance of χάρις cannot be more closely defined from the context, but as the gift of Christ is generally referred to as ζωή, it does not seem too daring to suggest that χάρις and ζωή are in this respect identical (cf. Rom. 5.17–21).

It is most interesting to see how St John in this connection uses one of the main conceptions of gnostic thought, πλήρωμα.[4] The πλήρωμα of Christ, the mark of which is ever-increasing grace, is here placed over against that of

[1] John 3.16. [2] John 3.17; 12.47.
[3] John 16.27. [4] John 1.16.

gnosticism. One single historical person, Jesus Christ, and the redemptive work he accomplished, is put over against the tremendous mythological monster of gnosticism. The intensified χάρις shows that this work is still going on. The πλήρωμα of Christ continues to be revealed and realized— it is itself the Church.

36. δόξα (glory)

δόξα and δοξάζειν occur forty-four times in the Fourth Gospel but not at all in the First Epistle. In a few places in the first half of the Gospel δόξα means "honour", "praise", and it is used with a double meaning in 8.50. For the rest, however, the expression means "glory", "splendour";[1] δοξάζειν means "to glorify", and is mainly used in chapters 11–17, and this is very significant.

In classical Greek δόξα means "opinion", "view", but also "honour", "praise". In Hellenistic times the latter meaning becomes more prominent and a further one is added, that of "splendour", "glory". In the mystery religions δόξα eventually comes to signify a magic or bewitching power. δόξα corresponds to the Old Testament "*kabod*", which represents on the one hand the brilliance wherein Jahveh is revealed, and on the other hand the divine power whereof this brilliance is an expression. In the Synoptists and St Paul δόξα is used only about the risen Christ and his gifts, and in the accounts of the Transfiguration. The Fourth Gospel, seeing the whole of the life of Jesus in the light of the resurrection, adopts the same use.

1. δόξα *is an expression of the unity between the Father and the Son*
    - 11.4. "This sickness is not unto death, but for the glory of God, that the Son of God may be glorified thereby."
    - 13.31. "Now is the Son of Man glorified, and God is glorified in him."

[1] John 5.41, 44; 7.18; 9.24; 12.43.

IMPORTANT THEOLOGICAL CONCEPTIONS 153

17.4 ff. "I glorified thee on the earth, having accomplished the work which thou hast given me to do. And now, O Father, glorify thou me with thine own self with the glory which I had with thee before the world was."

12.41. "These things said Isaiah because he saw his glory; and he spake of him."

The latter example obviously refers to the revelation in the Temple in Isa. 6.1 ff and shows the tendency of St John to identify God's glory with that of Christ.

2. *The glory of Christ is made manifest through his death and resurrection*

7.39. "... for the Spirit was not yet given because Jesus was not yet glorified."

12.16. "When Jesus was glorified, then remembered they that these things were written of him."

12.23. "The hour is come that the Son of Man should be glorified."

17.1. "Father, the hour is come; glorify thy Son, that the Son may glorify thee."

3. *The glory of Christ is only revealed to those who believe*

1.14. "We beheld his glory, glory as of the only-begotten from the Father."

11.40. "Said I not unto thee, that if thou believedst, thou shouldest see the glory of God?"

2.11. "... and manifested his glory; and his disciples believed on him."

The meaning in the last instance is obviously not that the disciples did not come to believe on Jesus until he made this sign, but only that they were confirmed by it in the belief which they already had.

4. *The glory of Christ is revealed in the Church*

14.13. "Whatsoever ye shall ask in my Name, that will I do, that the Father may be glorified in the Son."

15.8. "Herein is my Father glorified, that ye bear much fruit; and so shall ye be my disciples."

16.14. "He (the Spirit) shall glorify me; for he shall take of mine and shall declare it unto you."

17.10. "... and I am glorified in them (the disciples)."
17.22. "And the glory which thou hast given me, I have given unto them; that they may be one, even as we are one."
17.24. "Father, that which thou hast given me, I will that, where I am, they also may be with me; that they may behold my glory, which thou hast given me."
12.28. "Father, glorify thy Name. ... I have both glorified it and will glorify it again."

The passages in 16.14 and 14.13 speak of the glory of Jesus as it is revealed in the cult of the Church; 15.8 should not be given a purely ethical interpretation: "to bear fruit" refers above all to faith. But there is also beyond doubt a reference to missionary work: the δόξα of Christ is made manifest through the spreading of the Church all over the world. In 17.22 the individual members of the Church are represented as partakers in the glory of Christ. δόξα signifies the unity between the Father and the Son and also the unity between Christ and the Church and among her several members.

The usual interpretation of 12.28 is that ἐδόξασα (I have glorified) refers to the earthly life of Jesus and δοξάσω (I will glorify) to his impending death and resurrection. Here, as often in this Gospel, the saying has a double, if not a triple, significance. Thus, in ἐδόξασα St John also refers to the death and resurrection of Jesus, which was already accomplished at the time of his writing: while δοξάσω refers to the continued revelation of Jesus in the Church, and particularly in the liturgy. The third possible interpretation is that ἐδόξασα signifies the revelation in the Church brought about through the resurrection, and δοξάσω the revelation which is to be made by the Parousia. Equally ambiguous is 17.24, which refers to the revelation of Christ in the Church as well as in eternity.

It is clear that δόξα in the Fourth Gospel is definitely an eschatological term, marked with the "plasticity" which is typical of the eschatological thinking of the Evangelist. It points out the unity between the Father and Jesus and refers to his work on earth, his death and resurrection, as at once

IMPORTANT THEOLOGICAL CONCEPTIONS 155

the expression of the power and glory of the Father, and the fulfilment of all eschatological expectations. This δόξα is concealed from the world but revealed to the faithful in the Church, experienced in the cult, and will finally be made known at the Parousia.

37. χαρά (joy)

χαρά and χαίρειν occur seventeen times in the Fourth Gospel, and once in the Epistle. In a few places "joy" is connected with different subjects: *Jesus* is glad that he was absent at the death of Lazarus; *the world* is rejoicing at the sorrow of the disciples; *Abraham* rejoiced to see the day of Christ; and *St John Baptist* rejoiced because of the bridegroom. All the other passages refer to the joy of the disciples and are to be found in the Last Discourse and also in 20.20.

14.28. "If ye loved me, ye would have rejoiced, because I go unto the Father."
15.11. "These things have I spoken unto you that my joy may be in you, and that your joy may be fulfilled."
16.20. "Ye shall weep and lament, but the world shall rejoice: ye shall be sorrowful, but your sorrow shall be turned into joy."
16.22. "I will see you again, and your heart shall rejoice and your joy no one taketh away from you."
16.24. "Ask and ye shall receive, that your joy may be fulfilled."
17.13. "Now I come to thee; and these things I speak in the world, that they may have my joy fulfilled in themselves."
20.20. "The disciples therefore were glad when they saw the Lord."
1 John 1.4. "And these things we write, that our joy (ἡ χαρά ἡμῶν) may be fulfilled."

The text of the last passage is disputed. Some MSS. have ἡ χαρά ὑμῶν (your joy), which appears to give a more natural meaning, but ἡμῶν corresponds to the "we" which is the subject all through 1 John 1.1, 5, representing the eyewitnesses of the incarnation. Thus the author shares with the reader the good news, and the joy that they bring.

The following conclusions may be drawn from the above passages:

1. Joy is the opposite of that sorrow (λύπη) which is prepared for the disciples by the world.
2. Joy is the opposite of the false joy of the world.
3. The foundation of joy is the glorification of Christ (14.28; 17.13), and his return to his disciples (16.22; 20.20).
4. Joy is inaccessible to the powers of the world (16.22).
5. Joy is experienced collectively in the Church.
6. Above all, joy is experienced in the liturgy (16.22, 24).
7. Joy is an anticipation of the joy of the fulfilment.

In the Fourth Gospel χαρά is presented as so vitally related to the death and "return" of Jesus that its character becomes altogether eschatological, and therefore also connected with the church—a characteristic which is emphasized by the collective and cultic nature of the joy. It is this "ecclesiastical" joy which is meant in 1 John 1.4; and in the following passages the character of χαρά is also nearly always eschatological. The picture of the woman in travail[1] refers to the agony from out of which the new age, with all its joy, is to come. Abraham and John the Baptist,[2] the first and last representatives of the Old Covenant, rejoice to see the fulfilment of all the promises in Jesus Christ. The passage about the common joy of the sower and the reaper[3] reflects the situation of the Church, wherein is found at once harvest-time (realized eschatology) and sowing-time (unfulfilled eschatology). The Thomas-passage shows how this eschatological joy which is experienced in the communion with the risen Lord is part of the cult. Another part of the cult is, of course, communion in prayer, with the promise of the joy of

[1] John 16.21.   [2] John 8.56; 3.29.   [3] John 4.36.

IMPORTANT THEOLOGICAL CONCEPTIONS 157

answer to prayer[1]; and finally we have the joy of reunion[2] which refers to the return of Jesus to his own, firstly at the resurrection, then in the liturgy, and finally at the Parousia.

Gulin describes the eschatology of the Fourth Gospel as "twisted eschatology", the mark of which is that, experienced as joy, it is transformed from something external and sensual to something internal and spiritual, from something collective to something individual. From what has been said above, it follows clearly that such a spiritualized and individual conception is false. With reference to 15.11 Gulin points to the "ethical side" of χαρά, which must mean that man could rejoice in his own works. In so doing Gulin treats ἀγάπη (love) and τὰς ἐντολὰς τηρεῖν (keeping the commandments) as purely ethical conceptions. Actually, they are closely linked up with πίστις, which does not, of course, exclude all ethical qualifications, for faith and ethics are inseparable. Gulin has, however, entirely failed to allow for the true eschatological significance of χαρά, which refers to the present as well as to the future. This becomes very clear in what he says about the "fulfilment of joy", where he attempts to show that in the Fourth Gospel χαρά is consistently used in a metonymical sense meaning that which is the object of joy. Among the different kinds of communion with Christ, Gulin also mentions communion through the sacraments, but when dealing with χαρά he deliberately ignores this. If he had not done this his results would have been more satisfactory, for it is precisely in the cult that the eschatological joy in the Fourth Gospel finds its chief expression.

38. εἰρήνη (peace)

εἰρήνη is only to be found three times in the Fourth Gospel: twice in the final discourses and once in the Thomas-passage; in the Epistle it does not occur at all. It is, however,

[1] John 16.24.   [2] John 16.22.

of importance in the Johannine theology, as it is used in certain vital contexts.

> 14.27. "Peace I leave with you; my peace I give unto you: not as the world giveth, give I unto you. Let not your heart be troubled, neither let it be fearful."
> 16.33. "These things have I spoken unto you, that in me ye may have peace. In the world ye have tribulation: but be of good cheer; I have overcome the world."
> 20.19, 21, 26. "Peace be unto you.' (εἰρήνη ὑμῖν).

In profane Greek εἰρήνη does not signify a feeling or mental state but a material condition, for example, *Pax Romana*. In the Old Testament *Shalom* means Jahveh's gift, which includes political, material, and spiritual peace, while it is never used with reference to any mental state or capacity. Without exception the reference is collective, to the Jewish nation, never to individuals.

From the passages quoted above the following conclusions may be drawn:

1. Peace is a gift from Christ.
2. Peace is the opposite of the false "peace" of the world.
3. The disciples have this peace in the midst of exterior unrest and oppression.
4. The foundation of peace is Christ's victory over the world, which is manifested in his death and resurrection.
5. Peace is experienced by the faithful in the cult in anticipation of that peace which will be theirs at the Parousia.

From this it follows that εἰρήνη expresses the peculiar character of the life which is led by the faithful with the risen Lord in the Church. In the Old Testament God gave peace to his chosen people through the priests.[1] Christ now gives peace to his disciples in this world. Thus εἰρήνη is firstly the fulfilment of the Old Testament *shalom* and then in its turn

[1] Num. 6.22–26.

IMPORTANT THEOLOGICAL CONCEPTIONS 159

an anticipation of the eternal peace.¹ The term is only used in the Fourth Gospel when Jesus is present in the closed circle of his disciples, which points to its cult-significance.

θαρσεῖτε (be of good cheer) in 16.33 is probably deliberately quoted from the word of consolation employed in the mysteries, θαρσεῖτε μύσται. By using it, St John shows that the redemption which man is seeking in many of the pagan rites is to be found in the Church. The greeting in chapter 20 is the late Jewish *shalom laken*. It seems likely that the Evangelist has here adopted a cult-formula already used in the Church.

39. ἀλήθεια (truth)

ἀλήθεια occurs in twenty-five places in the Fourth Gospel and in nine places in the First Epistle. Apart from this, the adjectives ἀληθής and ἀληθινός and the adverb ἀληθῶς are used several times, but we need not refer to this now. It may, however, be pointed out in passing that ἀληθινός is used with reference to the true light[2]; the true judgement[3]; true worshippers[4]; the true vine[5]; true God[6]; the true testimony[7] and Christ.[8] As an attribute of God ἀληθής is used in 3.33 and 8.26; applied to the testimony about Jesus in 5.31 ff, 10.41, and 21.24; likewise to the meat and drink which Jesus gives in 6.55; and finally to the commandments and teaching of Jesus in 1 John 2.8, 27.

1. *The truth is the message which Jesus delivers*
   8.40. "Ye seek to kill me, a man that hath told you the truth."
   8.45 ff. "But because I say the truth, ye believe me not. Which of you convicteth me of sin? If I say truth, why do ye not believe me?"

From the latter example we see that the opposite of truth is sin, not lies. Sin, however, to St John is identical with unbelief (cf. 8.44; 1 John 2.22).

[1] Rev. 7.14–17; 21.1–4.
[2] John 1.9; 1 John 2.8.
[3] John 8.16.
[4] John 4.23.
[5] John 15.1.
[6] John 17.3.
[7] John 19.35.
[8] 1 John 5.20.

2. *The message and the messenger are identical*
   - 1.14. "Full of grace and truth."
   - 5.33. "John hath borne witness unto the truth."
   - 14.6. "I am the way, and the truth, and the life."
   - 18.37. ". . . that I should bear witness unto the truth."

3. *The truth is received by the Chosen Ones*
   - 3.21. "He that doeth the truth cometh to the light."
   - 18.37. "Everyone that is of the truth heareth my voice."

4. *The truth is the mark of the Church*
   - 4.23, 24. ". . . the true worshippers shall worship the Father in spirit and truth."
   - 8.32. "And ye shall know the truth; and the truth shall make you free."
   - 16.7. "Nevertheless I tell you the truth; it is expedient for you that I go away. . . ."
   - 17.17. "Sanctify them in the truth: thy Word is truth."
   - 17.19. "And for their sakes I sanctify myself, that they themselves also may be sanctified in truth."
   - 16.13. "Howbeit when he, the Spirit of truth, is come, he shall guide you into all the truth."
   - 1 John 5.7. "And it is the Spirit that beareth witness, because the Spirit is the truth."
   - 8.44. "The devil . . . stood not in the truth, because there is no truth in him."

This brief summary may help us to understand the significance of the term ἀλήθεια which is so hard to define. It is at one and the same time the message and the messenger, that which constitutes the Church through the word and prayer, and also through the sacraments, although there is no direct reference to them in the text. This truth is the gift which the faithful receive in the Church; it gives them deliverance from sin[1] and a knowledge of God which inspires them to obey his commandments.[2] We can also say that those who receive the message about truth also receive the messenger, believing that he is the Truth—for these two are one.

[1] John 8.32; 16.13.   [2] 1 John 1.6; 2.4; 3.18, 19.

There can only be one meaning of ἀλήθεια in the Fourth Gospel: it is the truth about the death and resurrection of Jesus, to which witness is borne in 16.7 and 17.19. This is in accordance with the whole theology of the Fourth Gospel, the central point of which is the "lifting-up" of Jesus. Now if the real "truth" in the Fourth Gospel is the message of the death of Jesus and all that it means to the world, it then follows that this truth can only be received by man after his death, that is, in the Church. The many passages wherein the "truth" and the Spirit are connected with each other point to this conclusion.[1] "The Spirit of Truth" is the term used to describe the revelation of the risen Lord active in the Church, through whom true faith and true life are given to man.

Thus we cannot accept either Bultmann's vague definition that ἀλήθεια is equivalent to "divine reality" or Percy's theory that ἀλήθεια is something which appeals to man's conscience. This latter theory would lead us to conclude that it is finally the conscience of the individual which decides what is truth, a thought which is entirely foreign to the whole of the New Testament. It has been pointed out already that in the Fourth Gospel ἀλήθεια is a concept which embraces the whole of the great fact of Christian Redemption—the death and resurrection of Jesus. This truth can only be revealed and apprehended within the sphere of the life of the Church; that is, in the eschatological situation wherein the risen Lord reveals himself to his faithful ones as the Truth. Only in the Church, where the redemptive work of Jesus is an historical fact, can man, under the guidance of the Holy Spirit, come to the whole truth (εἰς τὴν ἀλήθειαν πᾶσαν).[2]

We are now in a position to understand the real significance of the question asked by Pilate: "What is truth?",[3] a question to which many different explanations have been

---
[1] John 14.17; 15.26; 16.13; 1 John 5.6.
[2] John 16.13.   [3] John 18.38.

given all down the ages. Generally it has been regarded as an expression of scepticism (Zahn, Loisy, Oehler) or scorn (Luther). Bultmann sees in it the neutrality of the State when faced with the question of the reality of God. To support such interpretations it is argued that the question is left unanswered by Jesus. But it can be clearly seen that the question of the governor is not left unanswered by the evangelist. True, the answer is not a verbal one; but it is given in action which makes clear to all men once and for all what truth is. The answer is the drama of the Cross, which follows immediately. Pilate's question "What is truth?" is, therefore, very far from being an unimportant or casual question. On the contrary, it is the most important of all questions, the real question about life and redemption which is now about to be answered. It is no mere coincidence that St John makes the Roman governor ask this question. At that moment Pilate is not only the representative of the Roman Empire with all its political and cultural resources, but also the representative of humanity seeking redemption. Obviously he does not himself realize the tremendously deep significance of his own question, just as he does not understand the answer given to it. He is here in the same position as the Jews, who ask for the Eucharist,[1] and the Samaritan woman who begs for Baptism.[2] Mankind's request and longing for salvation receive fulfilment through the death and resurrection of Jesus, that is, in the Church.

40. κρίσις (judgement)

κρίσις, κρίμα, and κρίνειν occur twenty-two times in the Fourth Gospel and once in the First Epistle. One Scandinavian scholar divides up the passages in which these words occur in such a way as to show that κρίσις at times means different things even in one and the same sentence; thus he

---

[1] John 6.34. [2] John 4.15.

IMPORTANT THEOLOGICAL CONCEPTIONS 163

is led to draw the conclusion that the word has the following different shades of meaning:

1. A judgement of the individual *in the present time* (a process of sifting) through the appearing of Jesus in the world.
2. A collective judgement *in the present time* through the death of Jesus.
3. A *final* judgement of the individual at the Second Coming of Jesus.

It may well be asked if there is any real foundation in the Scriptures for such an intricate pattern of judgement-scheme?

First of all we must sort out the texts wherein κρίσις has a secular significance, that is, where *man's* judgement is spoken of: 7.24, 51; 8.15; and 18.31. In all other places the judgement is a divine action, referred either to the Father or to the Son. Distinction may be made between the following groups:

1. *Judgement is the opposite to salvation*

    3.17. "For God sent not the Son into the world to judge the world; but that the world should be saved through him."

    12.47. "For I came not to judge the world, but to save the world."

2. *Christ is the judge*

    8.16. "Yea, and if I judge, my judgement is true."

    8.26. "I have many things to speak and to judge concerning you."

    5.22. "For neither doth the Father judge any man, but he hath given all judgement unto the Son."

    5.27. "And he gave him authority to execute judgement, because he is the Son of Man."

    5.30. "... as I hear, I judge; and my judgement is righteous."

3. *The crucial test in judgement is faith*

    3.18. "He that believeth on him is not judged: he that believeth not hath been judged already, because he hath not believed on the name of the only-begotten Son of God."

5.24. "He that heareth my word, and believeth him that sent me, hath eternal life, and cometh not into judgement."

12.48. "He that rejecteth me, and receiveth not my sayings, hath one that judgeth him."

4. *The judgement is in the present*

3.19. "This is the judgement that the light is come into the world, and men loved the darkness rather than the light."

9.39. "For judgement (εἰς κρίμα) came I into this world, that they which see not may see; and that they which see may become blind."

12.31. "Now is the judgement of this world: now shall the prince of this world be cast out."

16.11. "The prince of this world hath been judged."

5. *The judgement is at the same time a final judgement*

5.29. "... shall come forth, they that have done ill unto the resurrection of judgement (ἐν ἀνάστασιν κρίσεως)."

12.48. "The word that I spake, the same shall judge him in the last day."

1 John 4.17. "Herein is love made perfect with us, that we may have boldness in the day of judgement."

In all the references given above κρίσις means κατάκρισις and implies condemnation. This is the explanation of the fact that the faithful do not come to the judgement but pass out of death to life. The judgement is a present judgement, for it takes place in the eschatological situation of the Church through the preaching of the resurrection which in some kindles faith and in others reveals unbelief, just as was the case during the earthly ministry of Jesus. Simultaneously, however, the judgement is final, the "Day of Judgement" revealing to all men beyond any doubt who are for death and who are for life. Thus the κρίσις-idea in the Fourth Gospel is of an eschatological character, the eschatology being thought of as realized and yet still to attain to its fulfilment. It might perhaps be said that judgement according to the Fourth Gospel *is becoming* pronounced already now

IMPORTANT THEOLOGICAL CONCEPTIONS

de facto, and *will* one day at the Second Coming of Jesus be pronounced *de jure.* In this case the Johannine conception of judgement, in spite of the many external differences, is fundamentally the same as that underlying the great apocalyptic scene of the Final Judgement in Matthew 25.31-46: "I was an hungred, and ye gave me meat...". Man's attitude in the present determines his fate in eternity: that is the opinion of St John as well as of the Synoptists.

Only faith in Christ and life with him can save man from condemnation. But according to St John this faith and this life can only be had in the fellowship of the Church. The Saviour in the liturgy is the same as the Judge at the Parousia. Those who here, in the Church, have in faith received this Saviour and live in communion with him in the cult will not need to meet him as their Judge in the last day, for they have already "passed out of death into life".[1]

[1] John 5.24.

CHAPTER 6

THE IDEA OF ELECTION IN THE FOURTH GOSPEL

41. *The History of Exegetical Investigation*

IN THE course of our study we have repeatedly come across expressions behind which there seems to linger the idea that some people are predestined to belief, while to others this gift has not been granted. As examples of this we may quote such sayings as "born of God"[1]; to be "of God"[2]; to be "of the truth"[3]; the Father "drawing men to the Son"[4]; the Son "choosing men".[5] Since this particular question seems not to have attracted the scrutiny of scholars in modern times, this chapter will be devoted to a survey of the exegetical investigations regarding it which have been made down the ages.

1. *The Greek Fathers of the Church*

The oldest known commentary on the Gospels was written by the Valentinian gnostic *Heracleon*, and it deals with the Fourth Gospel. The entire commentary has been lost, but fragments of it have been preserved within Origen's Commentary on St John. Heracleon, in his exposition of 8.47, "He that is of God, heareth the words of God: for this cause ye hear them not, because ye are not of God", says that some men are from the devil, i.e. of the same nature as the devil (ὁμοουσίους τινὰς τῷ διαβόλῳ), a nature different from that of those whom he calls psychic or spiritual (ψυχικοὺς ἢ

[1] John 1.13. [2] John 8.47. [3] John 18.37.
[4] John 6.37, 44, 65. [5] John 6.70; 13.18; 15.16, 19.

πνευματικούς). This shows clearly how the gnostics consistently divided men into two groups, the hylics and the gnostics.

Origen is the most distinguished representative of the Alexandrian school of thought. In his exposition of 8.47 he attacks the gnostic interpretation of it, which he calls "the device of the different natures". To be of God is not something original to man, but rather a goal to which man must strive to attain: "The more man hears of the Word of God, the more he comes to be of God. Having received power to become children of God, let us do all that we can to be of God and hear his Word, and let us even make progress in being of God, so that we may also make progress in hearing his word." Of 13.18 it is said concerning Judas that Jesus had at one time great hopes of his becoming a good Apostle, and of 3.27, "A man can receive nothing, except it have been given him from heaven", we read: "Now the gifts are being bestowed by God to those who by faith and virtue are prepared to receive them." Origen, as the energetic upholder of free-will, consistently emphasizes man's possibilities of determining his own spiritual destiny.

Cyril of Jerusalem, in his seventh mystagogic catechism, ch. 13, follows up the tradition of Origen. Commenting on 8.44, "Ye are of your father, the devil", he says that some men are the children of the devil, not by nature, but by seduction. He points out the danger of interpreting 1 John 3.10 as if some by their nature would go to blessedness, others to destruction: "For it is by free-will and not by any compulsion that we come to this sacred adoption."

Cyril of Alexandria sees in 6.37, "All that which the Father giveth me shall come to me", a threat to the Jews and a promise that in their stead the Father will draw to himself those from among the Gentiles who are worthy; what kind of "worthiness" this should be, however, is not clear. In connection with 6.65, "No man can come unto me, except it be given unto him of my Father", he speaks of those who because of their own foolishness have shown themselves unworthy of eternal life, and who have not received the enlightenment given by God.

Ammonius of Alexandria emphasizes to an even greater extent man's free-will. In his Commentary on 6.64, "Jesus knew from the beginning who they were that believed not", we read: "The Father draws those who according to their own free-will are good, but he lets the evil be." This verse does not make void our right of self-determination but makes it clear to us that we need help. For man is not drawn against his will, but as the partaker of much help from God. "The God-given teaching as to what is the true good is the mystery of Christ." And of 8.47 he says: "Those who believe are of God, not by nature but because they receive from him their quality of godly fear, becoming related to him by means of virtue and obedience." Commenting on 10.29, "My Father which hath given them unto me is greater than all . . .", Ammonius points out that the evil is not in the nature of man but in his distorted will.

John Chrysostom, the most distinguished member of the School of Antioch, attempts to unite the principle of man's free-will to the thought of divine election. Of 1.11, "He came unto his own, and they that were his own received him not", he says that God will not force anyone, but that he wants servants who of their own free-will and choice follow him, thanking him for their position as servants. With reference to 1.12 he says that the work of God is to forgive, that of man to show faith. In opposition to the determinist views of the Manichees, Chrysostom, commenting on 6.44, "No man can come to me except the Father . . . draw him", says that Jesus is here showing that not everyone comes to him, but only those who rejoice in the assurance of God's marvellous help; while of 6.65 he says that faith is not the possession of every man. Jesus knows beforehand those to whom the Father has given the gift of faith, but it is not a question of blind chance as to who receives this gift, for only those will receive faith who are worthy of it. Chrysostom draws attention to the way in which Jesus in 10.27–29, "My sheep hear my voice", etc., exhorts those who have come to hear him to "strive to become his sheep".

Theodore of Mopsuestia, in his exposition of 1.13 ("... born of God"), speaks about those men who are born after a spiritual manner with divine power through their likeness to and kinship with God; while in 17.6 he speaks of the hindrances set up by free-will to Christ's power of kindling faith among men.

Theophylactus sees in the expression "born of God" a reference to Baptism, and concerning 6.37, "All that which the Father giveth me shall come unto me", he says that faith in Christ comes not by mere chance but as a gift of God, given by the Father to those who are worthy of it and righteous. In 6.44 we read that Jesus does not oppose the doctrine of man's free-will but reminds his hearers that if man is to have faith he needs much help from God. Commenting on 6.70, "Did not I choose you the twelve, and one of you is a devil?", he says: "God does not make us better by compulsion and force, nor does his election compel to goodness our free-will 'which is evil'. God's election lies in the fact that he encourages us to do that which is good and holds out to us his own goodness for example and help. In our reason and in our free-will lies the seed of our salvation and we ourselves decide whether we walk worthily of our election or not."

Theophylactus agrees with Chrysostom in seeing in 10.27, 29 an appeal to those who do not yet believe to become the sheep of Jesus. Judas, although he was sanctified and made a sheep of God, fell away from this state of his own free-will and choice. The nature of man is in itself neither evil nor good, but it is altogether determined by free-will.

Thus the Greek Fathers with one accord stress the free-will of man. Their position is determined on the one hand by their conscious opposition to gnosticism and its consistent determinism, on the other hand by their endeavour to emphasize man's personal responsibility. They perceive clearly the theological problem contained in the idea of election in the Fourth Gospel, but their method of confronting it with their own indeterminism based on philosophical and practical-religious motives is hardly convincing.

2. *St Augustine and the Middle Ages*

The most distinguished representative of the Western mode of interpretation is *St Augustine*. Even in the limited field of research with which we are at present concerned he has given the lead to all the medieval investigations of the subject. First of all it is worth noticing that he takes the Johannine idea of election seriously. In his exposition of 8.28, "When ye have lifted up the Son of Man, then shall ye know that I am he", etc., we read: "Jesus saw among his audience some whom he recognized, whom he himself had chosen together with the rest of his saints before the beginning of the world, knowing beforehand that they, after his passion, would come to believe". St Augustine also opposes the gnostics' dualistic conception of mankind. Commenting on 8.47 he says: "Jesus does not distinguish between different human natures, so that there should be in man one human nature unspoiled by sin: but because he foreknew those who would come to believe on him, he said of them that they are of God, since they would be born anew of God." Of such it is also said: "He that is of God heareth the words of God", while the following, "For this cause ye hear them not because ye are not of God", refers to those who are not only spoilt by sin (for that is common to all men) but who, as he foreknew, would not come to believe but would die in their sins. It is in accordance with this pre-election that the Lord has spoken; it does not imply that he has found any man who, either through being born anew already is of God, or who, because of his nature, cannot ever be of God.

St Augustine interprets St John 10.4–5 ("the sheep follow

him: for they know his voice", etc.) as a statement about those pre-elected by God to blessedness and known beforehand by Christ. The same thought reappears in the exposition of 10.29; 11.50; and 12.44 ff. Commenting on 12.40 ("he hath blinded their eyes", etc.), he speaks about the danger of resisting the call to faith in Christ. Thus he considers it possible for man to resist God and sees in the Jews' attitude to Christ merely pride and hardness of heart. Man's free-will is also stressed in the exposition of 6.44 that his free-will is necessary if there is to be any genuine belief. The "drawing" of the Father consists in the transformation of the human will so that man desires to believe in Christ and does so joyfully.

When referring to 6.70, "Did not I choose you the twelve, and one of you is a devil?", we find St Augustine's powers of expression at their height: "Is the devil, too, among the chosen ones? Many words of praise are uttered about those who are chosen, or even about one numbered among the chosen, since through him something good has come to pass without his will or knowledge. Such is God's way of acting in sharp contrast to that of the evil ones. For the latter make a wicked use of God's good works, while God actually brings something good out of the evil works of evil men. Look how wonderfully God has created all the members of the human body, and how badly they are all used by evil men; the eyes are turned to satisfy lust, the tongue speaks falsehood, and the hands commit murder. And in the same manner men misuse the rest of God's creation: gold, for instance, they use for the purposes of bribery and oppression. The evil man makes an evil use of all God's good things, while the good man makes a good use of even the evil deeds of the wicked. Who is good but God alone? The better he is, the better use he makes of our evil deeds. Who was more evil than Judas? Nevertheless the Lord turned his great misdeed into a blessing when he allowed himself to be betrayed for the sake of our redemption."

Referring to 15.16, "Ye have not chosen me but I have

chosen you", St Augustine speaks of election as God's unspeakable grace: "What were we when as yet we had not chosen Christ and therefore did not love him? We were lost... we had not yet come to believe in him and his election of us. For if he had chosen those who believe already, then he would be choosing those who were already chosen.... You cannot say: 'Before I believed I performed good deeds, therefore I am one of the chosen.' What good work is there before faith?... What then shall we say when we hear: 'Ye have not chosen me', if not that we were evil and were chosen that we might become good through the grace of him who chose us?" He refers to the election of the faithful as having taken place before the beginning of the world, and the doctrine of the double predestination is put forward in connection with 10.26, "Ye believe not because ye are not of my sheep." The expression "Everyone that is of the truth"[1] refers, according to St Augustine, to the grace wherewith God calls men in accordance with his own counsel. Man is not of the truth because he hears the voice of Jesus; he hears it because he is of the truth, that is, because he is a partaker of this gift.

The Venerable Bede takes up many of St Augustine's comments, often quoting them literally. In reference to 6.65 he says that faith is given by the Father to the faithful in order that no one may glory in his faith, since this is not of his own merit but by the grace of God; while in connection with 13.18 we read that Judas was chosen, not to blessedness, but to become a traitor. In the Commentary on 15.19, "... because ye are not of the world, but I chose you out of the world", we read: "The chosen ones have been elected, not because of their nature which through sin is corrupt in its essence, but by grace." And in regard to 18.37: "Jesus reminds us of the grace by which he calls us in accordance with the pre-election of God." Thus Bede sees in the freewill of man an obstacle to faith which is surmounted by the election of God.

[1] John 18.37.

IDEA OF ELECTION IN FOURTH GOSPEL 173

Alcuin's Commentary on St John often contains a literal repetition of the exegesis of St Augustine and St Bede, which is also the case in the Commentary of *Strabo*, while *Johannes Scotus* puts forward a clearly formulated synergism. In his exposition of 1.12–13 we read: "No one is robbed of the possibility of faith in, and acknowledgement of, the Son of God, a faith which springs from the co-operation between the will of man and the grace of God." *Bruno Astensis* is the representative of a less strict doctrine of predestination. We read, for instance, in his Commentary on 6.65: "Jesus knew whom he had pre-elected for life or death. He called many but chose few"; and on 17.6: "They belonged to God because they were pre-destined for life." Regarding 6.44, however, we read: "The Father draws not by force but by love. God draws no one if he does not want to come and desire to be saved"; and commenting on 15.16: "Jesus did first choose the disciples and then they chose him."

Rupertus Tutiensis also favours the doctrine of predestination in his Commentary, as does *Ratramnus* in his work, *De Praedestinatione Dei*, where he refers to several Johannine texts.

St Thomas Aquinas in his Commentary on 1.12, 13 speaks of the assent of free-will to the reception of grace. Lack of faith springs from man's rejection of grace, which presupposes free-will. Such men are drawn by the Father through a "deeper inspiration". The divine election is of two kinds: (i) *ad praesentem justitiam*,[1] which includes Judas; (ii) *ad finalem gloriam*,[2] which excludes Judas. As a consequence, the meaning of "to be of God" and "of the truth" in 8.47 and 18.37 is twofold: (i) including all men *per creationem*; (ii) referring further to a few *per affectum et imitationem*.

Like the Greek Fathers, St Augustine and the medieval writers whom he inspired were keenly opposed to the gnostic conception of man. Their great interest was to defend the Biblical faith in creation with its emphasis on the vocation

[1] John 6.70.   [2] John 13.18.

and responsibility of man. It was therefore necessary for them to avoid all consistent determinism in their interpretation of the Johannine texts. But as it was impossible to get away from the idea of election in the Fourth Gospel, this idea was used instead as the basis for the doctrine of predestination—a doctrine which was a heritage from Hellenistic philosophy and which, in varying degrees of emphasis, is an important feature in theological tradition from the time of St Augustine onwards. For since his time, the constant problem facing Western theologians has been how to reconcile this doctrine with the idea of free-will which is essential for a due recognition of the personal responsibility of man.

3. *The Reformation and the Period of Orthodoxy*

Martin Luther, in spite of his many writings, does not deal extensively with the idea of election in the Fourth Gospel. In his Commentaries on St John 3—4, 6—8, and 14—15 there is, however, sufficient material to enable us to discover certain fundamental ideas held by him on this subject. He rejects the doctrine of predestination, at times even with considerable harshness. In 1529, in a sermon on chapter 17.6, "... the men whom thou gavest me out of the world: thine they were and thou gavest them to me", he writes that this particular text puts before men a temptation to accept this "foolish doctrine". He then goes on to declare that the text in question is a word of comfort to man in his fear of the wrath of God. He is on the other hand anxious to see election as a decision of God's grace, stripping man of all self-merit and giving him courage in suffering.

Election obviously implies the casting off of those who are impenitent. Luther deals with this aspect in a sermon on 6.37, "All that which the Father giveth me shall come unto me...": "As the Jews did not believe in Jesus, although they did both see and hear him, they prove themselves to be rejected by God." Concerning 6.44 we read that the drawing of men by the Father to the Son does not take place contrary to the will of man, but that it is an expression of the loving guidance of God. In 6.65 Luther finds excellent opportunity of stating the fundamental thought of the Reformation regarding faith as a gift of God, given through the word and not by the merit or power of man.

Melanchthon is anxious to call attention to the idea in 1.12-13 and 6.37 of election. He rejects any theoretical speculations regarding predestination but does not deny its reality. Nevertheless, he is of the opinion that it is better to consider the effect of predestination rather than its cause, and its effect is faith in Christ. St John 6.44 is, according to him, a bulwark against Pelagianism and Pharisaism, pointing out how God through his word leads men to Christ, not against their will but by the Holy Spirit who gives them new enlightenment and a new direction of mind. In 6.70 Melanchthon sees a warning given by Christ in advance, so that the falling away of some might not lead the other disciples into despair, but that they might know for a certainty that the Church endures for ever. Commenting on 10.14, "I know my sheep and am known of mine", he speaks of "the sheep" who have the inner testimony—*testimonium cordis*—by which they know Christ as their shepherd and life-giver. In considering 10.29, "No man is able to pluck them out of my Father's hand", he warns his readers not to confuse election with a stoic fate (*stoicum fatum*) but to see in it a promise of universal grace. Melanchthon further considers 15.16, "I have chosen you", to be a word of comfort to troubled disciples. Finally, in treating of 17.6, he repeats his warning against over much disputing concerning election.

Erasmus, in his Commentary on St John 1.12-13, speaks about those who become the children of God by faith, but his exposition of 6.44 does not sound quite so evangelical: "The gift of coming to the Son is only given to those who desire it, that is, to those who by their will and devout zeal deserve to be drawn to the Father and gain eternal life."

Here the connection with the medieval school of interpretation is apparent. Commenting on 17.6 he definitely puts forwards a form of predestination.

Calvin emphasizes strongly the Johannine idea of election which is often incorporated with the Calvinistic teaching regarding predestination. Thus he says of 1.13 that for man to be born of God is a necessary condition for faith. Faith does not depend on the will of man but on the election of God; this he states in his exposition of 6.37. According to Calvin this passage shows not only that all men do not come to believe in Christ, but also that God works with such success in his elect that not one of them is lost. Regarding 6.44 he says: "Faith is not dependent on the will of man but is given by God." "Not everyone is drawn to the Son, but God gives his grace to those whom he has chosen. This drawing is not by force, contrary to the will of man, but it is the work of the Spirit making unwilling and resentful men meek and responsive." "Those who receive the words of Jesus have therein a seal of their election." The saying in 10.16 speaks of the election of God as being so certain that not one of those whom he desires to save will be lost. The hidden counsel of God by which he is to save men is eventually manifested in the vocation he bestows when he, through the Spirit, endows with a new birth as his own children those who were beforehand born of flesh and blood. Speaking on 13.18 he says: "Judas was made the object of a temporal election (*electio temporalis*) while Christ here refers to an eternal election (*electio aeterna*) through which we become children of God and thus predestined for eternal life." Calvin reads 15.16, ". . . I have chosen you", as referring not to the common election of God (*electio communis*) but to the particular election (*electio particularis*) which was the charge committed to the disciples to preach the Gospel, while 17.6 to him is a sign of the eternal election of God and an indication of the way in which this election is itself hidden but made known unto us in Christ.

Egidius Hunnius has, in his Commentary on St John 6, included a lengthy excursus, *De Praedestinatione*, which however seems to be based on Pauline rather than Johannine material. He makes predestination and election identical, and describes them both as the foreknowledge of God. While rejecting the theory of a double predestination, he emphasizes the idea that God's purpose behind the election is unalterable. In his Commentary on 15.16 we read that the election excludes all human merit. It is part of God's redemptive plan and is not absolute. It follows that a man might fall from grace. All men are not converted to Christ and this is due either to their not hearing or to their misinterpreting God's word. Therefore they are not drawn by the Father but receive punishment instead.

The main work of orthodox exegesis in Germany is the *Harmonia Quattuor Evangelistarum* (1652) by Martin Chemnitz, Polycarpus Lyserus, and Johan Gerhard. In its exposition of 6.44 we read that no one can come to Christ of his own freewill. The drawing of the Father is the *causa efficiens* of faith, by which he opens our hearts, gives us a new birth, and makes us partakers of the faith which binds us to Christ unto life eternal. God, however, does not draw man to Christ in a violent manner, as is supposed by the fanatics, but through the word and the sacraments administered through the Ministry of the Church. 6.70 is spoken of as referring to the election to the Apostolate and 13.18, "I know whom I have chosen", as the election to Redemption. Judas had received the first but not the latter. Referring to 8.47 it is written: "He who believes the word of God and by it is born anew, so that he does no sin, he is of God. But he who does not hear the word of God or, having heard it, goes away and kills his brother, he is of the devil." 10.29 points out the certainty of redemption for those who believe, for the Father has given to the Son all those who are destined for redemption. The Son receives and preserves them, he knows his own and gives to them eternal life and not one of them shall perish. According to 13.18 God has rejected Judas and all those who go to condemnation because of their own final impenitence, which he anticipated. 15.16 speaks on the one hand of the election to the Apostolate and to membership in the Church, on the other hand of election to blessedness, both of which are of grace through Christ. In the exposition of 17.6 we find a strong attack upon Calvin's doctrine of predestination: "The election comes about when Christ works through the word and the sacraments. It is not for the Christian to ask whether or not he is part of God's hidden predestination, but only if he is in Christ."

Hugo Grotius represents a much more vague conception of election than the one typical of the early Reformation. This is largely due to the influence of idealistic trends of thought. Thus to Grotius the expression "born of God" in 1.13 does not refer to the *"adoptio"* which takes place here in time, by which we are made like unto God, not in respect of power but of goodness. Commenting on 6.37 he writes: "The Father draws those who at any rate when they have heard the word of God try to cultivate a spirit of devotion", and on 6.65: "Faith is only given to those who are devout, humble, and eager to learn."

Abraham Calovius in his exposition of 6.44 speaks about our natural incapacity to come to God, and our innate resistance which is broken down by the grace of God. In 3.18 ("He that believeth on him is not judged . . .") he sees evidence not of eternal predestination but of the calling through Christ.

The popular orthodox commentator, *Christoph Starke*, in his treatise on 1.12–13 emphasizes the free-will of man. Man becomes the child of God by faith; and God's "drawing" is his gracious act when he, through the Gospel, takes away the darkness of reason, bestowing in its stead a clear conception of his own holiness and of man's misery and also of the means by which man may be restored. Man can, however, through his unwillingness, frustrate God's working.

In reference to 10.16, we read that Christ gives to all the chance of becoming sheep in his flock. Starke, however, reckons also with a hidden election, which we learn to recognize if we live by faith in Christ.

F. A. Lampe follows up the exegetical tradition emanating from Calvin. With regard to 1.12-13 he concludes that the elect are the children of God. "But", he asks, "how are they to become that which they already are?" In his reasoned answer he mentions a double *adoption*—the general one which is shown by man's belonging to Christ, and the special one which implies a higher degree of sonship. Concerning 6.37, "All that which the Father giveth me shall come unto me, and him that cometh to me I will in no wise cast out", he speaks of a double *election*, an eternal one and a temporal one, signifying the process of a deeper entry into God's redemptive purpose. Election precedes faith and no man has the power or the desire to resist the drawing of the Father.[1] To be "of God"[2] is to be chosen to a new birth, and 10.16 refers, according to Lampe, to those who are predestinated.

Maldonatus is anxious to stress freedom of will in opposition to the Reformers and in line with medieval tradition. Men are drawn by the Father not by force but because they themselves will to be drawn. He rejects, however, the Augustinian doctrine of predestination. To be "of God" is to live in accordance with his precepts and will. Predestination is part of the divine purpose. About 15.16 we read that the call to the Apostolate was not given on any ground of merit, while those who are predestinated may earn eternal life. In connection with 17.6 mention is made of the predestinated, which term, according to Maldonatus, means "those who will to believe".

According to *Quesnel*, the drawing of the Father brings about the reorientation of our perverted will. In connection with 15.16 he speaks of an election to the kingdom of God, but this does not prevent him from enumerating twelve

[1] John 6.44.   [2] John 8.47.

conditions necessary for our becoming the friends and intimates of Jesus.

Thus the contribution made by the Reformation era to the interpretation of the Johannine idea of election is considerable. Luther himself detached the idea of election from its philosophical accretions and made use of it in his practical cure of souls. His followers expressly warned men not to get engrossed in unfruitful theoretical speculations about election. The representatives of Lutheran orthodoxy saw in the election the result of God's work in the Church through the word, the sacraments, and the ministry. Calvin follows along the philosophical line. Thus the Johannine idea of election provides him with material for his accentuated doctrine of predestination. Roman theologians follow the Augustinian tradition which is, however, taking on an increasingly synergistic character.

4. *Pietism and the Age of Enlightenment*

From the age of Pietism onwards the interest of the exegetes in the Johannine idea of election lessens consistently, in accordance with the contemporary tendency to overemphasize the subjective side of man's relation to God. *Bengel* indeed speaks of election as the decisive difference between the believers and the "world", insisting that in order to belong to Christ one must be of the Truth.[1] He is, however, equally anxious to point out that man can fall away from his election.[2] The power to become a child of God does not precede the adoption which in itself bestows this power. Thus any thought of predestination is rejected. We become children of God by faith and by faith alone.

Scholars during the Age of Enlightenment follow the subjective line of thought. *J. L. von Mosheim* attacks the doctrine of predestination: man is himself able to decide what his reaction to God's influence is to be.[3] The sayings

---

[1] John 18.37. [2] John 6.70. [3] John 6.37.

in 13.18, 15.16, and 17.6 are interpreted as referring to the calling of the disciples to preach the Gospel. Von Mosheim, however, has not ceased to see in faith a supernatural power, even though it may be represented in moralistic guise. Referring to 1.13 he speaks of a secret birth which will serve to further the purpose of man's moral improvement. *Baumgarten* in his interpretation of 6.37, 44 is anxious to emphasize the free-will of man. There is no trace of any interest in the idea of election. *Semler's* conception of faith is marked by a definite concentration on the intellectual side. The drawing of the Father is identical with the knowledge of his good pleasure and the thought of a divine election is emphatically denied. He is strongly opposed to the Augustinian tradition. 15.19 is given a moralistic interpretation; to be of the Truth (18.37) is identified with the striving after the truth and perfection.

5. *Various Schools during the Nineteenth Century*

Schleiermacher shows no interest whatever in the question of election. His homilies consistently leave out all passages with any such reference. The drawing of men by the Father is an expression of God's merciful providence to all men. About 6.65 we read that the Father will finally put everyone under his dominion. The meaning of the words of Jesus in this connection is that no one can come to Christ until the time appointed by the Father. Immediately afterwards, however, this time is declared to be dependent upon the reaction of the human heart of each individual. From the words in 10.16, ". . . they shall become one flock, one shepherd", Schleiermacher develops his apokatastasis-theory: all mankind is to become one flock. *De Wette* goes one step further in subjective interpretation, seeing in the drawing of the Father only an expression of the interior divine work of redemption and of man's receptivity to faith. *Lücke*, the disciple of Schleiermacher, in his exposition of 3.21, insists that before Christ there were two kinds of men in the world, men of truth, and men of untruth (cf. light and darkness). The coming of Jesus into the world reveals their respective characters. There is, however, a spark of light in every man: "they loved darkness rather than light", but everyone has the power to make that innate spark burn brighter. With regard to 6.44 we read that the irresistible character of the divine mercy must not be made the basis of dogmatic speculation.

Nor do the Pietists of the nineteenth century allow themselves to get engrossed in the problem of election. *Tholuck*, writing about 6.37, says that those who come to Christ are driven on by a hunger for salvation which is partly inspired by the Father. The drawing of the Father is that powerful interior and exterior influence by which God turns the attention of man to the divine. That man possesses free-will is consistently emphasized. Referring to 17.6 *Tholuck* speaks of the elect as those who have a longing for heaven.

Hengstenberg denies the idea of absolute predestination but he nevertheless affirms that the final reason why some men do not come to Christ is not to be found in their own will. To become "sheep" does not depend on any quality inherent in man but on the election of God, and the election implies that Christ puts his mark on "children of wrath". 17.6 does not refer to eternal but only to temporal predestination. The drawing of the Father is co-ordinated with subjective factors. Stronger still is the subjective tendency in *Keil*, the disciple of Hengstenberg, who gives to the drawing of the Father a psychological interpretation, while in 15.19, "I have chosen you out of the world", etc., he sees vaguely a certain Church-consciousness: Jesus has chosen his disciples out of the world and placed them in a new fellowship.

The rationalist *H. Paulus* has no interest at all in this question, while *R. Köstlin*, the exegete from the Tübingen school, describes election as the deliverance by the grace of

God of a certain number of men from the thraldom under sin which is brought about by the perverted will of evil men. Köstlin sees in the Johannine texts a predestination which is supplemented by the God-given receptivity to that which is good. In the men who are of God faith is preceded by a "hunger" and a "thirst", while those who lack this craving are not of God, not the "sheep" of Jesus. By faith there comes the realization of what is already planted in man by God; human power and will are of no significance for the election. More emphatically still does *Hilgenfeld*, with reference to 1.12, point out that the predestination to that which is good is entirely independent of the human will.

A representative of the neo-orthodox movement, too, like *Luthardt*, sees in the Johannine texts two types of men, different in natures. The difference, however, is said to be of an ethical character. Behind the saying "How can ye believe which receive honour one of another" in 5.44, Luthardt detects moral incapacity. The new birth reveals to man that he is in faith. The free-will of man is presupposed in 6.37, and 6.44 is subjected to a psychological interpretation, implying discontent with man's relation to God and a striving after a right relation to God in Christ.

Olshausen in his exposition of 6.37 insists that faith has its roots in God's hidden counsel, while unbelief has not. 10.16 is said to refer to two groups of man, but there is no rigid line drawn between the two: transition in both directions is quite possible.

Godet rejects the idea of predestination and insists on the free-will of man. From a consideration of 3.21, "He that doeth truth cometh to the light", etc., it follows that before Christ there were already men who fought against their evil inclinations and tried to realize ethical ideals. 6.37 does not refer to an eternal election but to God's working in him when a man decides for faith. To be of God does not exclude but rather includes man's free self-determination. Those among the heathen who obey the inner light will recognize in Jesus their ideal and will follow him. In 15.19 Godet sees the call to faith but no predestination. *Clausen* directly attacks the doctrine of predestination.

6. *Modern Interpretations*

Among the scholars of recent decades there has been very little interest in the idea of predestination in the Fourth Gospel. *Wellhausen* makes a brief reference to it, *Tillmann* and *Wikenhauser* make vague attempts to link up with the tradition from St Augustine, while *Bernhard Weiss* openly opposes it. The same is the case with *Lagrange*, while *Westcott, Zahn, Spitta, Bugge, Schlatter, Joh. Jeremias, Boehmer, Ubbink*, and *Trench* do not deal with the subject at all.

Loisy, however, consistently insists on the doctrine of predestination; and *Weinel*, who sees, in the Johannine texts we have been considering, proofs of Hellenistic mysticism rather than of Christian belief, speaks of election with a bias towards predestination in his mind. *Bernard* points to the idea of predestination as appearing in the divine "must" (δεῖ), while *Moe* represents a rather diffused and no longer absolute predestination.

Büchsel declares that the drawing of men by the Father implies no obligation—for that would cancel the free-will of man—but that it is rather to be seen as God's personal influence. To be "of the truth" is not a natural inclination but it gives to man a character which decides his actions. *Feine* rejects all deterministic and dualistic interpretations and sees in the Johannine idea of election an expression of the true and original Christian faith when confronted with historical reality. *Hirsch*, too, reflects the idea of predestination. *Lüthi*, commenting on 10.29, speaks about the merciful election of the Father as revealed to the Son, while still insisting on man's free-will: it is possible for him to reject his election and thus be lost. *Smilde* cherishes the same ideas.

IDEA OF ELECTION IN FOURTH GOSPEL 185

Hoskyns in his interpretation of 17.6 rejects the doctrine of predestination, affirming that man comes to God by faith. Faith, however, is not dependent on the capacity of man but is the work of God. *Odeberg* says that it is wrong to ask whether the cause of faith lies in the will of God or in that of man himself. Unbelief springs from the fact that man has lost his inclination towards God. *Kolmodin* does not consider the drawing of the Father to be irresistible but sees in it only a condition for faith, while *Oehler* in the same passage sees not a theological speculation but experience drawn from missionary enterprises.

H. J. Holtzmann in his text-book on the theology of the New Testament devotes one part to "determinism" in the Fourth Gospel. He regards this determinism as founded not only on direct sayings of Jesus but also on the "metaphysical dualism" which he considers an integral part of the whole trend of thought in the Fourth Gospel. He is, however, obliged to admit that this determinism "is not carried to its conclusion as *gratia inadmissibilis*". Finally, he states that the Fourth Gospel does not present the simple combination of religious determinism and practical indeterminism which, in his opinion, is characteristic of Jesus and of St Paul.

Bultmann too speaks of some kind of determinism which makes the character of the revelation more distinct and which induces man to give up his self-assertion and allow himself to be drawn by God. This thought is very characteristic of Bultmann's theology, wherein revelation is said to be nothing else than man's attainment of self-consciousness, and of his own choice. To call this "determinism" is merely a play upon words. Bultmann's theology is anthropocentric to an alarming extent, while the theology of the Fourth Gospel is altogether theocentric and Christocentric. Bultmann arranges all his arguments to fit the main dogma of dialectic theology—the dogma of choice, which is, as a matter of fact, a conception entirely foreign to the trend of thought in the Fourth Gospel. If ever there are any references to a choice in this Gospel it is not man who chooses God but God who chooses man. The Johannine and ecclesiastical term for this is simply "election".

42. *The Johannine Idea of Election and the Old Testament*

This study of the interpretation of the election-texts in St John has left us with a rather confused impression. The theologians who have really wrestled with the problem of election have tried, as a rule, to come to a solution of it with the help of philosophical theories about predestination or determinism. Others, adhering to indeterminism, have taken great trouble to explain away or reinterpret the passages about election. Of late years the problem has been looked upon as insoluble, or uninteresting, and has consequently been pushed into the background.

Our survey has shown, however, that it is impossible to solve the question of election in the Fourth Gospel by referring to philosophic-metaphysical speculations. It is a concept at the very heart of religion, which can only be understood in its religious context. We have previously referred to the intimate connection between the Fourth Gospel and the Old Testament. Hence it is natural to assume that we must view the Johannine idea of election against the background of the Old Testament picture of Israel as the Chosen People of God. That line we are about to follow now.

Galling has pointed out two traditions of election in the Old Testament, one linking up with the Exodus-motif and leading on to that of the Covenant (Moses, Sinai), and the other centring round the patriarch-motif. Common to both these traditions is the fact that they represent God's election of Israel as an historical reality, once manifested in the past, with consequences affecting also the present and the future. Galling's attempt to examine more closely the origin and relations of the two traditions is of no particular interest to our present purpose and can therefore be left on one side, but he has provided us with an important starting point for our appreciation of the Johannine election-texts in their relation to the Old Testament.

In the prophets and particularly in Isaiah we often meet with the idea of the "remnant", the chosen remnant of the people appointed by Jahveh as an instrument for the salvation of the whole of Israel. Under the pressure of political disaster and religious decline the thought of such a remnant became dominant quite early among the prophets; a remnant which in itself personified the whole people and became the bearer of its promises and of its responsibilities. Later on this "remnant" came to be further concentrated in a single person, represented in the scriptures in the picture of the "Suffering Servant" of the Lord,[1] but also linked up with the heir of David, the King-Messiah. The more important the eschatological motive becomes in the religious thought of Israel, the more does the Jewish Messiah-concept become detached from its political and individual characteristics. Thus the main significance of the election no longer belongs to the past (Moses or Abraham), nor to the present (Jerusalem, the Temple and the cult), but to the future, when the people of God is to be raised up out of its degradation, and its true character is to be revealed to all the world. The idea of the chosen people is identical with that of the coming Messiah, who in his own person includes and perfects the eschatological people of God.

Referring to Galling's theory of the two election-traditions in the Old Testament, we may conclude that both of them are contained in the Fourth Gospel. It has been already pointed out in paragraph 27 that Moses as well as the patriarchs play an important part in the theology of this Gospel: Moses is represented as the type and precursor of Jesus, who himself fulfils the election begun through Moses.[2] The great signs of the years in the wilderness also belong to the Exodus-tradition—the sign of the manna, of the water,

[1] Isa. 42.1–12; 49.1–13; 50.4–9; 52.13—53.12.
[2] John 1.17, 45; 5.45–47; 7.19–24.

and of the fiery serpent—all of which have their complete fulfilment in Jesus. The passages about Abraham,[1] Jacob,[2] and the "fathers"[3] belong to the patriarch-tradition. The passage in 8.31–59 is of the greatest interest. Here the "Jews" as the "seed of Abraham" insist that they are the children of God, thus expressing the true Jewish idea of election. Jesus, however, points out that because of their disobedience to the Son they have lost their election: they are no longer children of God but children of the devil. This is most clearly manifested in their desire to kill the Son of God. But Jesus will fulfil the kingdom of God through those who believe on him, to whom he gives deliverance from sin and death. On the other hand there are in the Fourth Gospel instances of a direct attack upon the political and cultic foundations of the idea of election.

When St John presents Jesus as the fulfilment of the promises once given to Moses and the patriarchs, this must also be true with regard to the election which in itself includes all other promises and gifts. Numerous descendants, defence against enemies, deliverance from any anxiety, the giving of the law, the promise of the "prophet" to come—all this was only an expression of the fact that Israel was the people which God had chosen and loved. And now St John desires to show that this election has come to its complete realization and assumed its final character through Jesus and the Church founded by him.

43. *Chosen by Christ*

Under this heading we may gather all the texts wherein Christ is spoken of as choosing men to be his disciples. Clearly the condition which enables Jesus to make this choice is that he himself is the Chosen One, to whom God has given the task of introducing chosen men into the eschatological context of the Kingdom of God, while simultaneously

---

[1] John 8.31–59.   [2] John 1.51; 4.5–15.   [3] John 7.22.

IDEA OF ELECTION IN FOURTH GOSPEL 189

realizing in his own person this eschatological kingdom. There are, in the Fourth Gospel, many references to Jesus as the Chosen One, such as "the Father that dwelleth in me he doeth the works"; while according to some MSS. Jesus is spoken of in 1.34 as ὁ ἐκλεκτὸς τοῦ θεοῦ (the chosen of God). The verb used here to express the choice of Jesus is ἐκλέγομαι, which is also used in the following texts:

6.70. "Did I not choose you the twelve? and one of you is a devil."
13.18. "I speak not of you all: I know whom I have chosen."
15.16. "Ye did not choose me, but I chose you, and appointed you, that ye should go and bear fruit, and that your fruit shall abide (μένῃ): that whatsoever ye shall ask of the Father in my name, he may give it to you."
15.19. "But because ye are not of the world, but I chose you out of the world, therefore the world hateth you."

As has been made clear in the historical survey, there have been many attempts to evade the question of election in these passages by making them refer solely to the choosing of the Apostles. Support for such an interpretation might be obtained from 6.70 and 13.18, although the latter text obviously excludes Judas Iscariot, while in 6.70 he is expressly spoken of as chosen by Christ. As for 15.16, 19 it is quite impossible to limit their validity to the twelve only. Everything—the organic connection with the Vine-theme; the use of the "ecclesiastical term" μένειν; "the prayer in the name of Jesus"; the opposition to the hateful "world"; and finally the fact that the expression occurs in the "Church plan" outlined in the final discourses—indicates that the issue at stake is the discipleship in the Church and not merely the election of the Twelve. 14.22 ["Lord, what is come to pass that thou wilt manifest thyself unto us, and not unto the world?"] continues on the same lines and draws a clear picture of the situation after the death and resurrection of Jesus. The continued revelation is given only to those who are chosen.

Although the election in 6.70 and 13.18 primarily refers to the Apostles, it is nevertheless apparent that it has also wider implications; in particular this may be concluded from the previously mentioned connection of these texts with those regarding the manna-sign and the washing of the feet. The faithful disciples are the type of the faithful in the Church, while the traitor Judas is the prototype of those who are unfaithful to their election. For the election does not diminish the personal responsibility of man. This is an argument often put forward without justification against the scriptural legitimacy of the idea of election. On the contrary, the election intensifies the responsibility. Those who are chosen must realize their election in faith and life and so "bear fruit", a fruit which "abideth".

Judas, too, belonged to the chosen ones. The saying in 6.70 does not, of course, mean that God had predestined him to become a traitor, but is only an expression of the fact that Jesus knew beforehand what would happen (cf. 2.24–25; 6.64). The Johannine Jesus knows men beforehand. He knows their faith or unbelief and is therefore never taken by surprise. When Judas was chosen as a disciple it was that through his actions the scriptures might be fulfilled and that the death of Jesus might appear, not as a triumph for the traitor or the "world", but as a consequence of God's purpose of redemption: "Not one of them perished but the son of perdition; that the scripture might be fulfilled." Any attempt to give a psychological "explanation" of the person of Judas and his actions fails because of the firm conviction in the Gospel that he is nothing but an instrument in the devil's hand, forced to serve the purpose of God's redemptive work.[1] When he has completed his act of betrayal he disappears from St John's story. It is significant that Judas leaves the band of disciples immediately before Jesus begins his final discourse in which he depicts the situation of the Church in the world. Before that, Judas has been pointed

[1] John 13.2, 27; 18.2–5.

IDEA OF ELECTION IN FOURTH GOSPEL

out as the traitor and dismissed from the circle of disciples. After receiving the sop he at once (εὐθύς) goes out: "And it was night" (ἦν δέ νύξ). The same eternal sternness rests over this ἦν as over that of the Prologue but here with an added note of anxiety and fear. The "night" is the world of the lost and the damned, outside the fellowship with Christ, outside the Church.

Here follow a few texts which deal with election from another point of view:

> 10.16. "And other sheep I have, which are not of this fold: them also I must bring, and they shall hear my voice; and they shall become one flock, one shepherd."
>
> 10.26–27. "But ye believe not, because ye are not of my sheep. My sheep hear my voice, and I know them, and they follow me."
>
> 11.52. "Not for the nation only, but that he might also gather together into one (συναγάγῃ εἰς ἕν) the children of God that are scattered abroad."

The first two passages belong to the "Church-text" about the shepherd and the sheep, representing the election of Jesus as a gathering together of the faithful "sheep"; 11.52 is of the same type. The chosen ones have no natural or innate quality which predestines them to blessedness. If it were so, the redemptive work of Christ would be unnecessary. But Jesus must die so that those who are his sheep and the children of God, i.e. those to whom God gives the possibility of faith, might understand who he is, listen to his voice, and follow him. It follows that they also perceive their own situation, their responsibilities, and their possibilities as the chosen of Christ. The word about "following" again emphasizes the responsibility of the elect.

Finally, there is a third group of texts which also should be mentioned in this context:

> 6.37. "All that which the Father giveth me shall come unto me; and him that cometh to me I will in no wise cast out."

6.44. "No man can come to me except the Father which sent me draw him: and I will raise him up in the last day."
6.65. "No man can come unto me, except it be given unto him of the Father."
10.29. "My Father which hath given them unto me, is greater than all; and no one is able to snatch them out of the Father's hand."
17.9. "I pray . . . for those whom thou hast given me; for they are thine."

The sayings in chapter 6 are organically one with the great discourse on the Bread of Life. Thus they belong to the sacramental doctrine of the Fourth Gospel and show that it is the Father who "draws" to the Son whoever he wills. To "come to Jesus" means to believe in him. The drawing of the Father is thus another expression of the election which, it is true, is in this particular instance ascribed to the Father and not to the Son. This, however, is mainly of the same significance as the passages in chapters 10 and 11 treated above. 10.29, too, is part of the same context, although the text here is not altogether reliable. At all events this passage shows the security of the elect in the keeping of God. From 17.9 it is clear that they are the object of the intercession of Christ.

It is significant that all these passages regarding the election are to be found in some of the most "ecclesiastical" texts of the Fourth Gospel—namely those concerning the Eucharist, the Shepherd, the Washing of the Disciples' Feet, the Vine, and the High-Priestly Prayer. From this it may be concluded that it is in the Church that Jesus gathers together his elect. The sheep do not choose their shepherd, nor the branches the tree from which they spring. The union between the disciples and Christ is never dependent on their own choice but on that of their Lord. Faith is not the result of man's work or merit, but a gift of God. On the other hand, unbelief reveals those who are not chosen or who have despised and rejected their election.[1] The general state-

---
[1] John 8.44–45; 10.26.

ment in 3.27, "A man can receive nothing, except it have been given him from heaven", gives renewed emphasis to the sovereignty of God over the undertakings of men, a sovereignty of which the Johannine idea of election is an expression.

Thus the election leaves the disciples of Christ without any merit of their own, but not therefore without personal responsibility. On the contrary, they are pledged to live the life of the elect, the life of faith and love: "A new commandment I give unto you, that ye love one another; even as I have loved you, that ye also love one another. By this shall all men know that ye are my disciples, if ye have love one to another."[1] "These things I command you, that ye may love one another."[2] In the First Epistle of St John particular emphasis is laid on this responsibility of the disciples.[3] On the other hand, the elect are given to enjoy that *peace* in the present and that *hope* with regard to the future which belongs to a life in the eschatological situation of the Church.[4] The passage about the many mansions in particular is a reminder that the election refers not only to this present time but also to that which is to come.

44. *"Born of God"*

There remain yet certain passages which seem very different from those treated above but which nevertheless have a connection with the idea of election in the Fourth Gospel. For they speak of men who are "born of God", an expression which has led to various interpretations on the lines of predestination.

> 1.12–13. "... to them gave he the right to become children of God, even to them that believe on his name: which were born, not of blood, nor of the will of the flesh, nor of the will of man, but of God."

[1] John 13.34, 35.
[2] John 15.17.
[3] 1 John 2.6, 28; 3.16–18.
[4] John 14.1–3, 27; 15.4, 5; 17.24–26.

3.3–7. "Except a man be born from above he cannot see the Kingdom of God. . . . Except a man be born of water and the Spirit, he cannot enter into the Kingdom of God. That which is born of the flesh is flesh; and that which is born of the Spirit is spirit. Marvel not that I said unto thee, ye must be born from above."=R.V. marg.

3.21. ". . . but he that doeth the truth cometh to the light, that his works may be made manifest, that they have been wrought in God."

8.47. "He that is of God heareth the words of God: for this cause ye hear them not, because ye are not of God."

18.37. "Everyone that is of the truth heareth my voice."

The first two examples refer to men who are "born" in some way other than through the ordinary physical birth—born "of God"; "from above"; of "water and the Spirit". From the last three examples it may be concluded that there is, according to the Fourth Gospel, a certain quality or receptivity in men who come to believe on Jesus. These are the people who "do the truth", "are of the truth", "are of God". To "come to the light" (Christ) and to "hear his voice" are merely different expressions of faith. This "birth" or "quality" seems to be the condition which enables a man to *believe on Jesus*—not a fruit of this belief. Is not this a doctrine of predestination?

We have already examined the passage in 3.3–7 from the point of view of its baptismal character. Thus, to be "born of water and the Spirit" or "from above" means to be baptized. Baptism is, then, according to St John, the way by which man enters into the Kingdom of God. But what does it mean, then, to be "born of *God*"—a birth which is so very markedly distinguished from that "of the will of the flesh"? Attached to this phrase "born of God" in 1.13 we find a reference to "the power to become the children of God" (ἐξουσίαν τέκνα θεοῦ γενέσθαι) given to those "that believe on his name". Here faith seems to be the condition for adoption as a child of God and it would be difficult to discover any actual difference in meaning between "to become the children of God" and "to be born of God". According to 1.12–13 the new life is a consequence of the faith of man, while in 3.3–7 "the birth from above" seems to be the primary fact. The explanation of this apparent discrepancy in Johannine thought lies in the fact that St John thinks theologically, not chronologically, about the spiritual life of man, just as he does about the life of Jesus. St John has not set out to lay down the exact time-sequence between the "birth in God" and faith in Christ. They are both a gift of God independent of any human merit and cannot actually be separated from one another. That the "birth of God" is some kind of reward, a power given to those who already believe, is as unthinkable as to believe that "the birth from above" (Baptism) is an asset and a way to salvation for man regardless of his belief.

We have already seen that real faith, faith in the glorified Christ, is only possible in the Church. Even the expression εἰς τὸ ὄνομα αὐτοῦ in 1.12 bears witness to the Church, thus showing that it is only in the Church that a man can be "born of God". "Born of God" and "born from above" or "born of water and the Spirit" must, for rational and linguistic reasons, mean the same thing and refer to Baptism which is in itself a gift of God, but which can only be received and kept by man in faith. Thus Baptism is an elective action on the part of God and faith is man's possibility of realizing this election, of realizing his right to become a child of God. It is clear that the Johannine idea of election is always accompanied by the thought of personal responsibility. Without exception the many passages in the First Epistle of St John which speak of those who are "born of God" point to faith, righteousness, and love as "signs" of man's being born of God.

There remain the passages about those who "do the truth", "are of the truth", and "are of God". That the "truth" is identical with Christ and his redemptive work has been shown above. But how is a man to "do the truth" or "be of the truth" before he comes to believe? And how can he be "of God" before he hears his words, that is, before he believes in him? These questions are quite irrelevant, as they imply that St John is setting out to arrange a time-table for the conversion of man. But here, too, the principle "theology, not chronology" may be applied. In the Epistle 3.9–10 the term "to be of God" is synonymous with "to be born of God". This shows that the terms "to be born of God" and "to be of the truth" are merely other expressions for the reality which is conveyed by the terms "born of God" or "children of God". They all refer to people who live in union with Christ in the Church. It is clear from 1 John 3.2, that this life is marked by an eschatological perspective—"Beloved, now are we children of God, and it is not yet made manifest what we shall be. We know that if he shall be manifested, we shall be like him; for we shall see him even as he is."

The term "born of God" and others of the same kind are thus expressions of the Johannine idea of election. They are inserted into the Church-theology of the Fourth Gospel and cannot be understood if interpreted from a purely individualistic point of view. By being "born of God" the individual is made part of the unity of the Church, as a sheep is of a flock and a branch of the vine. Only in that fellowship does he share in Christ's life and in the power of the Spirit: only there does he receive the possibilities of faith and love and the hope of eschatological fulfilment. The election to membership in the Church, which according to the Fourth Gospel is identical with Baptism, is thus one with the election to eternal life. And the life of election which is led by the disciples of Christ in the Church and which is marked by faith and love, is an anticipation of life at the consummation. Thus the idea of election is an integral part of both Church and eschatology in the Fourth Gospel.

IDEA OF ELECTION IN FOURTH GOSPEL 197

But from which world of thought has St John taken the term "born of God" and others like it, and why does he employ them? It would be hard to trace any links with the Old Testament. We must seek the origin of this terminology in Hellenism. This does not, of course, mean that in the Gospel these terms are marked by Hellenistic ideas. On the contrary, we have seen how the Evangelist, albeit with great difficulty, has made of them vehicles for the Biblical idea of election. Here, for the second time, he has taken Hellenistic terms and filled them with Christian meaning. His purpose is as usual a double one—polemic and apologetic. He attacks on the one hand the iron-bound faith in Providence which, together with unshakeable determinism, was characteristic of gnostic thought; and on the other hand the reliance of the Jews on their membership in the chosen people (cf. 8.33, 53—the seed of Abraham; 9.28—the disciples of Moses), who, nevertheless, considered themselves dispensed from fulfilling the obligations of their election. He is on the defensive when he shows how non-Biblical thoughts about the sovereignty of God and man's absolute dependence on him reach their fulfilment in the Christian revelation. For this revelation is not mainly a doctrine about divine election: it is this election put into action. It shows how God sends for the salvation of men his Chosen One who continually chooses new disciples, gathering them together into the Church—the instrument whereby he is to win all mankind. For this is the deepest significance of the election: God chooses the few that by them he may redeem many.

45. *The "Offence"*

The problem of the "offence" is theologically connected with the idea of election. The Offence (σκάνδαλον) is, so to speak, the negation of the election. Although the noun σκάνδαλον is not found at all in the Fourth Gospel and the verb comes only twice, the thing itself occurs very frequently, and thus demands our attention. The cause of the offence to the people—the "Jews"—is the words and works of Jesus.

1. *The offence caused by the words of Jesus*

In 3.4 we see how Nicodemus takes offence at the words of Jesus about being born from above: "How can a man be born when he is old?" In 6.41 we find that the Jews murmured (γογγύζειν) when Jesus spoke of himself as the Bread coming down from Heaven. In 6.52 they petulantly ask how Jesus can give them his flesh to eat, and in 6.60 ff we read that "many of his disciples" went away because of his "hard sayings" (σκληρὸς λόγος). When Jesus finds that they "murmur" because of it, he says: "Doth this cause you to stumble? (τοῦτο ὑμᾶς σκανδαλίζει) What then if ye should behold the Son of Man ascending where he was before?" Thus over against the offence which even the disciples find in the hard sayings of Jesus, is set the still greater offence of the "lifting-up" of Jesus. The same thought is expressed again in 16.32: "Ye shall be scattered every man to his own, and shall leave me alone."

In chapters 7—8 there are frequent disputes with the Jews who get very angry because of the words of Jesus and want to kill him,[1] or lay hands on him.[2] Controversy also arises among the people because of Jesus.[3] Even the "shepherd-discourse" causes offence and those who hear it strive among themselves as to its meaning.[4] The Jews, again, threaten to stone Jesus; or to capture him.[5] As the narrative goes on, the threats become more serious—a sign that the offence caused by the words of Jesus is ever increasing.

2. *The offence caused by the works of Jesus*

The Jews were offended because of the Cleansing of the Temple and demanded from Jesus a "sign" of his authority.[6]

[1] John 7.1, 19; 8.37, 40, 43, 59.
[2] John 7.30, 32.
[3] John 7.43.
[4] John 10.19.
[5] John 10.31; 10.39; 11.8.
[6] John 2.18.

They persecuted him because he, on the sabbath, cured the sick man by the Pool of Bethesda, and also threatened to kill him.[1] The healing of the man born blind led to his being cast out of the Synagogue.[2] The worst offence, however, was that caused by the raising of Lazarus, which led Caiaphas to pronounce his prophecy about the death of Jesus, and to have steps taken against him in consequence of it.[3] Lazarus, too, was threatened with death, and the anger of Judas regarding the wasted ointment at Bethany belongs to the same category.[4] There is also a steady increase in the resentment felt by the Jews and in the ways in which it finds expression. The greatest work, the raising of Lazarus, produces the greatest rage and the most serious threats. This reminds us that the "mighty works" of Jesus do not awaken popularity among the multitude but rather turn them against him in hate. Thus the whole story is leading on to the great drama of the Cross, the biggest "stumbling-block" of all.

In his account of the earthly life of Jesus St John refers throughout to the "offence" as the reaction of the "Jews" to Jesus, his words and works. Therefore σκανδαλίζεσθαι becomes the complete opposite of πιστεύειν. It is that force of unbelief which drives Jesus to his death. Judas, the one among the Twelve who has taken offence, consequently becomes the traitor. It does not cease when the earthly life of Jesus is ended. The "lifting-up" of the Son of Man proves to be the greatest of all offences. This means that in the Church, too, the disciples of Jesus must wrestle with "offence" and its bitter fruits: hate, mocking, persecution unto death. Such is the situation outlined in 16.1–4, where the prediction of the sufferings of the disciples for the sake of Jesus begins with the words: "These things have I spoken unto you, that you should not be made to stumble" (μὴ σκανδαλισθῆτε).

[1] John 5.16–18.
[2] John 9.22, 34, 35.
[3] John 11.50–53, 57; 18.14.
[4] John 12.5, 10.

To be "offended at" Jesus, that is the way of the world—the mark of unbelief. In contrast to the election and the life of the elect in union with Christ in the Church of the redeemed, the scandal is part of a demonic situation marked by enmity to Christ and finally leading to condemnation and eternal death.

By a forceful emphasis on the thought of God's election and the consequent "offence", St John has attempted to solve the problem of unbelief. This had become actualized both in the Jews' rejection of Jesus during his earthly life and in their indifference or hostility to the young Church. The idea of election gives emphasis to the Church's conviction that she is the true Israel. It stimulates her undauntedness when faced with the threats of the world and strengthens her certainty of eventually reaching the eschatological fulfilment. This certainty is not the result of human speculation regarding God's omnipotence and the frailty of man, as is the case with determinism and the doctrine of predestination: it is altogether rooted in faith, a wholehearted acknowledgement of the free choice of God's mercy. When Christ acts through his words and the sacraments, then God chooses in every new situation those who come to believe, but the rest take offence. Thus the tension between faith and unbelief, election and "offence", is to continue until the end of time when God will gather together all his elect in the world of fulfilment.

CHAPTER 7

CONSUMMATUM EST

THE FOREGOING examination of certain theological ideas in the Fourth Gospel has confirmed our previous conclusions as to the connection between the Church and eschatology. It ought further to have shown that this ecclesiastical-eschatological mode of interpretation gives us a better understanding of the real meaning of these ideas, as also of the peculiar character of the whole theology which they represent.

The idea of election is another part of the Johannine theology where Church and eschatology meet. It has been shown how all attempts to interpret it in an individualistic manner lead, without fail, to philosophical speculations about determinism and predestination, quite alien to the theology of the Fourth Gospel. For St John's doctrine of election aims at showing that the gathering together of the elect in the Church is a preparation for, and an anticipation of, their final gathering together in the eschatological fulfilment.

What conclusions may we now finally draw from the material concerning eschatology and the Church already presented in this book? Previous examinations of this subject have not for the most part taken into consideration the indissoluble connection between the two. Consequently, the main emphasis has been laid either on Church-consciousness, seeing in the Johannine revelation of the Church a corrective of the strong inclination in that Church towards an eschatological perspective: or on eschatology, dissolving it into individualism and mysticism when it was no longer connected with an ecclesiastical community. The present work has aimed at pointing out the organic connection in this Gospel between eschatology and the idea of the Church, and at showing their inter-dependence. The Johannine Church has its roots in eschatology, which in its turn is firmly anchored in the Church.

1. The eschatological foundation of the idea of the Church, as revealed in the Fourth Gospel, prevents us from regarding it as merely an institution of this world, although that is clearly one aspect of her nature. She has her ministry, her cult, her confession, and her missionary activity, all of them visible and belonging to this world; and this must be part of her vocation, because she works among men and through them in the world. She is the extension of the continuing Incarnation. Anyone who despises or denies this is guilty of the same docetic error against which St John fights with so great determination. The Johannine Church is, however, above all of an eschatological nature, having her foundation and origin in the death and resurrection of Jesus which is the great mystery of Redemption. In her the risen Lord fulfils his redemptive work until the end of time.

Only in the Church is there the possibility of faith. For faith is always belief in the risen Lord who continues his revelation in the Church. *Eternal* life is only realized in the Church: and eternal life is, in its turn, the fulfilment of all *created* life. It is expressed on the one hand in the cult, which is the meeting place between the risen Lord and his faithful ones, and on the other hand in the mutual love of Christians, which is a manifestation of Christ's own love for his disciples. No one has more strongly than St John underlined the truly Christian saying: "*extra ecclesiam nulla salus.*"

The Church, although herself limited in respect of time and power, gives to the believer already, now, life eternal. The Church is limited in respect of time because her *origin* is based on historical fact, i.e. on the death and resurrection of Jesus; while the completion of her task will come about at the end of time, at the Parousia. She is limited in respect of *power* because her work has to be done in this world of sin and death where temptations, errors, and dangers continually impose limitations on her work. The struggle of Jesus against the unbelief of "the Jews", which is an outstanding feature in the Fourth Gospel, reflects also the Church's struggle against "the world". When that battle is over the fulfilment will be a reality: it is towards that fulfilment that the Johannine Church is always pointing in her teaching, her cult, and indeed by the very fact of her existence.

2. The ecclesiastical basis of the Johannine eschatology has preserved St John from the two dangers which always threaten all eschatological speculations: the mystic's individualistic experience of timelessness and the apocalyptic's attempt to date and map out the last things. The Johannine theology is, as we have seen, neither mystical nor apocalyptic, while everywhere the idea of the Church accompanies, deepens, and makes concrete the eschatological tendencies. Eschatology is, like the Church, dependent on the historical fact of redemption, i.e. on the death and resurrection of Jesus, and its consequences for the future of the individual as well as of mankind as a whole. This has kept it free from individualistic arbitrariness and superficial speculations. In the Church, and above all in the Liturgy, the Christian experiences proleptically the age to come. Because the eschatological ideas are thus made concrete, the final fulfilment and his own share in it becomes a certainty to every believer.

Another conclusion that might be drawn from the above examination is that neither the question of the Church nor that of eschatology can be treated as secondary problems within Johannine theology, nor can they be limited to certain *parts* of the Gospel. It is the Gospel *as a whole* that has provided the material for the illumination of this question. Our survey of the most important theological terms ought to have shown that the question of the Church and of eschatology is of decisive importance for the whole of Johannine theology.

Our present study of this Gospel as a theological and historical problem should have brought us to a new and truer understanding of the whole book. We have seen that there is need for a new testing as to what is and what is not of main importance in this Gospel. The old issues regarding its dependence on or independence of the Synoptic Gospels, and whether its aim is to complete or replace them, are no longer in the forefront. All attempts to find definite facts about the person of the author, his character, the length of his life, and his artistic ambitions seem likewise pointless and even at times ridiculous. The relationship between the beloved disciple and the evangelist and the identity of the former are other questions to which critical scholarship is never likely to find a satisfactory answer. It can, however, come to a far more important result.

The opinion that the beloved disciple is an ideal figure is becoming increasingly common among scholars of today. Whether he is also an historical figure is beyond the knowledge of anyone. The important thing is that the Fourth Gospel itself represents him as the eyewitness of what he describes, the guarantee of the truthfulness of all that he records in his Gospel. His anonymity is, we think, neither mere chance nor an expression of some kind of humility on the part of the author. On the contrary it seems to suggest a by no means modest claim, for by his anonymity, he is pointing out, with great deliberation and consistency, that his account is not the work of any single author but that it is the work of the Church. Sometimes the beloved disciple at the foot of the Cross of Jesus has been taken to represent Gentile Christianity as opposed to Jewish Christianity here represented by Mary. There are, however, strong reasons for dismissing such an interpretation, as it is founded on the existence of a contrast between Jewish and Gentile Christianity quite alien to the Fourth Gospel as a whole. It would, however, seem reasonable for us to assume that the beloved disciple is a representative of the Church herself—the Church which is the faithful witness of the "lifting-up" of Jesus and of his continued work in the world. The Fourth Gospel does not aim at being a "personal" testimony about Jesus, nor an exposition by a learned teacher of the mysteries of redemption manifested before a chosen band of disciples. Its one desire is to be the Church's own witness about herself and about that Lord who is working in and through her.

This study has now come to its close. While the work on it has been in progress, one of the passages in the Fourth Gospel not yet considered here has come to fascinate the author more and more as an illustration of his main theme: Church and eschatology in the Fourth Gospel. It is the account of the disciples in the boat and of Jesus walking to them on the water.[1] The relationship between this little story and that of the great miracle of the feeding gives us reason to suppose that the former, thus linked up with a text of sacramental character, must be a "Church-text". The details of St John's narrative are very much the same as those of the Synoptists: i. the disciples get into the boat while Jesus remains alone on the shore; ii. evening had come; iii. they were hard pressed by the waves; iv. Jesus came walking to them on the water; v. the disciples were afraid; vi. Jesus comforted them; vii. Jesus went up into the boat. Here St John leaves the Synoptic tradition and adds: "They were willing therefore to receive him into the boat: and straightway the boat was at the land whither they were going." The idea of the life of the Church as a dangerous voyage is not foreign to the rest of the New Testament and in St John 21.4–13 the shore where stands the risen Lord is the destination towards which the disciples strain with their catch. This gives us a picture of the eternal world where the disciples are allowed to enjoy the fellowship of a common meal with the risen Lord.

[1] John 6.16–21.

Thus St John, like the Synoptists, in the voyage of the disciples, pictures the difficult position of the Church in an evil and hostile world, showing at the same time how the risen Lord, in a wonderful and inconceivable manner, comes to the help of his disciples. St John does not, however, stop short at this. He is anxious to point out that as soon as Jesus came to his disciples in the boat, they found themselves already at their destination. A better expression of the peculiar character of the Johannine eschatology and its relation to Church-consciousness could hardly be found: those who are with Christ in the Church are already living in eternity. The distance between this world and that which is to come has been annihilated. For the powers of the world to come are already at work in the Church, and the promises of eternal life are fulfilled in anticipation. This does not make the Parousia and the final fulfilment superfluous to Christian thought, but it helps to keep the Christian hope of eternal life living among men in time.

The idea of the world to come where God will give to his faithful ones life in incorruption, in joy, and in peace is an essential feature in all true religion. By means of theological speculations and rites and myths of various kinds this longing for eternal life was kept alive in man. But never did it find a more vivid and pure expression than in the religion of the Old Testament. It was expressed in its liturgy, its prophecies, and in the law, and through these spiritual manifestations retained ascendancy over the people. Eventually this longing came to be more and more linked up with the expectations regarding the coming Messiah, who was to gather together the scattered people of God, establish the eternal Kingdom, and restore the corrupted Creation. Now the author of the Fourth Gospel states that all this has come to pass in Christ Jesus. In him is the fulfilment of the eschatological expectations of Jews and Gentiles. Through him the new age of eternity has come and is manifested in his Church. It is indeed true that the old age with its errors, its suffering, and its death has not fully passed away, but the new Kingdom has, nevertheless, come, the promises are fulfilled, and life eternal is already given in an anticipatory manner to those who believe in Christ and live with him in his Church. The turning point of history and of all the ages came in that hour when Jesus Christ, the Son of God, was lifted up on the Cross and from that Cross raised his triumphant cry to all nations and all ages: It is finished—τετέλεσται—CONSUMMATUM EST.

ABBREVIATIONS

The following abbreviations are used in the Bibliography:

AASF	Annales Academiae Scientiarum Fennicae.
AbhThANT	Abhandlungen zur Theologie des Alten und Neuen Testaments.
AmJSL	The American Journal of Semitic Languages and Literatures.
AmJTh	The American Journal of Theology.
AMU	Arbeiten und Mitteilungen aus dem neutestamentlichen Seminar zu Uppsala.
ARW	Archiv für Religionswissenschaft.
ASNU	Acta Seminarii Neotestamentici Upsaliensis.
AUL	Acta Universitatis Latviensis.
BFchrTh	Beiträge zur Förderung christlicher Theologie.
BHTh	Beiträge zur Historischen Theologie.
BJRL	Bulletin of the John Rylands Library.
BWANT	Beiträge zur Wissenschaft vom Alten und Neuen Testament.
BzR	Beiträge zur Religionswissenschaft.
CQR	The Church Quarterly Review.
CN	Coniectanea Neotestamentica.
CR	Corpus Reformatorum.
CThAP	Cahiers Théologiques de l'Actualité Protestante.
DTh	Deutsche Theologie.
EMM	Evangelisches Missions-Magazin.
EMZ	Evangelische Missions-Zeitung.
EvTh	Evangelische Theologie.
Exp	The Expositor.

ABBREVIATIONS

FchrLD	Forschungen zur christlichen Literatur- und Dogmengeschichte.
FRLANT	Forschungen zur Religion und Literatur des Alten und Neuen Testaments.
GCS	Die griechischen christlichen Schriftsteller der ersten drei Jahrhunderte, herausgegeben von der Kirchenväter-Commission der Königl. Preussischen Akademie der Wissenschaften.
GThF	Greifswalder Theologische Forschungen.
HNT	Handbuch zum Neuen Testament, herausgegeben von H. Lietzmann.
ICC	The International Critical Commentary on the Holy Scriptures of the Old and New Testament.
IKZ	Internationale Kirchliche Zeitschrift.
JBL	Journal of Biblical Literature.
JQR	Jewish Quarterly Review.
JThS	The Journal of Theological Studies.
KuM	Kerygma und Mythos. Ein theologisches Gespräch, herausgegeben von H. W. Bartsch. (Theologische Forschung I.) 1948. E.T., Kerygma and Myth, 1953.
Lab	The Labyrinth. Further Studies in the Relation between Myth and Ritual in the Ancient World, ed. Hooke. 1935.
MaR	Myth and Ritual. Essays on the Myth and Ritual of the Hebrews in Relation to the Culture Pattern of the Ancient East, ed. Hooke. 1933.
MC	The Modern Churchman.
MPG	Patrologiae cursus completus, series graeca, ed. Migne.
MPL	Patrologiae cursus completus, series latina, ed. Migne.
NAbh	Neutestamentliche Abhandlungen.
NachrGGW	Nachrichten von der Königl. Gesellschaft der Wissenschaften zu Göttingen, Philol.-hist. Klasse.
NedThT	Nederlands Theologisch Tijdschrift.

ABBREVIATIONS

NF	Neue Folge.
NKZ	Neue Kirchliche Zeitschrift.
NS	Nouvelle Série.
NtlF	Neutestamentliche Forschungen.
RB	Revue Biblique.
RechScRel	Recherches de Science Religieuse.
RHR	Revue de l'Histoire des Religions.
RThPh	Revue de Theologie et de Philosophie.
SbHAW	Sitzungsberichte der Heidelberger Akademie der Wissenschaften.
SbPAW	Sitzungsberichte der Preussischen Akademie der Wissenschaften.
SBU	Symbolae Biblicae Upsaliensis.
SEÅ	Svensk Exegetisk Årsbok.
SGKA	Studien zur Geschichte und Kultur des Altertums.
SymbOsl	Symbolae Osloenses.
ThB	Theologische Blätter.
ThR	Theologische Rundschau.
ThS	Theologische Studien.
ThSK	Theologische Studien und Kritiken.
ThZ	Theologische Zeitschrift.
TU	Texte und Untersuchungen zur Geschichte der altchristlichen Literatur.
UUÅ	Uppsala Universitets Årsskrift.
UzNT	Untersuchungen zum Neuen Testament.
WA	Martin Luthers Werke. Kritische Gesamtausgabe. Weimar.
YCS	Yale Classical Studies.
ZAW	Zeitschrift für die alttestamentliche Wissenschaft.
ZkathTh	Zeitschrift für katholische Theologie.
ZNW	Zeitschrift für die neutestamentliche Wissenschaft.
ZsystTh	Zeitschrift für systematische Theologie.
ZThK	Zeitschrift für Theologie und Kirche.

BIBLIOGRAPHY

Aall, A., Der Logos. Geschichte seiner Entwicklung in der griechischen Philosophie und der christlichen Literatur. I–II. Leipzig 1896–1899.
Aebert, Bernh., Die Eschatologie des Johannes-Evangeliums. Eine systematische Untersuchung auf Grund seiner religionsgeschichtlichen Voraussetzungen. Diss. Breslau. Würzburg 1936.
Aicher, G., Der Prozess Jesu. Kanonistische Studien und Texte, herausgegeben von Dr A. M. Koeniger, Band 3. Bonn 1929.
Alcuin, Commentaria in S. Johannis Evangelium. MPL 100, 733–1008.
Althaus, P., Die letzten Dinge. Entwurf einer christlichen Eschatologie. 3. Aufl. Gütersloh 1926. 4. Aufl. Gütersloh 1933.
Ammonius of Alexandria, Expositio in Evangelium S. Johannis. MPG 85, 1391–1524.
Anz, W., Zur Frage nach dem Ursprung des Gnostizismus. Ein religionshistorischer Versuch. TU XV: 4. Leipzig 1897.
Arvedson, T., Das Mysterium Christi. Eine Studie zu Mt 11:25–30. AMU VII. Diss. Uppsala 1937.
Askwith, E. H., The Historical Value of the Fourth Gospel. Exp VII: 8, 1909, pp. 71–81, 244–263, 365–375, 431–441, 530–542. VII: 9, 1910, pp. 86–96, 132–138, 228–241, 440–449, 538–547. VII: 10, 1910, pp. 38–52, 254–265.
Asmussen, H., Die Kirche und das Amt. München 1939.
Asting, R., Die Heiligkeit im Urchristcentum. Diss. Göttingen 1930.
Augustine, In Ioannis Evangelium Tractatus CXXIV. MPL 35, 1579–1976.
Bacon, B. W., The "Other" Comforter. Exp XIV, 1917, pp. 274–282.
Baldensperger, W., Der Prolog des vierten Evangeliums. Sein polemischapologetischer Zweck. Freiburg in B. 1898.
Barth, Chr., Die Errettung vom Tode in den individuellen Klage- und Dankliedern des Alten Testaments. Basel 1947.

Bauer, W., Das Johannesevangelium. HNT 6. 3. Aufl. Tübingen 1933.
— Rechtgläubigkeit und Ketzerei im ältesten Christentum. BHTh 10. Tübingen 1934.
Baumgarten, S. J., Auslegung des Evangelii St. Johannis herausgegeben von Joh. Sal. Semler. Halle 1762.
Bede, In S. Joannis Evangelium Expositio. MPL 92, 633–938.
Belser, J., Die Geschichte des Leidens und Sterbens, der Auferstehung und Himmelfahrt des Herrn. 2. Aufl. Freiburg in B. 1913. E.T., History of the Passion, Death, and Glorification of our Saviour, Jesus Christ, freely adapted into Eng. St Louis and London 1929.
Bengel, A., Gnomon Novi Testamenti I. 2. Ed. Tubingae 1759.
Bentzen, A., Messias—Moses redivivus—Menschensohn. Skizzen zum Thema: Weissagung und Erfüllung. AbhThANT 17. Zürich 1948. E.T., King and Messiah. London 1955.
Bernard, J. H., A Critical and Exegetical Commentary on the Gospel according to St. John, I–II. ICC. Edinburgh 1928.
Bert, G., Das Evangelium des Johannes. Versuch einer Lösung seines Grundproblems. Gütersloh 1922.
Bertling, O., Der johanneische Logos und seine Bedeutung für das christliche Leben. Leipzig 1907.
Bertram, G., Die Himmelfahrt Jesu vom Kreuz aus und der Glaube an seine Auferstehung. Festgabe für Ad. Deissmann, Tübingen 1927, pp. 187–217.
— Die Leidensgeschichte Jesu und der Christuskult. Eine formgeschichtliche Untersuchung. FRLANT NF 15. Göttingen 1922.
Beyschlag, W., Die Christologie des Neuen Testaments. Ein biblisch-theologischer Versuch. Berlin 1866.
Bickermann, E., Die römische Kaiserapotheose. ARW 27, 1929, pp. 1–34.
Blumenthal, M., Die Eigenart des johanneischen Erzählungsstieles. ThSK NF 1, 1934/35, pp. 204–212.
Boehmer, J., Das Johannesevangelium nach Aufbau und Grundgedanken. Eisleben 1928.
Boismard, M.-E., Le chapitre XXI de Saint Jean. RB 54, 1947, pp. 473–501.
Bornhäuser, K., Die Gebeine der Toten. Ein Beitrag zum Verständnis der Anschauungen von der Totenauferstehung zur Zeit des Neuen Testaments. BFchrTh 26: 3. Gütersloh 1921.

Bornhäuser, K., Das Johannesevangelium. Eine Missionsschrift für Israel. BFchrTh II: 15. Gütersloh 1928.
Bornkamm, G., Die neutestamentliche Lehre von der Taufe. ThB 17, 1939, cols. 42–52.
— Der Paraklet im Johannesevangelium. Festschrift Rudolf Bultmann. Stuttgart 1949, pp. 12–35.
— Die Sturmstillung im Matthäus-Evangelium. Jahrbuch der theol. Schule Bethel 1948, pp. 49–54.
Bousset, W., Kyrios Christos. Geschichte des Christusglaubens von den Anfängen des Christentums bis Irenaeus. FRLANT NF 4. Göttingen 1913.
— Hauptprobleme der Gnosis. FRLANT 10. Göttingen 1907.
— Die Religion des Judentums im späthellenistischen Zeitalter. HNT 21. 3. Aufl. Tübingen 1926.
Brandt, W., Dienst und Dienen im Neuen Testament. NtlF II: 5. Gütersloh 1931.
— Das ewige Wort. Eine Einführung in das Evangelium nach Johannes. (Die urchristliche Botschaft IV.) Berlin 1936.
— Die jüdischen Baptismen oder das religiöse Waschen und Baden im Judentum mit Einschluss des Judenchristentums. ZAW Beiheft 18. Giessen 1910.
Braun, F.-M., Le lavement des pieds et la réponse de Jésus à Saint Pierre (Jean XIII, 4–10). RB 44, 1935, pp. 22–33.
— Neues Licht auf die Kirche. Die protestantische Kirchendogmatik in ihrer neuesten Entfaltung. Einsiedeln/Köln 1946.
Brooke, A. E., A Critical and Exegetical Commentary on the Johannine Epistles. ICC. Edinburgh 1912.
Brun, L., Die Gottesschau des johanneischen Christus. SymbOsl V, 1927, pp. 1–22.
Bruno Astensis, Commentaria in Joannem. MPL 165, 451–604.
Bucer, M., In sacra quattuor Evangelia Enarrationes. Basel 1536.
Büchsel, F., Der Begriff der Wahrheit in dem Evangelium und den Briefen des Johannes, BFchrTh 15: 3. Gütersloh 1911.
— Das Evangelium nach Johannes. (Das Neue Testament Deutsch 4.) Göttingen 1946.
— Der Geist Gottes im Neuen Testament. Gütersloh 1926.
— Johannes und der hellenistische Synkretismus. BFchrTh II: 16. Gütersloh 1928.
— Johannes und die Synoptiker. ZsystTh 4, 1926/27, pp. 240–265.
— Die Johannesbriefe. (Theol. Handkommentar zum Neuen Testament XVII.) Leipzig 1933.

Buchsel, F., Mandäer und Johannesjünger, ZNW 26, 1927, pp. 219-231.
— Theologie des Neuen Testaments. Geschichte des Wortes Gottes im Neuen Testament. Gütersloh 1935.
Bugge, F. W., Johannes-Evangeliet. Christiania 1893.
Bullinger, H., In divinum Iesu Christi Domini nostri Evangelium secundum Joannem commentariorum libri X. Tiguri 1556.
Bultmann, R., Analyse des ersten Johannesbriefes. Festgabe für Ad. Jülicher, Tübingen 1927, pp. 138-158.
— Die Bedeutung der neuerschlossenen mandäischen und manichäischen Quellen für das Verständnis des Johannesevangeliums. ZNW 24, 1925, pp. 100-146.
— Die Eschatologie des Johannes-Evangeliums. Glauben und Verstehen, Tübingen 1933, pp. 134-152.
— Das Evangelium des Johannes. (Meyer, Kritisch-exegetischer Kommentar über das Neue Testament, 2. Abt. 10. Aufl.) Göttingen 1941.
— Der religionsgeschichtliche Hintergrund des Prologs zum Johannes-Evangelium. ΕΥΧΑΡΙΣΤΗΡΙΟΝ II. FRLANT NF 19: 2, pp. 3-26. Göttingen 1923.
— Neues Testament und Mythologie. KuM 1948, pp. 15-53; E.T., pp. 1-44.
— Zu J. Schniewinds Thesen, das Problem der Entmythologisierung betreffend. KuM 1948, pp. 135-153; E.T., pp. 102-103.
Bunch, T. G., "Behold the Man!" A Review of the Trials and Crucifixion of Jesus. The Biblical Record in the Light of Hebrew and Roman Law. Nashville 1946.
Buri, F., Die Bedeutung der neutestamentlichen Eschatologie für die neuere protestantische Theologie. Ein Versuch zur Klärung des Problems der Eschatologie und zu einem neuen Verständnis ihres eigentlichen Anliegens. Diss. Bern 1934.
Burkitt, F. C., Church and Gnosis. A Study of Christian Thought and Speculation in the Second Century. Cambridge 1932.
— The Mandaeans. JThS 29, 1928, pp. 225-235.
Burney, C. F., The Aramaic Origin of the Fourth Gospel. Oxford 1922.
— The Poetry of Our Lord. An Examination of the Formal Elements of Hebrew Poetry in the Discourses of Jesus Christ. Oxford 1925.
Calovius, A., Biblia Novi Testamenti illustrata I. Dresden—Leipzig 1719.

Calvin, J., Commentaries in Evangelium Ioannis. CR 47, cols. 1-458.
Campenhausen, H. v., Die Idee des Martyriums in der alten Kirche. Göttingen 1936.
— Die Schlüsselgewalt der Kirche. EvTh 4, 1937, pp. 143-169.
— Zur Auslegung von Joh. 13. 6-10. ZNW 33, 1934, pp. 259-271.
Carpenter, J. E., The Johannine Writings. A Study of the Apocalypse and the Fourth Gospel. London 1927.
Carrington, P., The Primitive Christian Catechism. A Study in the Epistles. Cambridge 1940.
Caspari, W., Beweggründe der Erwählung, nach dem Alten Testament. NKZ 32, 1921, pp. 201-215.
Cassian, Archimandrite, Die Lehre des Neuen Testaments von der Kirche. IKZ 30, 1940, pp. 1-12.
— Kirche oder Reich Gottes. Zur johanneischen Eschatologie. In Extremis 1939, pp. 186-202.
Cerfaux, L., Le thème littéraire parabolique dans l'évangile de saint Jean. CN XI, 1947, pp. 15-25.
Chadwick, G. A., Asking in Christ's Name. Exp III; 6, 1887, pp. 191-198.
Chemnitz, M., Harmonia quattuor evengelistarum a D. Martino Chemnitio primum inchoata, D. Polycharpo Lysero post continuata atque D. Johanne Gerhardo tandem felicissime absoluta I-II. Frankfurt—Hamburg 1652.
Chrysostom, John, Commentarius in sanctum Joannem Apostolum et Evangelistam. MPG 59, pp. 23-482.
Clark, K. W., "Realized Eschatology". JBL 59, 1940, pp. 367-383.
Clemen, C., Religionsgeschichtliche Erklärung des neuen Testaments. Die Abhängigkeit des ältesten Christentums von nichtjüdischen Religionen und philosophischen Systemen. 2. Aufl. Giessen 1924. E.T., Primitive Christianity and its non-Jewish Sources, trans. from 1st German ed. Edinburgh 1912.
Connick, C. M., The Dramatic Character of the Fourth Gospel. JBL 67, 1948, pp. 159-169.
Corell, A., Det historiska och det homiletiska Nu. SEÅ X, 1946, pp. 186-191.
Craig, C. T., Realized Eschatology. JBL 56, 1937, pp. 17-26.
— Sacramental Interest in the Fourth Gospel. JBL 58, 1939, pp. 31-41.

Cramer, J. A., Catenae graecorum patrum in Novum Testamentum II. In Evangelia S. Lucae et S. Ioannis. Oxonii 1846.
Creed, J. M., Sacraments in the Fourth Gospel. MC 16, 1926, pp. 363-372.
Cullmann, O., Christus und die Zeit. Die urchristliche Zeit- und Geschichtsauffassung. Zürich 1946. E.T., Christ and Time. The Primitive Christian Conception of Time and History. London 1951.
— Le cult dans l'église primitive. CThAP 8, 2md éd. Paris 1945.
— Die ersten christlichen Glaubensbekenntnisse. ThS 15. Zürich 1943. E.T., Earliest Christian Confessions. London 1949.
— Eschatologie und Mission im Neuen Testament. EMM 85, 1941, pp. 98-108.
— Der johanneische Gebrauch doppeldeutiger Ausdrücke als Schlüssel zum Verständnis des vierten Evangeliums. ThZ 4, 1948, pp. 360-372.
— Le retour du Christ. CThAP 1, Neuchâtel 1943.
— La signification du baptême dans le Nouveau Testament. RThPh 30, 1942, pp. 121-134.
— Urchristentum und Gottesdienst. AbhThANT 3. Zürich 1944. 2. vermehrte und veränderte Aufl. 1950. E.T., Early Christian Worship. London 1953. (S.C.M. Studies in Biblical Theology, 10.)
— Das wahre durch die ausgebliebene Parusie gestellte neutestamentliche Problem. ThZ 3, 1947, pp. 177-191.
Cyril of Alexandria, Commentarius in Evangelium Ioannis. MPG 73-74, 756.
Cyril of Jerusalem, Catechesis VII illuminandorum. MPG 33, 605-622.
Dahl, N. A., Das Volk Gottes. Eine Untersuchung zum Kirchenbewusstsein des Urchristentums. Diss. Oslo 1941.
Dalman, G., Jesus—Jeschua. Die drei Sprachen Jesu. Jesus in der Synagoge, auf dem Berge, beim Passahmahl, am Kreuz. Leipzig 1922. E.T., Jesus—Jeshua. Studies in the Gospels. Authorized trans. London 1929.
— Die Worte Jesu I. 2. Aufl. Leipzig 1930. E.T., The Words of Jesus. Authorized Eng. version from 1st German ed. Edinburgh 1902.
Davies, W. D., Paul and Rabbinic Judaism. Some Rabbinic Elements in Pauline Theology. London 1948.
Delafosse, H., Le quatrième Évangile. Paris 1925.

Delbrueck, R., Antiquarisches zu den Verspottungen Jesu. ZNW 41, 1942, pp. 124–145.
Delff, H., Die Geschichte des Rabbi Jesus von Nazareth. Leipzig 1889.
— Das vierte Evangelium. Ein autentischer Bericht über Jesus von Nazareth. Husum 1890.
Denney, J., The Death of Christ. Its Place and Interpretation in the New Testament. 6th ed., London 1907.
Dibelius, M., Die alttestamentlichen Motive in der Leidensgeschichte des Petrus- und des Johannes-Evangeliums. ZNW Beiheft 33, Abhandlungen... W. W. v. Baudissin... überreicht, Giessen 1918, pp. 125–150.
— Rom und die Christen im ersten Jahrhundert. SbHAW 1941/42: 2. Heidelberg 1942.
Dillersberger, J., Das Wort vom Logos. Vorlesungen über den Johannes-Prolog. Salzburg—Leipzig 1945.
Dindorf, W., Epiphanii episcopi constantiae opera I. Leipzig 1859.
Dobschütz, E. v., The Eschatology of the Gospels. Exp VII: 9, 1910, pp. 97–113, 193–209, 333–347, 398–417. (Reprinted in book form in "The Eschatology of the Gospels", London 1910.)
— Zum Charakter des 4. Evangeliums. ZNW 28, 1929, pp. 161–177.
Dodd, C. H., The Apostolic Preaching and its Developments. Three Lectures with an Appendix on Eschatology and History. London 1936.
— The First Epistle of John and the Fourth Gospel. BJRL 21: 1. Manchester 1937.
— The Parables of the Kingdom, 3rd ed., London 1936.
Dölger, F. J., ΙΧΘΥΣ. Das Fischsymbol in frühchristlicher Zeit I. Religionsgeschichtliche und epigraphische Untersuchungen. Zugleich ein Beitrag zur ältesten Christologie und Sacramentenlehre. Rome 1910.
Dupont, G., Le Fils de l'Homme. Essai historique et critique. Thèse. Geneva—Paris 1924.
Dürr, L., Ursprung und Ausbau der israelitisch-jüdischen Heilandserwartung. Ein Beitrag zur Theologie des Alten Testaments. Berlin 1925.
Eck, O., Urgemeinde und Imperium. Ein Beitrag zur Frage nach der Stellung des Urchristentums zum Staat. BFchrTh 42: 3. Gütersloh 1940.

Eisler, R., The Enigma of the Fourth Gospel. Its Author and its Writer. London 1938.
— ΙΗΣΟΥΣ ΒΑΣΙΛΕΥΣ ΟΥ ΒΑΣΙΛΕΥΣΑΣ. Die messianische Unabhängigkeitsbewegung vom Auftreten Johannes des Täufers bis zum Untergang Jacobs des Gerechten nach der neuerschlossenen Eroberung von Jerusalem des Flavius Josephus und den christlichen Quellen I–II. (Religionswissenschaftliche Bibliothek IX.) Heidelberg 1929–30. E.T., The Messiah Jesus and John the Baptist, according to Flavius Josephus' recently rediscovered "Capture of Jerusalem" and other Jewish and Christian Sources. London 1931.
— Zur Fusswaschung am Tage vor dem Passah. (Ev. Joh.: 13. 2–16.) ZNW 14, 1913, pp. 268–271.
Ely, M. R., Knowledge of God in Johannine Thought. New York 1925.
Engnell, I., Studies in Divine Kingship in the Ancient Near East. Diss. Uppsala 1943.
— The 'Ebed Yahweh Songs and the Suffering Messiah in "Deutero-Isaiah". BJRL 31, 1948, pp. 54–93. Manchester 1948.
Erasmus, Paraphrasis in Euangelium secundum Ioannem. 1523.
Fascher, E., Ich bin die Tür! DTh 1941, pp. 37–66, 1942, pp. 33–57, 118–133.
Faulhaber, D., Das Johannes-Evangelium und die Kirche. (Kirche im Aufbau 7.) Diss. Heidelberg, Kassel-Wilhelmshöhe 1935
Faure, A, Die alttestamentlichen Zitate im 4 Evangelium und die Quellenscheidungshypothese ZNW 21, 1922, pp. 99–121.
Faye, E. de, Gnostiques et gnosticisme. Étude critique des documents du gnosticisme chrétien aux IIe et IIIe siècles. 2e éd. augmentée. Paris 1925.
Feigel, F. K., Der Einfluss des Weissagungsbeweises und anderer Motive auf die Leidensgeschichte. Ein Beitrag zur Evangelienkritik. Tübingen 1910.
Feine, P., Theologie des Neuen Testaments. 3. Aufl. Leipzig 1919.
Fiebig, P., Die Fusswaschung. Angelos 3, 1930, pp. 121–128.
Filson, F. V., Who was the Beloved Disciple? JBL 68, 1949, pp. 83–88.
Flemington, W. F., The New Testament Doctrine of Baptism. London 1948.
Franke, A. H., Das alte Testament bei Johannes. Ein Beitrag zur Erklärung und Beurtheilung der johanneischen Schriften. Göttingen 1885.

Frankfort, H., Kingship and the Gods. A Study of Near Eastern Religion as the Integration of Society and Nature. Chicago 1948.

Fridrichson, A., Bemerkungen zur Fusswaschung Joh 13. ZNW 38, 1939, pp. 94–96.

— La pensée missionnaire dans le Quatrième Évangile. AMU VI, 1937, pp. 39–45.

Foerster, W., Herr ist Jesus. Herkunft und Bedeutung des urchristlichen Kyrios-Bekenntnisses. NtlF II: 1. Gütersloh 1924.

— Von Valentin zu Heracleon. Untersuchungen über die Quellen und die Entwicklung der valentinianischen Gnosis. ZNW Beiheft 7. Giessen 1928.

Gächter, P., Das dreifache "Weide meine Lämmer". ZkathTh 69, 1947, pp. 328–344.

Gagneius, Joh., Clarissima et facillima in quattuor sacra Iesu Christi Evangelia, necnon in Actus Apostolicos Scholia. Paris 1552.

Galling, K., Die Erwählungstraditionen Israels. ZAW Beiheft 48. Giessen 1928.

Gardner-Smith, P., The Christ of the Gospels. A Study of the Gospel Records in the Light of Critical Research. Cambridge 1938.

— Saint John and the Synoptic Gospels. Cambridge 1938.

Garvie, A. E., The Beloved Disciple. Studies of the Fourth Gospel. London 1922.

Gaugler, E., Das Abendmahl im Neuen Testament. (Gegenwartsfragen Biblischer Theologie II.) Basel 1943.

— Die Bedeutung der Kirche in den johanneischen Schriften. Diss. Bern 1925.

— Das Christuszeugnis des Johannes-Evangeliums. EvTh Beiheft 2, pp. 34–67. München 1936.

— Heilsplan und Heilsverwirklichung nach Epheser 1.3–2.10. IKZ 20, 1930, pp. 201–216.

— Die Kirche, ihr Wesen und ihre Bestimmung. IKZ 17, pp. 136–155.

Gavin, F., The Jewish Antecedents of the Christian Sacraments. London 1928.

Godet, F., Commentaire sur l'évangile de Saint Jean I–III. 2e éd. Paris—Neuchâtel 1876–77. E.T., Commentary on the Gospel of St John. With a critical introduction. Trans. from the 2nd French ed. 3 vols, Edinburgh 1876, 1877. (Clark's Foreign Theological Library, 4th series, vols. 51, 53, and 56.)

Goetz, K. G., Das Abendmahl eine Diatheke Jesu oder sein letztes Gleichnis? UzNT 8. Leipzig 1920.

Goguel, M., Eschatologie et apocalyptique dans le christianisme primitif. RHR 105/106, 1932, pp. 381–434, 489–524.
— L'Eucharistie des Origines à Justin Martyr. Thèse. Paris 1910.
— La Foi à la Résurrection de Jésus dans le christianisme primitif. Étude d'histoire et de psychologie religieuses. (Bibl. de l'École des Hautes Études, Sciences religieuses 47.) Paris 1933.
— Jean-Baptiste, Paris 1928.
— La notion johannique de l'Esprit. Thèse. Paris 1902.
Goldammer, K., Navis Ecclesiae. Eine unbekannte altchristliche Darstellung der Schiffsallegorie. ZNW 40, 1941, pp. 76–86.
Goltz, E. v. der, Das Gebet in der ältesten Christenheit. Eine geschichtliche Untersuchung. Leipzig 1901.
Goodenough, E. R., The Political Philosophy of Hellenistic Kingship. YCS 1, 1928, pp. 55–102.
Goossens, W., Les origines de l'Eucharistie. Sacrement et Sacrifice. (Universitas Catholica Lovaniensis II: 22.) Diss. Gembloux —Paris 1931.
Goppelt, L., Typos. Die typologische Deutung des Alten Testaments im Neuen. BFchrTh II: 43. Gütersloh 1939.
Grant, R. M., The Bible in the Church. A Short History of Interpretation. New York 1948.
Greeven, H., Gebet und Eschatologie im Neuen Testament. Diss. Greifswald—Gütersloh 1931.
Greiff, A., Das älteste Pascharituale der Kirche, Did. 1–10, und das Johannesevangelium. JohStud I. Paderborn 1929.
Gressmann, H., Der Messias. FRLANT NF 26, Göttingen 1929.
Grether, O., Name und Wort Gottes im Alten Testament. ZAW Beiheft 64. Giessen 1934.
Grill, J., Untersuchungen über die Entstehung des vierten Evangeliums I. Tübingen u. Leipzig 1902. II. Tübingen 1923.
Grotius, H., Annotationes in Novum Testamentum. I: 2. Editio nova. Halae 1769.
Gulin, E. G., Die Freude im Neuen Testament I–II. AASF XXVI: 2, XXXVII: 3. Helsinki 1932 and 1936.
— Das geistliche Amt im Neuen Testament. ZsystTh 12, 1934/35, pp. 296–313.
Hamp, V., Der Begriff "Wort" in den aramäischen Bibelübersetzungen. Ein exegetischer Beitrag zur Hypostasen-Frage und zur Geschichte der Logos-Spekulationen. Munich 1938.

Hanson, S., The Unity of the Church in the New Testament. Colossians and Ephesians. ASNU XIV. Diss. Uppsala 1946.
Harnack, A. v., Brod und Wasser: Die eucharistischen Elemente bei Justin. TU VII: 2, pp. 117–144. Leipzig 1891.
— Die Terminologie der Wiedergeburt und verwandter Erlebnisse in der ältesten Kirche. TU 3. Reihe XII: 2, 1918, pp. 97–143.
— Das "Wir" in den johanneischen Schriften. SbPAW 1923, pp. 96–113.
Harris, R., The Origin of the Prologue to St John's Gospel. Cambridge 1917.
Haussleiter, J., Johanneische Studien. Beiträge zur Würdigung des vierten Evangeliums. Gütersloh 1928.
Headlam, A., The Fourth Gospel as History. Oxford 1948.
Hebert, A. G., The Throne of David. A Study of the Fulfilment of the Old Testament in Jesus Christ and His Church. 3rd ed., London 1945.
Heckel, T., Wahrheit im Johannesevangelium und bei Luther. Betrachtungen und Texte. Schriften der Luther-Agricola Gesellschaft in Finnland 5. Helsingfors 1944.
Heim, K., Zeit und Ewigkeit, die Hauptfrage der heutigen Eschatologie. ZThK NF 7, 1926, pp. 403–429.
Heitmüller, W., Das Johannes-Evangelium. (Die Schriften des Neuen Testaments neu übersetzt und für die Gegenwart erklärt. 3. Aufl. Bd IV, pp. 1–184.) Göttingen 1918.
— "Im Namen Jesus". Eine sprach- und religionsgeschichtliche Untersuchung zum Neuen Testament, speciell zur altchristlichen Taufe. FRLANT 1; 2. Göttingen 1903.
Henderson, R. A., The Washing of the Feet. A New Interpretation. Th 10, 1925, pp. 126–133.
Hengstenberg, E. W., Das Evangelium des heiligen Johannes I–II. Berlin 1861–63. E.T., Commentary on the Gospel of St John. 2 vols, Edinburgh (Clark's Foreign Theological Library, 4th series, vols. 5 and 7.)
Heracleon, Fragmenta Commentarii in S. Johannis Evangelium. MPG 7, 1293–1322.
Hilgenfeld, A., Das Evangelium und die Briefe Johannis nach ihrem Lehrbegriff dargestellt. Halle 1849.
— Die Ketzergeschichte des Urchristentums, urkundlich dargestellt. Leipzig 1884.
Hirsch, E., Studien zum vierten Evangelium BHTh 11. Tübingen 1936.

Hirsch, E., Das vierte Evangelium in seiner ursprünglichen Gestalt verdeutscht und erklärt. Tübingen 1936.
Hoffmann, G., Das Johannesevangelium als Alterswerk. Eine psychologische Untersuchung. NtlF IV: 1. Gütersloh 1933.
Holtzmann, H. J., Lehrbuch der Neutestamentlichen Theologie I-II. 2. Aufl. Tübingen 1911.
Hoskyns, E. C., The Fourth Gospel. Ed. by F. N. Davey. 2nd ed., London 1947.
Howard, W. F., Christianity according to Saint John. London 1947.
— The Fourth Gospel in Recent Criticism and Interpretation. 2nd ed., London 1935.
Huber, H., Der Begriff der Offenbarung im Johannes-Evangelium. Ein Beitrag zum Verständnis der Eigenart des vierten Evangeliums. Göttingen 1934.
— Das Herrenmahl im Neuen Testament auf Grund der neuesten Forschung dargestellt und beurteilt. Diss. Bern—Leipzig 1929.
Huby, J., De la connaissance de Foi dans saint Jean. RechScRel 21, 1931, pp. 385-421.
Hulen, A. B., The Call of the Four Disciples in John 1. JBL 67, 1948, pp. 153-157.
Hunnius, E., Commentarius in Evangelium de Iesu Christo secundum Ioannem. Editio tertia. Frankfurt am Main 1595.
Jeremias, Joachim, Die Berufung des Natanael (Joh. 1,45-51). Angelos III, 1930, pp. 2-5.
— Erlöser und Erlösung im Spätjudentum und Urchristentum. DTh II, 1929, pp. 106-119.
— Jesus als Weltvollender. BFchrTh 33: 4. Gütersloh 1930.
Jeremias, Joh., Das Evangelium nach Johannes. Eine urchristliche Erklärung für die Gegenwart. Leipzig 1931.
Johansson, N., Parakletoi. Vorstellungen von Fürsprechern für die Menschen vor Gott in der alttestamentlichen Religion, im Spätjudentum und im Urchristentum. Diss. Lund 1940.
Johnson, A. R., The One and the Many in the Israelitic Conception of God. Cardiff 1942.
— The Rôle of the King in the Jerusalem Cultus. Lab, 1935, pp. 71-111.
Johnston, G., The Doctrine of the Church in the New Testament. Cambridge 1943.
Jonas, H., Gnosis und spätantiker Geist. I, Die mythologische Gnosis. FRLANT NF 33. Göttingen 1934.

BIBLIOGRAPHY

Jost, W., ΠΟΙΜΗΝ. Das Bild vom Hirten in der biblischen Ueberlieferung und seine christologische Bedeutung. Diss. Giessen 1939.
Keil, C. F., Commentar über das Evangelium des Johannes. Leipzig 1881.
Kempf, T. K., Christus der Hirt. Ursprung und Deutung einer altchristlichen Symbolgestalt. Rome 1942.
Kittel, G., Die Probleme des palästinischen Spätjudentums und das Urchristentum. BWANT 3: 1. Stuttgart 1926.
— Religionshistorien och urkristendomen. Stockholm 1933.
Kittel, H., Die Herrlichkeit Gottes. Studien zu Geschichte und Wesen eines Neutestamentlichen Begriffs. ZNW Beiheft 16. Giessen 1934.
Klauser, T., Taufet in lebendigem Wasser! Zum religions- und kulturgeschichtlichen Verständnis von Didache 7, 1–3, Pisciculi . . . F. J. Dölger . . . dargeboten, Münster in W. 1939, pp. 157–164.
Klein, G., Zur Erläuterung der Evangelien aus Talmud und Midrasch. ZNW 5, 1904, pp. 144–153.
Köstlin, R., Der Lehrbegriff des Evangeliums und der Briefe Johannis. Berlin 1843.
Kraeling, C. H., Anthropos and Son of Man. A Study in Religious Syncretism of the Hellenistic Orient. (Columbia University Oriental Studies 25.) Diss. New York 1927.
Krebs, J., Der Logos als Heiland im ersten Jahrhundert. Ein religions- und dogmengeschichtlicher Beitrag zur Erlösungslehre. (Freiburger Theol. Studien II.) Freiburg in B. 1910.
Kreyenbühl, J., Das Evangelium der Wahrheit. Neue Lösung der johanneischen Frage. I–II. Berlin 1900–05.
Krüger, G., Handbuch der Kirchengeschichte. I, Das Altertum. 2. Aufl. Tübingen 1923.
Kruse, H., Studien zur offiziellen Geltung des Kaiserbildes im römischen Reich. SGKA XIX: 3, 1934.
Kümmel, W. G., Kirchenbegriff und Geschichtsbewusstsein in der Urgemeinde und bei Jesus, SBU I, 1943.
Kundsin, K., Charakter und Ursprung der johanneischen Reden. AUL I: 4, 1939.
— Topologische Ueberlieferungsstoffe im Johannes-Evangelium. FRLANT NF 22. Göttingen 1925.
Kuss, O., Die Theologie des Neuen Testamentes. Eine Einführung. Regensburg 1937.

Lagrange, M.-J., Évangile selon Saint Jean, 8me éd., Paris 1948.
— La gnose mandéenne et la tradition évangélique. RB 36, 1927, pp. 321-349, 481-515, RB 37, 1928, pp. 5-36.
Lampe, Fr A., Commentarius Analytico-Exegeticus tam literalis quam realis Evangelii secundum Joannem I-III. Amsterdam 1724.
Leipoldt, J., Johannesevangelium und Gnosis. Neutestamentliche Studien G. Heinrici . . . dargebracht, UzNT VI, pp. 140-146. Leipzig 1914.
Leisegang, H., Die Gnosis. Leipzig 1924.
— Der heilige Geist. Das Wesen und Werden der mystischintuitiven Erkenntnis in der Philosophie und Religion der Griechen. I: 1, Die vorchristlichen Anschauungen und Lehren von ΠΝΕΥΜΑ und der mystisch-intuitiven Erkenntnis. Leipzig—Berlin 1919.
— Pneuma Hagion. Der Ursprung des Geistbegriffs der synoptischen Evangelien aus der griechischen Mystik. (Veröffentlichungen des Forschungsinstituts für vergleichende Religionsgeschichte an der Universität Leipzig IV.) Leipzig 1922.
Lietzmann, H., Ein Betrag zur Mandäerfrage. SbPAW 1930, pp. 596-608.
— Messe und Herrenmahl. Eine Studie zur Geschichte der Liturgie. (Arbeiten zur Kirchengeschichte herausgegeben von K. Holl und H. Lietzmann 8.) Bonn 1926.
Lindblom, J., Das ewige Leben. Eine Studie über die Entstehung der religiösen Lebensidee im Neuen Testament. Uppsala—Leipzig 1914.
— Skandalon. Eine lexikalisch-exegetische Untersuchung. UUÅ 1921, Teologi 2.
Linssen, H., ΘΕΟΣ ΣΩΤΗΡ. Die Entwicklung und Verbreitung einer liturgischen Formelgruppe. Diss. Bonn. Münster in W. 1929.
Linton, O., Das Problem der Urkirche in der neueren Forschung. UUÅ 1932, Teologi 2. Diss. Uppsala 1932.
Lofthouse, W. F., The Father and the Son. A Study in Johannine Thought. London 1934.
Lohmeyer, E., Das Abendmahl in der Urgemeinde. JBL 56. 1937, pp. 217-257.
— Christuskult und Kaiserkult. SgemVortr 90. Tübingen 1919.
— Die Fusswaschung. ZNW 38, 1939, pp. 74-94.
— Galiläa und Jerusalem. FRLANT NF 34. Göttingen 1936.

Lohmeyer, E., Die Idee des Martyriums im Judentum und Urchristentum. ZsystTh 5, 1927/28, pp. 232–249.
— Kultus und Evangelium. Göttingen 1942.
— Kyrios Jesus. Eine Untersuchung zu Phil 2,5–11. SbHAW 4, 1927/28. Heidelberg 1928.
— Die rechte Interpretation des Mythologischen. KuM 1948, pp. 154–165; E.T., pp. 124–137.
— Vom urchristlichen Abendmahl. ThR NF 9, 1937, pp. 168–227, 273–312, NF 10, 1938, pp. 81–99.
Loisy, A., Le mandéisme et les origines chrétiennes. Paris 1934.
— Le quatrième évangile. 2me éd., Paris 1921.
Loos, H. van der, Allegorische Exegese. NedThT 2, 1947/48, pp. 129–137.
Lösch, S., Deitas Jesu und Antike Apotheose. Ein Beitrag zur Exegese und Religionsgeschichte. Rottenburg a. N. 1933.
Lücke, F., Commentar über das Evangelium des Johannes I–II. Bonn 1833–34.
Lundberg, P., La typologie baptismale dans l'ancienne église. ASNU X, Diss. Uppsala 1942.
Luthardt, C. E., Das johanneische Evangelium nach seiner Eigenthümlichkeit I–II. Nürnberg 1852–53. E.T., St. John's Gospel Described and Explained According to its Peculiar Character. 3 vols., Edinburgh 1865. (Clark's Foreign Theological Library, 4th series, vols. 52, 55, 57.) Also: St. John the Author of the Fourth Gospel, revised, translated and the literature much enlarged (from "Das Joh. Ev".) Edinburgh 1875.
Luther, M., Auslegung des dritten und vierten Kapitels Johannis in Predigten 1538–1540. WA 47, pp. 1–231.
— Auslegung . . . über das Sechste, Siebende und Achte Capitel des Euangelisten Joannis, 1530–1532. WA 33.
— Das XIV und XV Capitel S. Johannis. WA 45, pp. 465–733.
— Wochenpredigten über Joh. 16–20. 1528/29. WA 28, pp. 31–500.
Lüthi, W., Johannes. Das vierte Evangelium ausgelegt für die Gemeinde. 3. Aufl. Basel 1943.
Lyons, D. B., The Concept of Eternal Life in the Gospel according to Saint John. Diss. Washington 1938.
Macgregor, G. H. C., The Gospel of John. (The Moffat New Testament Commentary.) London 1933.
Maldonatus, J. Commentarii in Quattuor Evangelistas II. Denuo edidit J. M. Raich. Moguntiae 1874.

Marmorstein, A., Iranische und jüdische Religion mit besonderer Berücksichtigung der Begriffe "Wort", "Wohnen" und "Glorie" im IV Evangelium und in den rabbinischen Literatur. ZNW 26, 1927, pp. 231-242.
Masson, C., Le prologue du quatrième Évangile. RThPh NS 28, 1928, pp. 297-311.
Meinertz, M., Jesus und die Heidenmission. NAbh I: 1, 2. 2. Aufl. Münster i. W. 1925.
Melanchton, F., Annotationes in Evangelium Ioannis. CR 14, cols. 1043-1220.
— Enarratio in Evangelium Ioannis. CR 15, cols. 1-440.
Menoud, P.-H., L'Évangile de Jean d'après les recherches récentes. CThAP 3, 2me éd. Neuchâtel 1947.
— La foi dans l'Évangile de Jean. (Les Cahiers Bibliques de foi et vie I: 2, pp. 27-43.)
Messel, N., Der Menschensohn in den Bilderreden des Henoch. ZAW Beiheft 35. Giessen 1922.
Meyer, E., Sinn und Tendenz der Schluss-szene am Kreuz im Johannesevangelium. SbPAW 1924, pp. 157-162.
Michaelis, W., Zur Herkunft des johanneischen Paraklet-Titels. CN XI, 1947, pp. 147-162.
— Die sakramente im Johannesevangelium. Bern 1946.
Michel, O., Unser Ringen um die Eschatologie. ZThK 13, 1932, pp. 154-174.
— Das Zeugnis des Neuen Testaments von der Gemeinde. FRLANT NF 39. Göttingen 1941.
Middleton, R. D., Logos and Shekinah in the Fourth Gospel. JQR 29, 1938/39, pp. 101-133.
Moffat, J., The Lord's Supper in the Fourth Gospel. Exp VIII: 6, 1913, pp. 1-22.
Montgomery, J. A., The Christian Creed and History. (The Twenty-first Annual Hale Memorial Sermon.) Evanston, Ill. 1935.
Moore, G. F., Judaism in the First Centuries of the Christian Era, the Age of the Tannaim I-III. Cambridge 1927-30.
Mosheim, J. L. von, Erklärung des Evangelii Johannis. Weimar 1777.
Mowinckel, S., Psalmenstudien II. Das Thronbesteigungsfest Jahwäs und der Ursprung der Eschatologi. Kristiania 1922.
— Die Vorstellungen des Spätjudentums vom heiligen Geist als Fürsprecher und der johanneische Paraklet. ZNW 32, 1933, pp. 97-130.

Müller, D. H., Das Johannes-Evangelium in Lichte der Strophentheorie. (Sitzungsberichte der Kaiserl. Akad. der Wissenschaften in Wien, Phil.-Hist. Klasse, 161. Band, 8. Abh.) Vienna 1909.
Müller, W., Die Vorstellung vom Rest im Alten Testament. Diss. Leipzig 1939.
Nielen, J. M., Gebet und Gottesdienst im Neuen Testament. Eine Studie zur biblischen Liturgie und Ethik. Freiburg in B. 1937.
Odeberg, H., The Fourth Gospel, interpreted in its Relation to contemporaneous Religious Currents in Palestine and the Hellenistic-Oriental World I. Diss. Uppsala—Stockholm 1929.
— Ueber das Johannesevangelium. ZsystTh 16, 1939, pp. 173–188.
Oehler, W., Das Johannesevangelium, eine Missionsschrift für die Welt. Gütersloh 1936.
— Zum Missionscharakter des Johannesevangeliums. BFchrTh 42 : 4. Gütersloh 1941.
Oepke, A., Das missionarische Christuszeugnis des Johannesevangeliums. EMZ 1941, pp. 4–26.
Oesterley, W. O. E., Early Hebrew Festival Rituals. MaR 1933, pp. 111–146.
— The Jewish Background of the Christian Liturgy. Oxford 1925.
Olivier, A., La Strophe sacrée en St Jean. Contribution à la critique textuelle de l'Apocalypse, du IVe Évangile et de la Ie Épître. Paris 1939.
Olshausen, H., Biblischer Commentar über sämtliche Schriften des Neuen Testaments II. 3. Aufl. Königsberg 1838.
Origen, Commentarii in Evangelium Joannis, MPG 14.
— Origenes Werke IV, Der Johanneskommentar. GCS. Herausgegeben von E. Preuschen. Leipzig 1903.
Otto, R., Reich Gottes und Menschensohn. Ein religionsgeschichtlicher Versuch. München 1934. E.T., The Kingdom of God and the Son of Man: A Study in the History of Religion. Trans. from revised German ed. London 1938. (Lutterworth Library, vol. 9.)
Overbeck, F., Das Johannesevangelium. Studien zur Kritik seiner Erforschung. Aus dem Nachlass herausgegeben von C. A. Bernoulli. Tübingen 1911.
Patai, R., Man and Temple in Ancient Jewish Myth and Ritual. London 1947.

Paulus, H. E. G., Philologisch-kritischer und historischer Commentar über das Neue Testament. IV, Das Evangelium des Johannes 1. Lübeck 1804.
Percy, E., Untersuchungen über den Ursprung der johanneischen Theologie zugleich ein Beitrag zur Frage nach der Entstehung des Gnostizismus. Diss. Lund 1939.
Phythian-Adams, W. J., The Call of Israel. An Introduction to the Study of Divine Election. London 1934.
— The People and the Presence. A Study of the At-one-ment. London 1942.
Pickl, J., Messiaskönig Jesus in der Auffassung seiner Zeitgenossen. München 1935. E.T., The Messias. St Louis and London 1946.
Power, E., John 2.20 and the Date of the Crucifixion. Biblica 9, 1928, pp. 257–288.
Preisker, H., Geist und Leben. Das Thelos-Ethos des Urchristentums. Gütersloh 1933.
Pribnow, H., Die Johanneische Anschauung vom "Leben". GThF IV. Greifswald 1934.
Prucker, E., Γνῶσις Θεοῦ. Untersuchungen zur Bedeutung eines religiösen Begriffs beim Apostel Paulus und bei seiner Umwelt. Cassiciacum IV, 1937.
Prümm, K., Herrscherkult und Neues Testament. Ein Beitrag zum sprachlichen Problem der Pastoralbriefe und zur Frage nach den Wurzeln des paulinischen Christusbekenntnisses ΚΥΡΙΟΣ ΙΗΣΟΥΣ. Biblica IX, 1928, pp. 3–25, 129–142, 289–301.
Puech, H.-C., Le Mandéisme. Histoire Général des Religions III, 1945, pp. 67–83.
— Le Manichéisme. Histoire Général des Religions III, 1945, pp. 85–116.
Quasten, J., Das Bild des Guten Hirten in den altchristlichen Baptisterien und in den Taufliturgien des Ostens und Westens. Das Siegel der Gottesherde. Pisciculi . . . F. J. Dölger . . . dargeboten, Münster in W. 1939, pp. 220–244.
— Der Gute Hirte in hellenistischer und frühchristlicher Logostheologie. Heilige Ueberlieferung . . . I. Herwegen . . . dargeboten, Münster 1938, pp. 51–58.
Quesnel, P., Das Neue Testament unsers Herrn Jesu Christi mit erbaulichen Betrachtungen über ieden Vers. Frankfurt a. M. 1718. E.T., The New Testament, with Moral Reflections upon every Verse. London 1719–25.

BIBLIOGRAPHY

Quispel, G., La conception de l'Homme dans la gnose valentinienne. Eranos-Jahrbuch XV, 1947, pp. 249–286.
Rad, G. v., Das Gottesvolk im Deuteronomium. BWANT III: 11. Stuttgart 1911.
— Das theologische Problem des alttestamentlichen Schöpfungsglaubens. ZAW Beiheft 66, 1936, pp. 138–147.
Rahner, H., Navicula Petri. Zur Symbolgeschichte des römischen Primats. ZkathTh 69, 1947, pp. 1–35.
Raney, W. H., The Relation of the Fourth Gospel to the Christian Cultus. Giessen 1933.
Ratramnus, De Praedestinatione Dei libri duo. MPL 121, 11–80.
Reicke, B., Drei Bemerkungen zur urchristlichen Taufe. Amt und Gemeinde II, 1948, pp. 97–100.
— Die Mahlzeit mit Paulus auf den Wellen des Mittelmeers Act 27.33–38. ThZ 4, 1948, pp. 401–410.
Riesenfeld, H., Jésus Transfiguré. L'arrière-plan du récit évangélique de la transfiguration de Notre-Seigneur. ASNU XVI. Thèse. Uppsala. Lund 1947.
Rigg, W. H., The Personality of John the Apostle and the Fourth Gospel. CQR 1925, pp. 231–258.
Ringgren, H., World and Wisdom. Studies in the Hypostatization of Divine Qualities and Functions in the Ancient Near East. Diss. Uppsala. Lund 1947.
Rupertus Tutiensis, In Evangelium S. Joannis Commentariorum libri XIV. MPL 169, 205–826.
Rust, E. C., The Christian Understanding of History. (Lutterworth Library XXX.) London 1947.
Sagnard, F., La gnose valentinienne et le témoignage de Saint Irénée. (Études de Philosophie Médiévale 36.) Paris 1947.
Sasse, H., Jesus Christ, the Lord. Mysterium Christi, ed. G. K. A. Bell and D. A. Deissmann, 1930, pp. 93–120.
— Der Paraklet im Johannesevangelium. ZNW 24, 1925, pp. 260–277.
Schaefer, O., Der Sinn der Rede Jesu von den vielen Wohnungen in seines Vaters Hause und von dem Weg zu ihm. ZNW 32, 1933, pp. 210–217.
Schencke, W., Die Chokma (Sophia) in der jüdischen Hypostasenspekulation. Ein Beitrag zur Geschichte der religiösen Ideen im Zeitalter des Hellenismus. (Videnskapsselskapets Skrifter II, Hist.-Filos. Klasse 1912: 6.) Kristiania 1913.
Schlatter, A., Der Evangelist Johannes. Wie er spricht, denkt und glaubt. Gütersloh 1930.

Schlatter, Das Evangelium nach Johannes. (Schlatters Erläuterungen zum Neuen Testament III.) Stuttgart 1928.
— Der Glaube im Neuen Testament. 2. Aufl. Stuttgart 1896.
Schleiermacher, F., Homilien über das Evangelium des Johannes in den Jahren 1823 und 1824 gesprochen I–II. (Fr. Schleiermachers sämmtliche Werke II: 8–9.) Berlin 1837–47.
Schmid, L., Johannesevangelium und Religionsgeschichte. Diss. Tübingen 1933.
Schmidt, H., Die Thronfahrt Jahwes. SgemVortr 122. Tübingen 1927.
Schmidt, K. L., Eschatologie und Mystik im Urchristentum. ZNW 21, 1922, pp. 277–291.
— Der johanneische Charakter der Erzählung vom Hochzeitswunder in Kana. Harnack-Ehrung, Leipzig 1921, pp. 32–43.
Schmidt, N., Recent Study of the Term "Son of Man". JBL 45, 1926, pp. 326–349.
Schnackenburg, R., Der Glaube im vierten Evangelium. Diss. Breslau 1937.
Schneider, J., Doxa. Eine bedeutungsgeschichtliche Studie. NtlF III: 3. Gütersloh 1932.
— Die Einheit der Kirche nach dem Neuen Testament.(Aus der Welt der Bibel V.) Berlin.
— Eschatologie und Mystik im Neuen Testament. ZThK NF 13, 1932, pp. 111–129.
— Zur Komposition von Joh. 10. CN XI, 1947, pp. 220–225.
Schniewind, J., Antwort an Rudolf Bultmann. Thesen zum Problem der Entmythologisierung. KuM 1948, pp. 85–134; E.T., pp. 45–101.
Schrenck, E. von, Das ewige Leben nach johanneischer Anschauung. Diss. Jurjew. Naumburg a. S. 1897.
Schwartz, E., Aporien im vierten Evangelium. NachrGGW 1907, pp. 342–372, 1908, pp. 115–188, 497–560.
Schweitzer, A., Die Mystik des Apostels Paulus. Tübingen 1930. E.T., The Mysticism of Paul the Apostle. London 1931, 2nd ed. 1953.
Schweizer, E., EGO EIMI . . . Die religionsgeschichtliche Herkunft und theologische Bedeutung der johanneischen Bildreden, zugleich ein Beitrag zur Quellenfrage des vierten Evangeliums. FRLANT NF 38. Göttingen 1939.
— Das Leben des Herrn in der Gemeinde und ihren Diensten. AbhThANT 8. Zürich 1946.

Scott, E. F., The Fourth Gospel, its Purpose and Theology. Edinburgh 1906.
— The Hellenistic Mysticism of the Fourth Gospel. AmJTh 20, 1916, pp. 345–359.
Scotus, Johannes, Commentarius in S. Evangelium secundum Joannem. MPL 122, 297–348.
— Homilia in Prologum S. Evangelii secundum Joannem. MPL 122, 283–296.
Semler, S., Paraphrasis Evangelii Ioannis I–II. Halae—Magdeburgicae 1771–72.
Simon, T., Der Logos. Ein Versuch erneuter Würdigung einer alten Wahrheit. Leipzig 1902.
Sjöberg, E., Der Menschensohn im äthiopischen Henochbuch. (Acta Reg. Soc. Hum. Litterarum Lund XLI.) Lund 1946.
Smilde, E., Leven in de Johanneische Geschriften. Diss. Amsterdam—Kampen 1943.
Smith, J. M. P., The Chosen People. AmJSL 45, 1928/29, pp. 73–82.
Söderberg, H., La religion des cathares. Diss. Uppsala 1949.
Soltau, W., Kannte der 4, Evangelist den Lieblingsjünger Jesu? ThSK 88, 1915, pp. 371–380.
Spitta, F., Das Johannes-Evangelium als Quelle der Geschichte Jesu. Göttingen 1910.
Stærk, W., Zum alttestamentlichen Erwählungsglauben. ZAW 55, 1937, pp. 1–36.
Stählin, G., Skandalon. Untersuchungen zur Geschichte eines biblischen Begriffs. BFchrTh II: 24. Gütersloh 1930.
— Zum Problem der johanneischen Eschatologie. ZNW 33, 1934, pp. 225–259.
Starke, C., Synopsis Bibliothecae Exegeticae in Novum Testamentum I. Leipzig 1758.
Stauffer, E., Die Theologie des Neuen Testaments. Stuttgart—Berlin 1941. E.T., New Testament Theology. London 1955.
Steffes, J. R., Das Wesen des Gnostizismus und sein Verhältnis zum katholischen Dogma. Eine dogmengeschichtliche Untersuchung. FchrLD XIV: 4. Paderborn 1922.
Strabo, Valafrid, Glossa Ordinaria, Evangelium secundum Joannem. MPL 114, 355–426.
Strachan, R. H., The Fourth Evangelist. Dramatist or Historian? London 1925.
Strack, H. L.—Billerbeck, P., Kommentar zum Neuen Testament aus Talmud und Midrasch II. Munich 1924.

Sundkler, B., Jésus et les Païens. AMU VI, 1937, pp. 1–38.
Tasker, R. V. G., The Old Testament in the New Testament. London 1946.
Taylor, L. R., The Divinity of the Roman Emperor. (Philological Monographs published by the American Philological Association I.) Middleton 1931.
Theodore of Mopsuestia, Commentarii in Novum Testamentum. In Evangelium Ioannis Commentarii Fragmenta. MPG 66, 727–786.
Theophylactus, Enarratio in Evangelium Ioannis. MPG 123, 1133–1348, MPG 124, 9–318.
Tholuck, A., Commentar zum Evangelio Johannis. Hamburg 1831. E.T., Commentary on the Gospel of St John. Trans. from the last German ed., Edinburgh 1860. (Clark's Foreign Theological Library, 3rd series, vol. 5.)
Thomas Aquinas, In Evangelia S. Matthaei et S. Joannis Commentaria I–II. Ed. IV (Marietti). Turin 1925.
Thornton, L. S., The Common Life in the Body of Christ. 2nd ed., London 1944.
Tillmann, F., Das Johannesevangelium, übersetzt und erklärt. 4. Aufl. Bonn 1931.
Titius, A., Die neutestamentliche Lehre von der Seligkeit und ihre Bedeutung für die Gegenwart. III, Die Johanneische Anschauung unter dem Gesichtspunkt der Seligkeit. Tübingen 1900.
Torrey, C. C., The Four Gospels. A New Translation. London 1934.
— Our Translated Gospels. Some of the Evidence. London 1936.
Trench, G. H., A Study of St John's Gospel. London 1918.
Ubbink, J. T., Het Evangelie van Johannes. Groningen 1935.
Vaganay, L., La finale du quatrième évangile. RB 45, 1936, pp. 512–528.
Völker, K., Mysterium und Agape. Die gemeinsamen Mahlzeiten in der alten Kirche. Gotha 1927.
Volz, P., Die Eschatologie der jüdischen Gemeinde im neutestamentlichen Zeitalter nach den Quellen der rabbinischen, apokalyptischen und apokryphen Literatur. 2. Aufl. Tübingen 1934.
— Das Neujahrsfest Jahwes (Laubhüttenfest). SgemVortr 67. Tübingen 1912.
Wagenführer, M. A., Der Kirchenbegriff des Neuen Testaments. Germanentum, Christentum und Judentum II, Leipzig 1942, pp. 273–306.

Weber, H. E., "Eschatologie" und "Mystik" im Neuen Testament. Ein Versuch zum Verständnis des Glaubens. BFchrTh II: 20. Gütersloh 1931.
— Die Kirche im Lichte der Eschatologie. NKZ 37, 1926, pp. 299–339.
— Die Vollendung des neutestamentlichen Glaubenszeugnisses durch Johannes. (Sonderabdruck aus Denkschrift über die VI. Konferenz von Religionslehrerinnen zu Elberfeld 1912.) Leipzig 1912.
Weinel, H., Biblische Theologie des Neuen Testaments. Die Religion Jesu und des Urchristentums. (Grundriss der Theol. Wissenschaften III: 2.) 2. Aufl. Tübingen 1913.
Weiser, A., Glaube und Geschichte im Alten Testament. BWANT IV: 4. Stuttgart 1931.
Weiss, B., Der Johanneische Lehrbegriff in seinen Grundzügen untersucht. Berlin 1862.
— Das Johannesevangelium als einheitliches Werk. Berlin 1912.
Wellhausen, J., Das Evangelium Johannis. Berlin 1908.
Wendland, H.-D., Die Eschatologie des Reiches Gottes bei Jesus. Eine Studie über den Zusammenhang von Eschatologie, Ethik und Kirchenproblem. Gütersloh 1931.
— Der Herr der Zeiten. (Kirche im Aufbau 3.) Kassel—Wilhelmshöhe 1936.
Wendland, P., Die hellenistisch-römische Kultur in ihren Beziehungen zu Judentum und Christentum. HNT 1: 2. 2. u. 3. Aufl. Tübingen 1912.
Wendt, H. H., Der "Anfang" am Beginne des 1. Johannesbriefes. ZNW 21, 1922, pp. 38–42.
— Das Johannesevangelium. Eine Untersuchung seiner Entstehung und seines geschichtlichen Wertes. Göttingen 1900.
E.T., The Gospel according to St John: An Enquiry into its Genesis and Historical Value. Edinburgh 1902.
Wensinck, A. J., The Semitic New Year and the Origin of Eschatology. Acta Orientalia I, 1923, pp. 158–199.
Westcott, B. F., The Gospel according to St. John. London 1896.
de Wette, W. M. L., Kurze Erklärung des Evangelium und der Briefe Johannis. Leipzig 1846.
Wetter, G. P., Altchristliche Liturgien: Das christliche Mysterium. Studie zur Geschichte des Abendmahles. FRLANT NF 13. Göttingen 1921.
— Charis. Ein Beitrag zur Geschichte des ältesten Christentums. UzNT V. Leipzig 1913.

Wetter, G.P. "Ich bin es". Eine johanneische Formel. ThSK 88, 1915, pp. 224–238.
— "Ich bin das Licht der Welt". Eine Studie zur Formelsprache des Johannesevangeliums. BzR I, 1913/14, pp. 166–201.
— Phôs (ΦΩΣ). Eine Untersuchung über hellenistische Frömmigkeit zugleich ein Beitrag zum Verständnis des Manichäismus. (Acta Reg. Soc. Hum. Litterarum XVII: 1.) Uppsala 1915.
— "Der Sohn Gottes". Eine Untersuchung über den Charakter und die Tendenz des Johannes-Evangeliums. FRLANT NF 9. Göttingen 1916.
— Die "Verherrlichung" im Johannesevangelium. BzR II, 1914/15, pp. 32–113.
Whitby, D., A Paraphrase and Commentary on the New Testament I. London 1706.
Widengren, G., The Great Vohu Manah and the Apostle of God. Studies in Iranian and Manichaean Religion. UUÅ 1945: 5. Uppsala 1945.
— Mesopotamian Elements in Manichaeism. (King and Saviour II.) Studies in Manichaean, Mandaean and Syrian-Gnostic Religion. UUÅ 1946: 3. Uppsala 1946.
Wikenhauser, A., Das Evangelium nach Johannes. (Das Neue Testament . . . herausgegeben von A. Wikenhauser und O. Kuss IV.) Regensburg 1948.
Windisch, H., Die Absolutheit des Johannesevangeliums. ZsystTh V, 1927/28, pp. 3–54.
— Angelophanien um den Menschensohn auf Erden. Ein Kommentar zu Joh. 1,51. ZNW 31, 1932, pp. 199–204.
— Die fünf johanneischen Parakletsprüche. Festgabe für Ad. Jülicher, Tübingen 1927, pp. 110–137.
— Jesus und der Geist im Johannes-Evangelium. Amicitiae Corolla . . . Presented to J. R. Harris, London 1933, pp. 303–318.
— Johannes und die Synoptiker. Wollte der vierte Evangelist die älteren Evangelien ergänzen oder ersetzen? UzNT 12. Leipzig 1926.
— Die johanneische Weinregel (Joh. 2,10). ZNW 14, 1913, pp. 248–257.
— Joh. 1:51 und die Auferstehung Jesu. ZNW 31, 1932, pp. 199–204.

BIBLIOGRAPHY

Wobbermin, G., Religionsgeschichtliche Studien zur Frage der Beeinflussung des Urchristentums durch das antike Mysterienwesen. Berlin 1896.

Wrede, W., Das Messiasgeheimnis in den Evangelien. Zugleich ein Beitrag zum Verständnis des Markusevangeliums. Göttingen 1901.

Wright, C. J., The Meaning and Message of the Fourth Gospel. A Study in the Application of the Johannine Christianity to the Present Theological Situation. London 1933.

Zahn, T., Das Evangelium des Johannes. (Kommentar zum Neuen Testament herausgegeben von Th. Zahn IV.) 5.–6. Aufl. Leipzig—Erlangen 1921.

Zimmern, H., Das babylonische Neujahrsfest. Der Alte Orient 25: 3. Leipzig 1926.

— Vater, Sohn und Fürsprecher in der babylonischen Gottesvorstellung. Leipzig 1896.

Zwaan, J. de, John wrote in Aramaic. JBL 57, 1938, pp. 155–171.

INDEX OF AUTHORS QUOTED IN THE TEXT

Alcuin, 173
Ammonius of Alexandria, 168
Augustine, 170 ff, 173, 174

Bacon, B. W., 87
Bauer, W., 45, 70
Baumgarten, S. J., 181
Bede, The Venerable, 172, 173
Belser, J., 70
Bengel, A., 180
Bernard, J. H., 184
Bertram, G., 70
Boehmer, J., 184
Boismard, M.-E., 10
Bousset, W., 45
Bruno Astensis, 173
Büchsel, F., 184
Bugge, F. W., 184
Bultmann, R., 2, 10, 23, 40, 44, 46, 53, 59, 60, 64, 70, 74, 79, 80, 81, 88, 108, 114, 115, 144, 145, 161, 162, 185
Buri, F., 81
Burney, C. F., 46

Calovius, A., 178
Calvin, J., 176, 178, 180
Campenhausen, H. von, 70
Cassian, Archimandrite, 82
Chemnitz, M., 177
Chrysostom, John, 168, 169
Clausen, 184
Craig, C. T., 70
Creed, J. M., 76

Cullmann, O., 33, 34, 54, 55, 59, 61, 62, 64, 65, 67, 70, 74, 75, 77, 84, 110, 146, 147
Cyril of Alexandria, 167
Cyril of Jerusalem, 167

Dodd, C. H., 81

Eisler, R., 70
Erasmus, 175

Fascher, E., 26
Faulhaber, D., 44, 83
Feine, P., 184

Galling, K., 186, 187
Gaugler, E., 81
Gerhard, Johan, 177
Godet, F., 183, 184
Goguel, M., 70
Greeven, H., 80
Grotius, H., 178
Gulin, E. G., 157

Henderson, R. A., 70
Hengstenberg, E. W., 182
Heracleon, 166
Hilgenfeld, A., 183
Hirsch, E., 70, 184
Holtzmann, H. J., 185
Hoskyns, E. C., 185
Howard, W. F., 82
Huber, H., 76, 82
Hunnius, E., 177

Jeremias, Joachim, 146
Jeremias, Joh., 184
Johansson, N., 88, 90
Josephus, 27

Keil, C. F., 182
Kolmodin, 185
Köstlin, R., 182, 183
Kümmel, W. G., 84
Kundsin, K., 56, 70

Lagrange, M.-J., 184
Lampe, F. A., 179
Lindblom, J., 143, 144, 145
Lohmeyer, E., 70
Loisy, A., 21, 162, 184
Lücke, F., 181
Ludin Jansen, H., 84
Luthardt, C. E., 183
Luther, M., 53, 162, 174-5, 180
Lüthi, W., 184
Lyons, D. B., 146
Lyserus, P., 177

Maldonatus, J., 179
Melanchton, F., 175
Michaelis, W., 61, 62, 64, 70
Michel, O., 80
Moe, 184
Moffat, J., 76
Mosheim, J. L. von, 180, 181
Mowinckel, S., 88

Odeberg, H., 45, 185
Oehler, W., 76, 162, 185
Olshausen, H., 183
Origen, 166, 167

Paulus, H. E. G., 182
Percy, E., 161
Pribnow, H., 142, 144
Prucker, E., 138

Quesnel, P., 179

Raney, W. H., 46
Ratramnus, 173
Rupertus Tutiensis, 173

Sasse, H., 87
Schlatter, A., 184
Schleiermacher, F., 181
Schneider, J., 80
Schrenck, E. von, 144
Schwartz, E., 71
Schweizer, E., 10, 26, 27
Scotus, Johannes, 173
Semler, S., 181
Smilde, E., 144, 184
Spitta, F., 71, 184
Stählin, G., 80, 81
Starke, C., 178-9
Strabo, Valafrid, 173
Sundkler, B., 33

Theodore of Mopsuestia, 169
Theophylactus, 169
Tholuck, A., 182
Thomas Aquinas, 173
Tillmann, F., 184
Trench, G. H., 184

Ubbink, J. T., 184

Wagenführer, M. A., 84
Weber, H. E., 82, 83
Weinel, H., 184
Weiss, B., 184
Wellhausen, J., 71, 184
Wendland, H.-D., 146
Westcott, B. F., 184
de Wette, W. M. L., 181
Wetter, G. P., 45
Wikenhauser, A., 184
Windisch, H., 56

Zahn, T., 162, 184

www.ingramcontent.com/pod-product-compliance
Lightning Source LLC
Chambersburg PA
CBHW070938240426
43667CB00036B/2270